PRAISE FOR 37 TONS

"I thoroughly enjoyed reading *37 Tons*. It was easy for me to identify with the writer's past, if not with the particulars of his endeavors, then certainly with the motivations that could lead to such an extreme way of living. As a person in recovery and having grown up in the inner city as well, I could really relate to the writer's upbringing and desire to succeed, and to succeed no matter what the cost. I had great appreciation for the extremely candid, straightforward tone.... Few people are able to achieve the degree of success and failure in their lives that Victorson has, especially in both the corrupt and legitimate business arenas. His ability to keep picking himself up and continue on into sobriety makes this an amazing story of strength and hope."   —*T. Brown, senior executive, banking*

"Beautifully told, heartbreaking, ... well done."
                     —*M. Arsinoe, artist*

"I was literally unable to stop reading *37 Tons*. Victorson has an incredible skill for telling stories and setting the scene so it's as if you're really there. The stories make wider analyses about society, such as the way class distinctions play out before our eyes without most people thinking about their complexities. In one instance, while coaching a youth soccer league, a fight breaks out on the field. The dynamic between white and Hispanic, rich and poor, is a microcosm of wider conflicts in the world in general. A brave account of emotional and psychological states of mind."
                     —*Peter Bolton, journalist*

"I just read every word and could not put it down!"
                     —*J. Kagen, Emmy Award-winning journalist*

37
TONS

DAVID VICTORSON

Six Beacon Street Publishers

Designed by Kim Llewellyn

ISBN 978–0–578–13864–0 (paperback)
ISBN 978–0–578–13837–4 (ebook)

Library of Congress Control Number: 2014904041

Printed in the United States of America.

FIRST EDITION

10 9 8 7 6 5 4 3 2 1

www.37tons.com

CONTENTS

ACKNOWLEDGMENTS

My spirit defeated, I had lost my voice. Writing this book brought my voice back, the memories of the birth of our son, smiling strangers, the beauty emanating from an aged face, each wrinkle signifying the wisdom of life.

Surrounding me is the grace of my family and brothers and sisters in the recovery community. My heartfelt thanks go out to them and to those who helped make this book a reality:

To my son for his encouragement and for never giving up on me.

To Kim Llewellyn, my wordsmith from hell, who forced me to dig deeper and to stay in the process no matter how painful.

And to all the characters along the way who taught me life's lessons that made me who I am today.

ONE

The End

heard the door of my hotel room being smashed open. As I jumped out of bed I was ordered on get to my knees. Six heavily armed Bolivian security police nervously stood over me. They handcuffed me, put a black cloth bag over my head, and shoved me down the hall to the elevator. As we passed through the lobby I heard one of the soldiers ask the man at the front desk if I had rented a safe deposit box. We got into a jeep and drove for about fifteen minutes. I didn't care what happened to me. I was tired of running, lying, and looking over my shoulder every minute.

When they took the bag off my head I was in a small dimly lit room. I was directed to sit in an armchair. These guards acted as if they were afraid of me. I knew eventually they would hand me over to U.S. marshals but for the time being they had to worry about repercussions from the Colombian cartel I worked for. They asked me who I was, why I had an Italian passport, and who I worked for. They left me alone handcuffed to the chair in the dark for about an hour. A short man in uniform came in and started yelling, he rushed at me in an aggressive hostile manner. I did not say a word or move a muscle. I just glared at him.

I was taken to a prison cell where I could see the snowcapped Mount Illimani, guardian of La Paz through a tiny barred window in the cement block. I stayed there handcuffed to a bed for three months while awaiting my extradition to the U.S. to begin serving four concurrent five-year prison sentences. I was a notorious fugitive from the U.S. after being convicted in Seattle of smuggling thirty-seven tons of marijuana.

1

I had plenty of time to think about how I had arrived in this Third World prison. Over the ten-year period before my arrest I had earned around thirty million dollars. I had tried to use that money to get me out of the black market and lead a normal life. I wanted that dream to come true but life had taught me many times that would never happen for me. I was part of the 1970s sex and drug subculture. I took drugs the same way I did everything else—relentlessly, with high risk and no regard for the consequences.

From the age of eighteen when I started dealing drugs, I always had to assess the people I was dealing with, watch what I told them about me, and keep a low profile. Having a lot of money sets you up for all kinds of wild speculations about where it came from. Friends and acquaintances could not be trusted with the true details of my life. After my arrest, many inaccurate and vindictive stories from any source other than me circulated in the press and in Marin County social circles. I had lived so many lives both legal and illegal and created myself as various characters that would blend into those lives—from an antiquities dealer of pre-Columbian artifacts in South America, an import-export broker in India, a trust fund baby in Nepal, a Ferrari dealer in Marin County, to a bass player in Miami, among many other cover stories.

I wondered how I had gone from being a normal kid from an impoverished inner-city Boston neighborhood in the 1960s to the "mastermind," as the *Seattle Times* reported in 1978, "behind the seizure of a freighter carrying thirty-seven tons of marijuana from Colombia to Seattle" in what was the largest known importation of marijuana to the West Coast at that time. A *Texas Monthly* article called me a "caustic, long-haired man who deals in marijuana and cocaine on a scale unmatched by anyone else in Marin County, the well-known drug capital of California."

I thought about my grandparents, the only family I ever felt close to, and what they would have thought about my life. Growing up in Dorchester, the back alleys, pool halls, and basketball courts had taught me a harsh way to live. No criminal or addict starts out as a child thinking *I know, let's grow up to become a criminal; no wait, a gambling or drug addict. However I get there, my ultimate goal is to end up in a Bolivian prison awaiting extradition.* Thinking back to that period in my life, I questioned why I felt so separate from everyone else. Why was I so hungry? When would I ever fit in with other people? How did it all begin?

TWO

Dorchester

My family lived in Dorchester, a tough neighborhood of southern Boston. On the street, our motto was "if you want a long life, don't live here." I was born on March 15, 1950, and named David. We lived on Lorne Street in a three-story wood-framed apartment house called a "triple decker," built during the late nineteenth and early twentieth centuries to house immigrant factory workers. My mother, father, sister, and I shared a second floor apartment with my bubbe, three aunts, and one uncle. All nine of us squeezed into the floor-through flat consisting of a kitchen, one bathroom, a living room, two bedrooms and a den, which was converted into a third bedroom.

My bubbe and her husband left Russia in their early twenties to immigrate to the U.S. for the opportunity of a better life. And this is where they ended up? They must have imagined life anywhere in the U.S. would be better than what they had in Russia. My grandparents raised four children in this neighborhood. My grandfather on my mother's side was an alcoholic who grew increasingly worse with time. Shortly after the birth of my mother, their fifth child, he abandoned the family, leaving my bubbe and five children to fend for themselves.

My bubbe was a hard-working woman. She had long grey hair down to her back that she put up in a hair net every morning. Her face was round and wrinkled, so much so that some of the wrinkles folded over when she smiled. Her back was hunched over. Despite her aged outward appearance, her blue eyes sparkled. The only time I saw her not working was at night, before bed, when she would sit at her dressing table and brush her long gray hair. She had had a physically hard life, but had a great spirit and set an example of kindness and humility that stayed with me.

I knew bubbe loved me and was happy to be around me and I felt the same way about her. Whenever I came up the stairs she would ask, "David, is that you?" I would say, "Yes, it's me." Then she would ask, "Are you hungry? Do you want to help me make the chicken liver?" I would help her by chopping the cooked chicken livers in a big wooden bowl while she added the chopped onions, hard-boiled eggs, and seasoning. With food shared among nine people I was always hungry and wise enough at four years of age to know when to be around the kitchen. I could then eat as much as I wanted because my bubbe and I were the only ones who knew how much there was to begin with. We worked together without saying much. It was comforting just being around her. I always did what she asked without question.

There was a dirt alley in back of the apartment building with run-down cars. People had thrown old dirty books and used condoms through their broken windows. On the other side of the alley was the Mattapan State Mental Hospital. Its expansive lawns and walking paths were surrounded by a chain-link fence, but the fence was easy to climb or find a hole in it big enough to sneak through. Ten feet inside the fence the smell of cleaning chemicals was overwhelming. But I liked the open space, uncluttered, without danger, the only area of green grass and trees I had ever seen. I liked to watch the light gray smoke rising from the buildings chimneys as it drifted up to the sky. I always wondered why there were wrought iron grills on the windows. There was a basketball court on the far side of the building that was empty most of the time where I could practice dribbling and shooting by myself.

My friends and I used to play stickball in the back alley with a small pink rubber ball and a broomstick for a bat. When the pitcher threw the ball, I hit that ball into orbit. When I saw the ball speeding toward me I felt at one with the universe. The broomstick connected with the ball perfectly. When I looked up and saw the ball a mile in the sky, I thought to myself, *This would be a home run at Fenway Park.* As I rounded the bases the boy in the outfield was still chasing the ball. The pitcher ran to cover home base. As I stepped on the plate he picked up the broomstick and whacked me in the face, giving me a bloody nose, letting me know that even though I had hit a home run I was not the winner. Only being the most ruthless and violent would make you the winner in this neighborhood. I didn't want anyone to see me cry, so I ran home as fast as I could, and upstairs to my bubbe, my sole protector. She laid me on my back on a pink hamper and using an old Russian remedy she magically stopped the bleeding.

On Friday nights our family observed the Jewish Sabbath. We placed two candlesticks in the middle of the kitchen table. When the sun set we would light the candles and say a prayer before we ate. We had great chicken soup. On the rare occasion I got the egg yolk from the soup, it was like a super treat just for me. When my family could afford chicken it was a single boiled chicken minus the head to be divided among nine people. The adults got the most, the kids what was left over. We ate every part, not the feet, but the neck and pupick, and sucked the bones dry. Food was not taken for granted.

I carried those early experiences of food deprivation and rare moments of gratification with me into adulthood. Years later I visited my girlfriend Carol's family at their home on Long Island. Her mom cooked breaded chicken breast filets. I was astounded. These must be very rich people who could eat only the white meat of the chicken and have as many pieces as they wanted.

My bubbe made rhubarb pies and baked homemade bread. I looked forward to the smells in the apartment when I came home and couldn't wait to taste what she had made. All the food she cooked tasted great. The kitchen had the warmest feeling of all the rooms in the apartment. We ate in the kitchen, and when we all sat down to eat, we opened up the table and added leaves. The oven was white porcelain as was the stovetop. White lace curtains hung at the window. My memories of my bubbe were always of her in her kitchen, and the best times of my childhood were spent there with her.

When I was about five or six my parents, sister, and I moved to our own house a few blocks away on Wales Street. I liked our new house. It had a porch, front yard, and a steep driveway on the side. I used to jump off the porch on to the dry orange and brown leaves that I had raked into a pile, and in the winter onto mounds of snow I had shoveled off of our front stairs. My backyard was a cracked concrete slab next to an old shed-like garage. Some people would call it a driveway, but for me it was my backyard. I made a basketball hoop from an old metal-rimmed basket used to carry fruit and tied it to the roof of the garage with a piece of old clothesline. I would practice year round, dribbling and shooting for hours at a time.

My mom was the youngest of five children. She loved the department store where she worked so much that she stayed late after work and went in on her days off to shop for marked down clothes. My childhood memories of her were of a woman who counted every cookie, carefully portioned out food, and bought clothes that were way too big for me so I would grow into them. Her favorite statement after dinner was "kitchen closed," so if you were still hungry you would have to wait till morning. I believe my mother loved me, but I still don't know why I believe that. She was not the comforting mother type but more the critical, disapproving type, the opposite of my bubbe. I wished my mother were more like her. I never felt a sense of comfort from her; whatever emotions she had were saved for my father.

My sister was born eleven months before me. We had nothing in common so I have very little memory of her while we lived in Dorchester. We went to the same grammar school but separated at middle school. She went to girls' Latin Junior High and I went to junior high in Mattapan. She seemed closer to my parents than I was. I was a boy out on the streets while she stayed home most of the time with my aunts.

I still went to visit my bubbe every chance I got. I was going to school and playing basketball so I saw her less and less. When I was ten years old I remember visiting my bubbe in the hospital. She seemed to have gotten smaller and weaker. I was walking down a corridor toward her room when an orderly was wheeling her out on a hospital bed. She was crying, asking, "Where am I going?" The orderly pushed the bed faster and rode along on the bars that held the wheels in place seemingly enjoying the ride while my bubbe was crying. My heart broke. She was blind and could not see or understand what was happening to her. I blamed it all on us being poor. Surely if we were rich she would not have been treated like a disposable human. There would have been someone with her to protect her. The orderly would have been afraid of getting fired because someone with money would have access to his boss and complain.

I just knew all this pain and suffering could be made more comfortable if my family had money. How unfair, my bubbe was a good woman, she loved all children, she spent most of her adult life with an apron on cooking and cleaning making a home for her children, all that with no help. The reward for her goodness seemed to me at that moment a lonely, terrifying ride down a dark corridor.

When my parents ignored me I felt hurt. If I was not picked first or second when we played pick-up games of basketball I felt like I was worthless. I blamed myself for my fears, I was told many times I was too sensitive and to get over it, so I learned to keep my fears locked up inside myself. I was always on guard in the neighborhood but when left alone at home, and the doors were locked, my inner fears turned to imagined terrors that could emerge from the basement or attic.

One Saturday night my parents went out to the movies, leaving my ten-year-old sister in charge of me. My sister and I went to our rooms around nine o'clock. I couldn't sleep, I kept hearing noises in the house, maybe sounds of someone breaking in, maybe just sounds the house made, or maybe monsters sleuthing their way upstairs to kill me. Whatever made those noises I did not want to meet, so I went downstairs to the kitchen, took the biggest knife I could find, and hid in a kitchen cabinet. Once crouched down inside the cabinet I closed the doors behind me. I clutched the knife and just keenly listened, anticipating at any moment a creature, human or subhuman, opening the door, discovering me, and tearing me limb from limb. I stayed like that for hours until I heard the key in the front door and my parents' voices. I opened the cabinet doors wide enough so they would notice me. When they saw me hiding there with the knife my mother asked, "What are you doing?" Then my father told me, "Put the knife back where you found it and go to bed." I went upstairs to my bedroom, got under the covers, and tried to sleep. Those terrifying feelings were not reasoned out; they were put on hold for another night. The only sense of relief I had was that now if a monster showed up, he would surely attack my parents first and maybe be full after eating them. We never talked about that night; to them it was normal, as if every child terrifies themselves and hides away with a weapon. Time after time I had to defend and console myself in whatever way possible.

I began life as a gentle soul. I know this because when I was around nine or ten years old, I was in my backyard dribbling my basketball from hand to hand, my mind blank, l saw out of the corner of my eye three teenage boys walking toward me. They were walking with a purpose, one foot in front of the other, staring straight at me. Without missing a beat they started pushing me around. They were saying something like, "Come on you little punk, put up your fists." As I put up my fists to fight, I felt tears on my face and my eyes got bleary. There was a sadness that overtook me. I was prepared to fight and get hurt, but at the same time I was saddened because I didn't know these kids or why they wanted to beat me up.

Those boys punched me a few times in the face. I covered my head and fell to the ground, curling up to protect as much of me as possible. They punched and kicked my body for a while and then went on their way. I was glad when they left. I knew street fighting. What had happened to me was nothing compared to what could have happened. I had watched fights many times on the street corners, at playgrounds, and at school. The street fighters in my neighborhood were well known. They were feared and respected.

Howard Ash was notorious for starting the bloodiest fights in the neighborhood. At seventeen, he was one of the oldest kids and always wore the same worn down boots and black jeans. Street fighting was a sport in my neighborhood, like a boxing match without any rules. A crowd gathered at the usual place on top of the hill, waiting for the fight to begin. Grown men, teenagers, and a few younger kids stood in a circle. Howard would fight another teenager who also had a reputation for being violent. The fight began with the two of them threatening each other with insults and profanities. The crowd grew as people walking by stopped to watch. They were both circling each other when suddenly Howard rushed in and kicked the other kid in the balls.

As the kid bent over in pain, he kneed him in the face, causing him to fall to the ground. Then he got on top of him and knelt just below his shoulders to keep his arms pinned down. He punched him repeatedly in the same eye until it was swollen shut, then the other eye. You could hear his fists pounding the guys face in. Then he reached over and picked up what looked like a rusty old tire iron and, with the full force of his upper body smashed it down on the guy's shoulder. You could hear the crack of a bone breaking. As Howard got off him, the guy rolled over, grabbing his shoulder with the arm that still worked. Howard stood over him as the guy stumbled to his feet. His face looked like a bloody piece of meat and you could tell he was in severe pain as he stumbled away. The fight lasted less than fifteen minutes. I felt tense watching and was hoping one of the adults would stop the fight but they didn't.

I observed the technical skills Howard used to dominate the fight thinking *I will fight like that if I ever have to.* Growing up in my neighborhood, if someone insulted you verbally or physically, you had to deal with it straight away or you would be considered weak. Being Jewish automatically made me an outsider and a target for abuse. There were no rules in a fistfight. The winner was decided when the loser was too hurt to fight any more. You could try to hide in the shadows and avoid as many confrontations as possible, and that's what I did.

Rabbi Shlomo Margolis was the head rabbi of my *shul*, the Hebrew word for temple. I went there every Saturday morning for services until my bar mitzvah. Congregation Chai Odom was an orthodox Jewish congregation. The men wore black suits, black hats, and black shoes. The women were not allowed to sit with the men so they sat upstairs. During the service the men davened, rocking back and forth reading from the Torah out loud in Hebrew. I recited the words even though I had no idea what they meant. After the service I would go with the Rabbi to his house along with other members of the congregation and hang out with his family. He lived on the same street as I did three houses down. I was accepted as part of his family and tried to fit in. His sons went to a private Hebrew academy. My family was the only one in the congregation that was not Orthodox. The boys and men sat in his living room while the girls and women prepared food in the kitchen.

The irony was that my mother never went to *shul* and my father only on high holidays, so I walked there alone most of the time. If you were to ask my parents, "Do you believe in God?" They would answer, "No, we believe in Mother Nature." Why I had to go there every Saturday morning was beyond me. I had this double life. On Saturdays I would be a good Jewish kid and every other day of the week I was out on the street, getting into fights, playing basketball, not interested in school.

I went to Hebrew school every day after school. As a Jewish boy I was supposed to learn enough Hebrew to be able to read from the Torah at my Bar Mitzvah. When I turned thirteen, I would become a man based on Jewish Law. The best part of Hebrew school for me was my teacher Miss Bernstein. She wore skirts short enough so that when she crossed her legs you could see that space between her legs where her panties were drawn tightly. Sometimes I would drop my pencil to get a better look, taking a mental snapshot. When I got older I would revisit those images as an erotic fantasy with Miss Bernstein as the star.

My grandfather died penniless. He was a socialist. Eugene Debbs, American union leader and one of the founding members of the Industrial Workers of the World, was his hero. He and my Uncle Harry owned a bookstore on Beacon Street in Boston. They wanted the local factory workers to learn how to read, so they were willing to sell them the books for eight cents that had cost them ten. My grandfather believed that you could not have a democracy with an illiterate populous.

Making money was never important to my grandfather. To offset his cost he also had a rare and collectible book business that was somewhat profitable. He was known at the City Room of the *Boston Globe* as the little man with the two satchels of books and periodicals perpetually tucked under his arms, a familiar and reliable sight.

Grandpa was a self-described orator and to me he was an eloquent speaker. My mother was disgusted by his self-involvement. Before every meal Grandpa would stand up and make a speech while my mother sat drooling waiting to eat. She also hated the fact that he was always broke and depended on my father to help him out.

He taught me to play chess. He would sit there smoking a cigar, explaining the history of the game and the strategies involved in winning. I remember one game when I was down to one pawn, one knight, and my king. He turned the board around, played my pieces, and won the game. He proved he could win even with a weak position. I learned never to give up, no matter what the odds were against you.

My grandfather took me to the movies on Sundays. We never saw comedies or adventure movies a kid would like. They had to be serious or have a message. Once he took me to see *Spartacus*, about an enslaved soldier who is forced to be a gladiator, played by Kirk Douglas. He was known as a champion of the poor, and rebelled against the Roman ruling class. After Spartacus had killed his opponent in a gladiator fight, a slave girl is thrown into his cell as a reward. Now he was put in the position of oppressor, the very principle he was fighting against; he was expected to rape her. It made me want to throw up. I had to close my eyes hoping he would do the right thing. Out of compassion he did not touch her, but instead became her friend. I was a relieved. At that age I wanted to believe in heroes.

That scene stayed with me for years. I still wondered why my grandfather would take a young kid to see such a violent movie. Years later I decided to look up some background on the movie and I found out that its screenwriter Dalton Trumbo had been blacklisted since 1946 for suspected Communist leanings and was one of the Hollywood Ten. President John F. Kennedy crossed picket lines to see the movie, helping to end blacklisting. The author of the novel on which it is based, Howard Fast, was also blacklisted, and originally had to self-publish it. That made all the sense in the world knowing my grandfather's politics. He probably took me to support his heroes, JFK and the blacklisted writers.

Some Sundays Grandpa and I would go to his favorite deli in the red light district of Boston. It would not be uncommon for some homeless person sitting on a doorstep to yell out, "Hey, Manny," as he was well known and respected in this lower class neighborhood. Most people in Dorchester aspired to be middle class and get out as soon as possible, but not him. He was right at home wherever he was. He could talk to anyone, Harvard Law School student or street hooker. Knowledge and wisdom were the only things that mattered to him. When he died the *Globe* did a big front page story on him. They wrote, "His books did more than is realized, perhaps to shape some reporter's career or influence his writing."

Being Jewish was very unpopular. Fortunately for me I did not look Jewish, and because I was athletic and mixed in with all the other kids, most people never suspected I was Jewish. I heard a lot of Jew jokes and just kept quiet. I never defended my heritage up until this one incident.

A group of Catholic boys saw me walking home wearing my yarmulke and ran after me. When they caught up to me, they asked me, "Why did you kill Christ?" Now, I'd never heard of Christ, so I had no idea what they were talking about. One of them took a long bicycle chain and wrapped it around my neck. He took off running, dragging me behind. An older guy nearby saw all this and yelled out "Hey, stop that!" They let me go and ran away.

The next time I saw my grandfather, I told him what had happened, that two of the kids were black and I had called them "niggers." He slapped me in the face and said a Jew must respect all races and religions. Jews had been persecuted throughout history and we had no right to be racist or bigoted. They had hurt me but I agreed with my grandfather. Even though I was outnumbered and they were the attackers, my grandfather focused on my racial slur being worse than their actions. I never forgot that lesson and made tolerance part of my code of ethics.

During my last year in middle school, I met Linda. She was outspoken and very cute, with blue eyes and black hair. I wanted to ask her out on a date, but she said she loved going to the movies, and I had no money for that. In those days the movies cost twenty-five cents and a bag of Wise potato chips five cents. There was no point in asking my mother for the money because she had always said no and looked at me as if I were stupid for asking. I was the only one of my friends who didn't have enough money to go to the movies or ask a girl out.

One day on the way home from school I found a silver necklace with a charm lying in the muddy street gutter. I polished it up carefully so it looked new. This was a real find. I had no money to buy Linda a present; the necklace gave me the opportunity to ask her to go steady. But I still had no money for a date. Out of frustration I decided to steal the money. There was no other way.

One afternoon while my mother and father were at work, I found the family money envelopes and slipped two dollars out of one. I put them back carefully, as if no one had touched them. But I knew when I got home my parents would find out. They kept track of every cent.

Off I went on my date to the movies and the neighborhood soda shop for ice cream sundaes. I felt on top of the world, happy, totally in the moment. As we walked toward her house, I pulled out the necklace and told her, "I have something for you." I handed it to her. She looked at it blankly. I was bewildered; the gift had no value to her. I felt all my efforts, stealing the money, planning a movie, polishing the necklace were not enough. This was not the reaction I was expecting. She kissed me anyway, but my mind was on the necklace. Up until that moment it was a fairy tale evening for me that I knew would end the second I got home. I never did ask Linda to go steady.

When I got home I knocked on the door. Both my parents were there to open it. My father was steaming. My mother didn't say anything other than "Go upstairs without dinner." Still cowering, I stood there and waited to hear what my father would say. He sent me to my room to think about what I had done. Later that night he came into my room with the metal filing box from which I had stolen the money. He opened it and took out the envelopes, which were labeled electricity, water, food, and other bills. There were dollar bills and change in each envelope. Then he explained to me in the calmest way he could that by stealing that money, I was taking family money needed to pay bills and save for the future. He also said "I am restraining myself. I am so mad I could kill you."

This was the first time I understood why we ate so little and never bought clothes that fit me. My dad was saving all his money so we could someday move to a better neighborhood. I already knew we were poor, I just didn't know how much it meant to him to save money. The irony for me was that if they ever did move to a better neighborhood, I did not know if I would go with them or not. I wasn't even sure if I would be invited, or if I wanted to. No one ever asked what I wanted. I never stole from them again.

In my parents own way frugality was their trade-off. By being so intent on a better future, they missed what was right in front of them and therefore did not take the time to be parents. This left a void in me where love and family should have been. What they did provide was just enough food to get by and a plan for what they wanted for a better future.

As I entered my teens, the neighborhood became more violent and rundown. There was a major exodus out of Dorchester by white families into the safer and more affluent suburbs around Boston. It was called "white flight." My family remained behind in the old neighborhood. The friends I grew up with, had all moved out and new people moved in. They were mostly black families and the kids were just like me only a different color. I had been a star basketball player in the white neighborhood but when my black friends enrolled in school and found the courts, the type of play changed from a passing game to a one-on-one confrontational game. It went from a team sport to a very personal competition. I adapted well. I liked their style. Like me, they had nothing else to do other than spend countless hours dribbling and shooting a basketball.

During the summer, we had a street league where players from all over the inner city came to play. I was the only white kid on my team. These games drew large crowds. Unlike white parents, the black parents were there every weekend talking trash about the players. I was known as a ball thief and when I blocked a pass or stole the ball they would yell at me "good hands." The Blue Hill Avenue basketball courts were made of old cracked cement. You had to learn to dribble around the cracks. The courts had a ten-foot-high chain-link fence around them, but the door was missing so you could come and go any time of day or night.

Pimps, drug addicts, and alcoholics used to hang around there, watching us play basketball and doing whatever else they were up to. We didn't want to know what they were up to because even if you looked at these guys they would come back with "What's wrong with you?" or "What the fuck are you looking at?" No matter, I often stayed late until the sun set and had to walk through an unlit pathway to Blue Hill Avenue. The early evening shadows made it hard to make out who was sitting on the park benches. I found many escape routes to get home and learned how to use everything from a hand-sized rock, rusty nail, or broken piece of glass as a weapon. If I were to have been attacked I was prepared to slash at the neck, nose, eyes, or ears of my attacker. To be mentally prepared, I would imagine being attacked and visualize what my defense would be. I kept those images with me while walking home until I was in the front door. You could not relax or take anything for granted. Without an edge you were vulnerable.

I spent a lot of time on the basketball courts but I really needed a way to earn spending money. All the other kids' parents gave them money for candy bars, cold drinks, and bus fare. I had no allowance, not even a dime from my parents. I had to find work even though at age twelve I wasn't old enough to have a real job.

I tried to get work at the Franklin Park Community Golf Course. I stayed away from the first hole where the manager's crew, all over sixteen, picked up their customers. I would go to the second hole and ask the golfers if they needed me to carry their golf bags for them. Sometimes I made three dollars a day, but that was rare. Usually they just said no in different ways—they would ignore me, look the other way, or say "You're too small." Or they would ask "How old are you?" I would say to myself, *These clowns have to be posers. Look at them wearing white shoes, plaid pants, and pink shirts.* Think about it, to get here you had to drive through a neighborhood of poverty. The people who actually lived around here couldn't even afford to buy golf balls, never mind the outfits, the green fees and clubs. I resented this display of arrogance. It was disrespectful. There weren't many places where city blocks had been turned into green lawns for a golf course and naturally reserved for those who could afford the privilege.

I finally found a job at the local drugstore in charge of the soda counter. I got paid under the table in quarters because I was underage. I made tuna sandwiches on toasted white bread and served all kinds of drinks, ice cream floats, sundaes, and banana splits. When there were no customers I stuffed myself on tuna sandwiches and drank vanilla cokes. Sundays were the busiest day for me. Sometimes as many as ten people would be sitting at my counter, so I made sure to feed myself before the crowd arrived.

I was also in charge of a counter with magazines and sundries for sale. One Sunday a man came up to my counter and asked me "Where are the prophylactics?" I relayed the question to the pharmacist behind his counter, yelling it across the crowded store. The man looked at me like I was a jerk and walked out. The pharmacist came over and took me aside, saying that if anyone asks that question again just walk over to him and repeat it quietly.

I saved up enough money to buy a squirt gun that shot around corners, something my parents would never have bought for me. When school started again I had to give up that job, and the free food that went with it.

My sister and I went to Sarah Greenwood Elementary School from kindergarten until fifth grade. Although I could have started school a year later my parents wanted both of us out of the house at the same time. When seat assignments were made or crayons passed out, I was always last. That's what happens when your last name begins with a "V" and you're the youngest and smallest kid in the class. So I always ended up in the back row or stuck with the crayon colors no one else wanted. Year after year that routine was repeated. In fourth grade math class I was sitting in the last seat of the last row of desks, daydreaming. I was wearing baggy blue jeans and I felt a throbbing coming from my penis. I felt it grow and get hard. I never had that happen before and wasn't sure what would happen next. Just at that moment the teacher called my name to come up to the front of the class and solve a math problem on the blackboard. I was caught off guard and made believe I did not hear her. But she persisted, so I grabbed my notebook, stood up, casually covered my erection with the notebook, and walked to the blackboard. It was an awkward moment; my hard-on persisted. I picked up a piece of chalk in one hand and solved the math problem while my other hand held the notebook over my crotch. I walked back to my seat the same way. When I sat back down the erection was gone and my penis went back to just being there.

I noticed while having this erection that the swelling felt good. It was as if my penis was trying to point me in a direction that it wanted to go. There was so much power down there. It just took over. On the way home from school I described what had happened to one of my friends. He had an older brother who had taught him how to jerk off. His suggestion was to take a bath at night, lock the bathroom door, fill the tub with warm water, soap up your dick, and rub it up and down until you ejaculate. The bath scene was so you would not get caught doing it in your room. I took him up on that idea. I took a bath every night after that and if no one was home I could be found in the bathtub at any time of day. My middle school was in Mattapan, a short bus ride up Blue Hill Avenue or a forty-five-minute uphill walk from my house. On one side of the hill was a dirt trail littered with rusted out tire rims, old washing machines, and dirty magazines. The magazines were moldy and covered with red ants and who knows what else. I tried to open one to look at the dirty pictures but the pages stuck together.

There were always fights and sometimes rapes right after school. When school was over we were supposed to go out the front door and then down the hill to get the bus or walk home, but if you walked this way, down the hill there was an area where daily fights took place. A small group of older boys, the ones that had been held back a school year, were the ringleaders and randomly chose two boys whom they would bully into fighting each other.

My first experience as a participant in this form of ghetto entertainment came as I was walking down the hill carrying my books.

Boys and girls from my class and others I didn't know, white and black, stood around in a circle. As I approached, two of the older boys, the Kelly brothers, grabbed me and pushed me into the middle of the circle. Then they randomly grabbed a kid named Joseph Podeko, who was overweight and taller than me. They pushed him into the middle of the circle with me. I just stood there holding my schoolbooks. The crowd was heckling Podeko, spurring him on, and shouting "Hit him!" So he came up to me and knocked my books down. I just stood there. I was no stranger to fighting. I just chose not to be part of the zoo. The crowd continued its jeering. Not knowing what to do, Podeko pushed me. One of the rules of respect I formed for myself was that if you touch me, you'd better kill me. So I put up my fists and started boxing, I kept punching him in the left eye and avoiding his flailing arms. I could tell he did not know how to fight. He kept his fists by his waist, leaving his head unprotected. A part of me felt sorry for him. The crowd wouldn't let us out of the circle until they got what they wanted, blood. We boxed for about ten minutes. His face was bleeding. He fell on his knees and started crying. I picked up my books and went home. From that point on, I never went out the school's front door. After school was out I would wait and exit through the gym down the back trail to Blue Hill Avenue. I don't have any warm feelings or fond memories of middle school, but I do have one memory that I will never forget.

One day after gym class I was going to the boy's locker room. From the showers, I heard a whimpering sound, like a dog begging not to be hit any more. I looked over and saw three older boys raping a younger boy. One was fucking his ass while another fucked his mouth. Then they just took turns on him. He was a soft kid. I had seen him around but never really talked to him. I remember his round freckled face to this day. I thought I should go get a teacher to stop this, but knew that was useless. The teachers were afraid of the students, especially the older boys. They tried to have as little contact with us as possible. The unspoken rule was that we had our society

they had theirs. Then I thought maybe I should try to stop this myself, but I didn't. The scene was so horrific to me I became frozen in
fear, so I just left. I saw him at school periodically and could not look
at him. I felt badly for him and understood that it could have happened to any of us. The boys who did this knew to pick on the
weaker kids. They just had an instinct for who would not fight back.

I did, however, get into a fight later with one of his attackers. This
jack-off carried a switchblade knife to school with him. He was two
years older than the rest of us because he kept getting held back year
after year. My desk was in the back row of the class. After class ended,
while getting up from my seat he walked up behind me and grabbed
me in a bear hug, I felt an insane rage come over me. With my arms
pinned and feet off the floor, I did the only thing I could do. I placed
both my feet against the wall and pushed us both backwards onto the
floor. I landed on top of him. Then I punched his face in an uncon-
trollable fast-paced attack. I wanted justice and not only to pay him
back for the raping of that kid, but to make him pay for all the wrong
in this world I had seen from the second I opened my eyes. It took
three of his friends to pull me off him. His face was all bloody and he
and his little rapist pals had nothing to say.

Sometimes after middle school I would go to the Blue Hill Avenue pool hall. It was on my way home from school or to the basketball courts and a convenient place to hang out. This pool hall had
candlestick bowling and a back room with pool tables and pictures of
naked woman on the walls. The men sat around card tables playing
poker and cribbage while smoking cigars. The air was always dense
with smoke and the smell of stale beer. The characters there were
loan sharks and bookies.

One day while in the pool hall one of these men asked me if I
wanted to play eight ball for fifty dollars. Gus was about six-foot four-
inches tall and weighed more than two hundred pounds including his
protruding beer belly. I told him I did not have fifty dollars so he said,
"How about if you win, I give you fifty dollars. If you lose we call it

even." I agreed to those terms and we shook hands. I won the game, at which point he pulled two twenties and a ten out of his pocket and said "If you can take this, it's yours." Of course, I could not take it. He was bigger and stronger than me and he was surrounded by his crew. I learned it was not good enough to win or earn money. You needed some kind of leverage to collect it.

Now, I arrived at that conclusion by myself at around age twelve. It was the beginning of a set of rules that I taught myself for survival. I had no adult to talk to or trust, so I took control. I couldn't wait to get out of middle school and away from all that madness.

The next year I went to Boston Technical High School, an all-boys school. In 1963, the Boston school system determined by the time you were in middle school which high school would suit your aptitude. I guess they thought I wasn't a candidate for higher learning. I took the train or bus to high school. My entire experience there could be summed up by saying that in my first week in high school a teacher was thrown out a fourth floor window by some students.

I made it onto the freshman basketball team. Our coach liked to throw basketballs at our heads during layup practice and while we were running floor drills. There was nothing to be done about that since more than three hundred kids had tried out for the team and you could be replaced in a minute. So I would mutter under my breath "asshole" when a basketball hit me in the face. We were state champions that year. The following summer our star basketball player, Marshall Lewis, got stabbed to death after a schoolyard game. He could have had a great future, but not in Dorchester, where instead he was killed at such a young age.

When I wanted to practice my basketball shots, I would go over to the state mental hospital courts behind my old house on Lorne Street. I would often be the only one on the courts. One afternoon after shooting by myself for a while, I was sitting on the lawn under a tree.

A woman patient, looking to be about thirty-five years old came up and sat on the grass next to me and said, "You are my favorite."

I said, "Thank you."

That's when she unzipped my pants, pulled my cock out, and jerked me off. I looked from a distance at this happening and thought to myself how bizarre it was, and then I came, and liked it. So there you have it: an older woman forcing herself on a twelve-year-old. At that age I had no idea what to think. I was ashamed but felt I did nothing wrong, so I buried the feeling of shame. Another rule I formed was that if something felt good, it did not matter where the source of enjoyment came from and that it was better to bury a feeling than wander around with a painful feeling in your gut.

Besides basketball, I would find all kinds of dangerous adventures around the neighborhood. In the winter, I sledded down steep hills standing up and when I hit a cross street where cars drove by I would lie down and try to go under them. I rode my bicycle through alleys and gang-infested dead end streets. One time I drove my bicycle off a ten-foot hill into open space to see if, when I landed, I could keep riding without falling. Instead, I got a concussion—or think I did. A side of me knew no fear, or maybe it was all of me, or maybe I just didn't care if I got hurt.

One day while walking home I got beat up pretty badly and had some teeth knocked out. My mother saw me come in with a bloody mouth and immediately blamed me for starting a fight when I hadn't even told her what had happened yet. This was a ritual between my mother and me. Whenever I told her about how I got hurt or that I was afraid of someone or something she would tell me it was my imagination or that I was just lying. I decided not to tell her anything anymore. She could not be trusted. My dad traveled during the week and when he got home he pretty much hung out with my mother. He only heard second hand from my mother the troubles I had gotten into that week.

When I was around twelve my parents sent me to a Boy Scout camp in New Hampshire. They dropped me off at the meeting place where there was a bus full of other kids going to the same camp. I was the youngest kid there and this was my first time away from home on my own. This became evident when we all were assigned tents each with four cots. We were told to change our clothes to go for a hike. In the tent the other boys just stripped right there in front of me and changed. I noticed they all had pubic hair and I had none. So I put on my raincoat and changed under the raincoat. The scout leader in charge of our group noticed what I was doing and asked me what was wrong. I did not answer. My punishment for not answering him and for being shy was instead of going with the other boys on the hike I had to stay behind in just my undershorts and clean the latrine. This punishment was designed to establish the pecking order. He was the boss. I got eaten alive by hoards of mosquitos and was never shy again.

I did not get the Boy Scout thing at all. I hated the great outdoors; I was a city kid. In the morning, dew covered the tent and sleeping bag. It made your clothes and skin feel wet and sticky. I was probably the worst Boy Scout ever to go to that camp. I found myself wandering off, ignoring the other kids, and just finding things to do by myself until the two weeks were up. That was my last experience as a Boy Scout.

The next summer I was sent to a Jewish camp. That was more to my liking. I was a star athlete there, maybe the only one who could run fast, catch a ball, and dive into the lake. The kids fit the image of the stereotypical unathletic Jewish boy perfectly. One day when we were playing softball, the ball was hit high into the outfield. The center fielder was wearing thick glasses, a baseball cap that was too big for his head, and moved clumsily. Well, he got under the ball okay, but when it came down he put his glove up hesitantly, missed the ball, and it knocked him on the head. It was so hilarious that I couldn't stop laughing. Well, I got into trouble for that. We went swimming every day in the lake, well, if you could call it swimming. The camp counselor would try to teach the kids how to dive off the dock only four inches off the water with little success. Sadly, they hit the water one after the other, on their stomachs, backs, in any position other than headfirst.

The girls' camp was on the other side of the lake. They would row their canoes over to our side for girls against boys softball games. Our team was so pitiful, the girls won. Once again I got eaten alive by mosquitos. When my parents picked me up from the bus, my mother noticed I was swollen with mosquito bites. She asked me "What did you do to yourself?" implying that I must have made the mosquitos bite me so I could come home looking pathetic. I just didn't answer.

My parents wanted me to have a normal life, be a Boy Scout, go to camp, get along with other kids. No doubt I fought that.

That was my last camp experience. The next summer I started hitchhiking out to Wolliston Beach. One day I met a girl there. She was sitting on the sand by herself and I was sitting beside her. Jewel Davies was my age with straight long red hair and a freckled face. She had an athletic body with breasts that looked a little too big for her frame. Nothing wrong with that I thought. She caught me looking at her and introduced herself. We sat and talked for a while. She lived in Quincy, a short walk to the beach. After about an hour talking in the sun she said "I have to go. Do you want to come over to my house?" I had no plans, so I said "Sure."

We walked to Jewel's house, an old Cape Cod white shingled home with a manicured lawn and a big tree in front. She asked me to wait outside while she changed and then we could take a walk. After about an hour she came out. She told me her parents were home and she did not want to bring me in to meet them so she suggested going to a place where she often hung out with her friends at an old cemetery. It was just a few blocks walk away through a very rich and safe neighborhood. The cemetery looked more like an arboretum. I could have moved in there. It was beautiful—tall trees, freshly cut grass, and fountains. I thought the dead people were lucky to be buried here. We found a big tree and sat down beside each other. She reached over and kissed me on the lips. Just like magic my penis started throbbing and grew, telling my brain that Jewel knew what to do with it. I kissed her back and felt her tongue in my mouth, so I did the same to her. This went on for a painfully long time. My cock kept telling me to move her hand onto it, but I was not sure how to do that. Should I just ask her or should I subtly move her hand there to show her it was okay to touch it? All these thoughts were going through my mind while we were kissing. Nothing more happened. She had to go home, so we made plans to meet at the beach the next day and then walk back to the cemetery to hang out.

I hitchhiked back home and immediately took a bath. Why not? I had to get the sand off of me. I wanted to talk to an adult male about my dilemma but I didn't know one I could trust with the subject, so I would have to solve this puzzle by myself. I thought back to the older woman at the asylum who jerked me off, to the rapes I had seen, and to my own masturbation in the bathtub. None of these experiences helped me understand if Jewel wanted to help me figure out what it was my cock wanted. The very sight of her gave me an erection, so she had something to do with this and I had to find out what. I met her at the beach the next day and the same scenario played out, a lot of kissing and me leaving with a pulsating cock. We continued to meet like that for a couple of weeks, always with the same ending. I liked her. She was smart and funny. She liked me. She said her favorite part of me was my stomach muscles. I had never noticed them before because any thoughts about my stomach were focused on how hungry I always felt.

I would think about Jewel constantly—what would her bare breasts look like? How would they feel? What was hidden under her panties? Why was I so driven to find out? When I didn't have an erection, all these questions had logical answers. When I did have an erection, she seemed to be the solution. I knew I would not be an aggressor. I had seen girls attacked and forced into sexual acts and I hated that. I could imagine how that might feel and I would never do that to another human being. That became my lifelong code toward women. So I had to communicate my sexual needs to her and let her volunteer to meet them. She could volunteer by telling me what she would do, or she could just do it; either way was fine. I had to get past this nonstop kissing routine.

Jewel invited me to the movies one hot summer afternoon. She said, "We don't have to watch the movie. It will be dark and cool."

I said okay and off we went. In those days you could see a double feature for the price of one, so we would have plenty of time. Jewel was wearing a skirt and I wore jeans. We sat down in the theatre and immediately started kissing. The theatre was dark and no one was sitting around us. After a while I felt her hand on the outside of my jeans rubbing back and forth. I noticed her legs were open so I put my hand on her thigh and moved it up. I felt a thick garment under her dress—not what I thought I would feel. She was wearing a girdle! It was so tight I could not fit my fingers under it so I just rubbed the fabric covering the space between her legs and it went on that way through the end of the second movie. On my way home I thought this is progress. Somehow it dawned on me she didn't know what she was doing any more than I did. I had assumed she had the answers, but by her actions she was as inexperienced as I was. I went to the beach a few days later and saw her sitting cozily on a blanket next to a slightly older guy. Immediately I assumed that he was her real boyfriend and my heart sank. I thought to myself there must have been something wrong with me—I was too young or didn't have any money. Whatever the reason, girls were certainly a mystery. We would be moving to Norwood soon and surely I would meet a girl there. This was just practice and now I am experienced.

Dorchester would not let go of me easily. Just before moving out of the neighborhood, I experienced one last horrifying degradation. While hitchhiking, I was picked up by a plumber in an old white van. We were headed in the direction of my house when he suddenly turned into a wooded area. I knew instinctively he was a dangerous man—big, unshaven, with muscular arms. Being a street smart kid, I looked for ways out of the van. He parked the van, got out, and walked around to the passenger door. With one arm he reached over and grabbed mine, pulling me out of the passenger seat. I thought of running but he stayed close to me. I knew I had to play this out to survive. He forced me down on the ground and sucked my dick until I came. I made my body limp as if I were dead. I was surprised that my cock got hard and I ejaculated. It was as if my penis was not part of me but acted on its own. I was ashamed of that, I felt like he got his way even though I had shut down. His parting words were "Isn't this better than a woman?"

I vowed in my mind that I would someday torture him by hammering a copper pipe up his ass then insert barbed wire. I would pull the barbed wire out slowly and as he screamed and bled and bled, then I would kill him. These thoughts of revenge kept me sane. The rage of what had happened stayed with me. I never told anyone about it. As years went by, the actual event disappeared from my conscious mind manifesting itself in paranoia. If a man, any man, touched me in any way, even a friendly slap on the back, I cringed and often reacted in a violent way. I learned to profile men by their size and strength to determine if they were a danger to me. This fear-driven caution of large men lasted throughout my life. I kept men who were bigger than me at an arm's length. I did not mind a handshake, but a hug was out of the question. Years later, when I was in therapy the memory of the plumber resurfaced. I told my dad what had happened. He said "You should not have been hitchhiking." I wanted him to say "If I had been there I would have protected you."

My father was the middle child, with a younger brother and an older sister. His brother became a lawyer who eventually defended Jack Ruby as part of the JFK assassination trial, and shortly thereafter died of alcoholism. His sister had four children. Her marriage ended in divorce and her children were put into foster care. No one in my family was willing to take them in.

I didn't know much about my father's family or how he grew up until his ninetieth birthday. I traveled up to Boston for the party and spent the weekend. We had not spent much time together over the years, let alone talk about family issues or questions I had about our lives together. One evening he told me his family was poor and his mother strict. One time his mother gave him some money and a list of groceries to buy at the local store. He had some money left over so he bought himself a few pieces of penny candy. When he got home his mother counted the change and asked where the rest was, when he told her about the candy she beat him with an ironing cord and scolded him for being so frivolous with money. My dad never volunteered much information about his growing up, but I could finally see where his tightness about money came from. I saw where he got his values about money and food, which later became his code.

My dad left home when he was eighteen years old by enlisting in the army. He was stationed in Manchester, England during the end of the Second World War. While working on an airplane, the engine blew up permanently damaging his left eye. When my father got out of the Army he sold window displays to department stores. The sales territory he was assigned by his company was all of New England, so he traveled a lot. When he was home he went out to play cards with his friends one night a week and went to the racetrack every Saturday. I watched him more than I talked to or spent time with him. Growing up I have almost no memories of us being together as father and son. I remember being afraid of him, as he seemed unpredictable and angry, always on the verge of going off.

I would like to describe more of my feelings and experiences with my dad but they just don't exist. Years later, out of the blue he said "I never took you to a baseball game or out fishing. I never liked sports." He said that to me in a matter of fact way with no remorse, expecting me to react, but I said nothing. Really, what would you say to that?

My father had told me I was a mistake. "We planned on having your sister. You came too soon." I don't remember exactly when he told me that but I do remember feeling alone at that moment. I wanted to undo that feeling but was never able to shake it. It got buried deep in my subconscious along with all the other hollow, dark memories and feelings.

My father's upbringing taught him to be the father he was. He had been raised in poverty. He did not want that for himself or for my mother so he worked hard, saved his money, and finally was able to achieve his goal of getting out of Dorchester.

THREE

Acting Middle Class

My dad bought us a three-bedroom ranch style house with a big yard in Norwood, a suburb thirty minutes outside Boston. I had my own room with a built-in desk. At first, I hated it there—the suburbs where quiet; there were no black kids; everyone seemed so orderly and neatly dressed. There were different rules to learn, codes of conduct for the middle class. Instead of settling differences with a fistfight you had to be slippery and talk your way to a victory. For me it was too late to learn all that. It seemed to me they all were weak. My parents were more comfortable living in the suburbs. I could tell by the way they relaxed with each other on the living room sofa watching television. In my family we all had separate lives. My sister and I never hung out together. Whatever was going on at work with my Dad he kept to himself. Whatever my mother was feeling she never talked about. I lived my life as if I was parenting myself.

I spent my junior and senior years at Norwood High School. My parents thought it would be a refuge from the chaos of Dorchester. Unlike Boston Tech, it was co-ed. During my first week at school I was walking down the hall to my next class, watching all the cute new girls walk by.

The school principle saw me and said, "We know your type. What are you grinning at?"

I answered, "Just enjoying the view."

He said, "We will be watching you." I kept walking wondering what his problem was. I was used to a tough life and had never been disciplined for just looking at someone. I made my own rules, lived my own life, and was not able to adjust, to just flip a switch and be like the white middle-class kids. I was not a good student. The only subject I paid attention to was math. The rest of the curriculum such as History, English, or Sociology had nothing that I could see was useful or would translate into money. So it was just a waste of time.

I made a few good friends at Norwood High, including my best friend Eric. We had the same sense of humor and were immediately comfortable being around each other. I met him walking to school. He lived a few blocks from me and we took the same street to school. Eric was one of the popular kids—six-foot-three with straight blonde hair, blue eyes, and a star on the football team. During a game Eric tackled a player breaking the kid's leg. After that Eric quit the team. He was a sensitive person who felt bad hurting someone else. His parents were great. There was always plenty of food at his house. His dad got us part-time jobs working at Prudential Insurance Company after school. We were filing clerks, but really did nothing. When we clocked in we were given boxes of files. We were supposed to file them in alphabetical order in a wall of filing cabinets. Instead we just took them in bulk out of the boxes and put them in one filing cabinet, then went to the back room to snooze.

On Christmas Eve in my senior year, Eric's family invited me to Midnight Mass. They walked into the church and sat in front. Eric and I sat in the back row. I wondered if I was being unfaithful to my Jewish heritage by being there. So when the congregation got on their knees to pray, I did not. Jews were not allowed to kneel down to pray. After the prayers and the sermon, the congregation all broke out in song. In my temple the songs were sung in Hebrew, but these were sung in English. I loved the singing and joined in during one song that sounded like "Star in the East." People turned to look at me like I was doing something wrong. This was my first time singing in public, and I guess I was too loud and pretty bad at it. Eric told me to quiet down, and later his parents said my singing was off key. I didn't feel bad about it though because I was feeling the music and honestly trying my best.

During our senior year we were going to a dance at a neighboring high school. I picked Eric up in my mother's dark blue Chevrolet Impala, along with four of our friends. We had a good time at the dance flirting with girls and clowning around. It was the middle of winter and the roads were icy. On the way home I was driving down a dark street when I smashed into a black Cadillac parked in a driveway half way out onto the street. When I hit the parked car my head smashed into the steering wheel. There were three of us in the front seat and three in the back. After checking that everyone else was all right I got out of the car and walked up the driveway to the house and knocked on the door. The owner of the car opened the door saw my face covered in blood and asked if I was all right. I was worried my parents would blame me and be furious so I asked him "What kind of an idiot would leave their car parked halfway out on the street?" He seemed more concerned about my bloody face than the cars. My friends came in and he called their parents, arranging to have them picked up. I would not let him call my parents or take me to the hospital, but I cleaned up the blood from my face in his bathroom. I had a cut on my forehead and my eye was swollen. I asked him to drive me home since I had to explain this to my parents in person.

He drove me to my house and we walked up the driveway and knocked on the door. My mother opened the door and asked, "Where's my car?"

I answered, "I totaled it."

My father then got up off the couch and asked, "Are you hurt?"

Blood was starting to drip down my face again, but I said, "No. I am sorry about the car."

The owner of the car was standing in the doorway and he chimed in that it was his fault for leaving his black Cadillac halfway out on the street. He and my father talked for a while about reporting the accident. I did not say anything else since I was getting dizzy and wanted to lie down. I went to my room and fell asleep. We never talked about it again. My mother got a new car but I was not allowed to drive it. My father told me I had to get my own car.

So I bought a broken down 1953 red Volkswagen bus for seventy-five dollars. I fixed it up with the little money I had and help from my friends. We got the engine working most of the time and built a bed and a counter with space for a small refrigerator. The outside was pretty rusty—nothing could be done about that—but at least I had a car of my own. I loved that bus even though it broke down almost every time I drove it.

There was a group of kids who didn't like me. I'm not sure why, maybe because I was Jewish. When I was presented with my varsity letters in basketball and track, this group booed. Even though I had made some friends in the past two years and tried to fit in, I started to get the same feeling in Norwood that I had in Dorchester. I just did not belong there either.

Dorchester had been tough to survive in. Physically, you needed a constant edge to keep you away from danger. I saw my future as a hardened man, trapped by poverty. Norwood, on the other hand, was physically safe but I felt like a stranger most of the time. I was very different from the other kids. They had no edge. They were childlike and comfortable and they had never had to defend themselves or live every day in fear.

Delores and I met at a dance in Walpole at the high school gym. She had a bubbly personality and spoke with a Southern accent. She had long black hair and dark eyes. We danced together and talked about her move from Louisiana to Massachusetts. Delores said I was the first boy she had met since coming to Walpole. At the end of the night I asked her out on a date for that Friday night.

I picked her up at her house and we went to the drive-in movies. That was the first of many weekend evenings I spent with her. We were always in the car either at the drive-in movie theatre or in the Friendly's restaurant parking lot. In 1966, "parking" was a teenager's national pastime. The car was the only place to be alone to make out. The parking lot at Friendly's was full of cars moving up and down with steamy windows. Boys were eagerly trying to unlock the key to the girl's willingness to get them off. Delores was not shy about it.

From our first date she gave me a hand job and continued this ritual on every date. She was so comfortable with my cock in her hand I knew she was more experienced than I was.

One Friday night my parents and sister were out. The house was empty. I was not allowed to bring friends over to my house. My mom was put out by teenage male energy. But this was one of those times I was willing to risk being caught. If I were to be caught my defense would be "Delores is not a guy." Then my mother would just shake her head in disgust and walk away. I knew I had only about a one-hour window before anyone would come home so I whisked Delores into the house right to the couch. We started kissing and in no time she had my cock in her hand. Then she laid down on the couch, pulled her skirt up, and her panties off. She laid there on her back with her legs open. I thought I knew what to do but just froze looking at her. She said "Hurry up." So I lay on top of her and tried to fit my cock into her vagina. I couldn't quite get it in and I started to enter the wrong hole, at which point she used her hand to guide me. After about ten seconds inside of her I came. Wow, that felt great. My body instantly relaxed. I had no thoughts, no emotions. I was calm, sleepy. Delores got up and went into the bathroom, panties in hand. My cock finally relaxed and I pulled my pants up. The relaxed feeling started to drift away as the reality set in that we'd better get out of my house before we got caught.

Delores and I dated through my senior year in high school. We had sex every time the opportunity presented itself. She seemed to like it, but she never asked me to do anything to please her. I wondered why. Maybe she had dated an older guy in Louisiana and he taught her how to please a man and she never expected anything for herself. I began to think sex was a selfish act. Each party had to ask for what they wanted from the other person. If they didn't ask for something, they got nothing.

I went to the senior prom with Delores. After the prom, all the seniors still dressed in prom attire went to the Friendly's parking lot. We were standing around and this kid from the hockey team came over to me and said "Did you fuck her? I did." I punched him in the face, put my fists down, and told him to walk away. Instead he punched me back on the chin. His punch was so weak I could not believe it actually landed. I told him that was a mistake and belted him a few times in the face and kidneys. Somehow he fell down and broke his leg. So the next day I was called to the principal's office. His parents were there, threatening to sue my parents and just raging on me. Nothing more happened but the white "wannabe" gang kids started to like me and invited me to hang with them and drink beer. I did not. These guys would not last five minutes in Dorchester.

During the summer before my senior year, I ran away from home late one afternoon, thinking I'd go back to Boston where I fit in better. I left my VW bus in the driveway, filled my empty guitar case with clothes, and took off on foot. My father found me on the road and told me to get into the car. For the first time I saw him cry. He was very sad. He had worked so hard to get us out of the ghetto into suburbia and I was rejecting it. He said "You have a beautiful room. Why are you leaving?" I said nothing but I knew it was too late. I did not care about a room. I wanted to be an accepted part of a family or community or, for that matter, by anyone to feel appreciated, a sense of belonging. But that time was over. I went back home with him but my heart was cold—I felt nothing. This became my tool for survival. I felt like I was made of stone, totally without emotion.

FOUR

Summer in Boston

fter graduating from high school in 1967, I applied to Cape Cod Community College and was accepted, as was every other lousy student who could not get into a four-year college. That summer before college began, I moved out of my house in Norwood to Boston. I rented a one-bedroom apartment in the slum with three other friends. We lived on the top floor of the five-story building. We put bunk beds in the bedroom and a stereo in the living room. We used to blast music, get stoned, and go up to the rooftop of the building and listen to the tunes as they traveled up our fireplace through the chimney to the roof.

One day when we came home our door was open and the stereo gone. There were a lot of junkies in that neighborhood so we assumed one of them stole it. We pooled our money and got another stereo. About two weeks later our door was kicked in and the second stereo was gone.

My roommates were suburban kids who were not used to living in such squalid surroundings, so they packed up and went home to their parents' houses. That was it for me. I wanted to hurt the junkie who was stealing from me. I put the door back on one hinge and waited for dark. Around seven p.m. in walks the junkie hoping to steal yet a third stereo. He was a skinny, tall white kid with a chain hanging from his belt loop to the pocket in his jeans. So I said to him "Hey, fuckface, where's the money from the stereos you stole?" He gave me the finger, at which point we were wrestling and pushing each other. Somehow in the struggle he fell out the open window.

37

About twenty minutes later an ambulance came and took him away. I thought I might end up in a fistfight to get my stereo or money. I had no intention of wanting him get hurt that bad. From that point on I became more controlled about how I sought revenge.

The other memorable incident that summer happened as I was walking late one night through Boston Commons. On my way back to my slum apartment I saw an older woman approaching me. She was blonde, kind of short and thick with big breasts. She said she had just been robbed and was terrified to walk home. She asked if I would walk her home.

So I said, "Well, where do you live?"

She said, "Beacon Hill."

I knew about Beacon Hill but I had never been there. It was where the bluebloods of Boston lived. I thought, *Why not help her out. What harm could come of that?*

When we got to her apartment she put her hand on my bicep and asked, "Why don't you come upstairs for some food?"

That sounded good to me. Food was hard to come by in those days.

When I entered the apartment she put on a Donovan album and served me a turkey sandwich. While I was eating she excused herself and went to her bedroom. When she came back she was wearing a black sheer top, cut low with no bra, her nipples sticking up. Around her waist was a garter belt holding up black stockings with red panties underneath. I had never seen anything like that before. The girls I knew just got naked. We ended up in bed with her on top first sucking my cock then fucking me, then playing with me, then back and forth kind of sexual aerobics. I was so surprised by this show going on that I detached and kind of just watched her enjoying my body hour after hour. I never came. At three in morning she said I had to go. I asked why, thinking I might sleep in a real soft bed with pillows and clean sheets. She told me she was married to a cop who worked the grave-yard shift and he would be home at six that morning. I summed it up like this: a married woman is likely to pick up a younger guy, fuck him all night, and try to get away with it. When her husband comes home she would fuck him too, and it would be no big deal to her. I knew women were different from men but this was something I had to remember.

One hot summer evening, I went out to buy an ice cream sandwich at the local deli a few blocks away. When I checked the prices, it was better to buy a box of four ice cream sandwiches than buy them one at a time. So I bought the box, thinking I would eat one now and bring the rest home. I was walking home looking aimlessly down at the cement when this homeless guy sitting on some church steps called me over to him. He had scraggly, long grey hair and a beard down to his chest. His clothes were old and ragged and his shoes were well worn.

He said to me with clear conviction, "When you walk, don't look down. Look up at the sky." That was all he had to say. Out on the streets I always looked down. I learned never to look directly at anyone when you are on the street. They might take it as an act of hostility. But this old man chose to pass on his wisdom to me. I did look up for the first time and noticed the black sky spotted with bright stars.

I walked over to the new Prudential Tower, the tallest building in Boston at the time, which had just been completed. I laid down on the sidewalk at the base of the building and looked up marveling at the amazing ingenuity it took. It was probably the vision of just one guy who knew he could do it. Everyone else might have called him insane, a dreamer, that it would never work, but he knew it would and he persevered till it was complete. I loved that. So I ate my ice cream sandwich and looked at the building straight up from my horizontal position. And an odd thing happened. I ate another ice cream sandwich. I argued with myself, one side saying, *You're not hungry, go home and put the rest in the freezer for another day,* the other, *eat them all, get as much pleasure as you can right away. They could be taken away. There is no tomorrow.* I was building a case for myself to binge and I did. Could it have been a reaction to the scarcity of food within my family?

As the summer of 1967 ended, I packed up my Boston apartment and moved to Hyannis. As a freshman at Cape Cod Community College I played basketball for the school, got drunk a lot, and had sex with a lot of girls like the rest of the guys in my group. But unlike my friends and teammates, I never went to class. Even though we all partied hard they managed to make it to their classes. I seemed to get drunker and more often. The other students wanted to make good grades so they could transfer to a four-year college after completing two years here and could rely on the support of their parents. I had no plan other than to make it to the next day. At eighteen I was on my own and had no emotional, financial, or educational guidance from my parents or other adult I could trust. I had gone to college because everyone else in my senior class had, so I just copied them.

While my parents paid my tuition I still needed money for food and other necessities. So I found a part-time job as a mason tender. It was grueling physical work and I loved it. I made good money and my boss fed me lunch every day. He thought I was strong but needed to bulk up. He wanted me to get bigger so I could work faster. His wife would make huge sandwiches for my lunch. I was invited to barbecues at their house and they always encouraged me to eat.

One Friday night I was walking down the main street in Hyannis with a group of teenagers. We were all stoned, just laughing and talking, but no one in the group stood out enough to draw attention, or at least we didn't think so. A cop was parked across the street, standing next to his police car.

He motioned to me and said, "Come over here."

I couldn't believe it. *Why me?*

I yelled back, "You get over here."

He then walked over to me, told me to put my hands behind my back, handcuffed me, and put me in the back seat of his police car. We drove about two hundred yards to the police station where I was charged with disorderly conduct and put in a cell. This was my first arrest. The cell wasn't bad. My cellmate was an older guy who was drunk. I was angry at first and then realized if I had been polite to the cop I would still be free and having fun. I was kept in the cell overnight and the next morning my friends came to pick me up. I did not really care that I got arrested, just that I missed out on a Friday night. I also learned to avoid cops.

I flunked out of Cape Cod Community College. The next year I transferred to Graham Junior College in Boston. I studied communications and liked all my classes, getting straight "A"s. One of my courses involved working in a television studio where I learned camera, sound, lighting, and directing. I absorbed myself in every aspect of mass communications, reading a lot about theories and practical applications. For the first time in my life I found a path I wanted to be on. I was sure I could get a job working for a television network when I graduated.

Now that I was in a new school I needed to find another part-time job. One day I was walking along Commonwealth Avenue thinking about how to earn money. By chance a pudgy hippie with curly blonde hair and a reddish beard called me over to him. He told me he had lids of pot for eight dollars each that I could sell for whatever price I wanted. He didn't care. He just wanted his money. He said "I'll front them to you. After you sell them you can find me here and pay me." I knew nothing of pot or drug dealing at that time. Did I worry about getting arrested or robbed? Wouldn't it have been normal to have those concerns? Well, the answer was no, not for me. I thought only of the profit I could make. So I took about ten bags and sold them to college kids along the Charles River for twenty dollars a bag. I found the hippie in a few hours, gave him his money, and immediately he gave me more to sell. I worked for him for a few months until I realized I could buy a kilo with my own money and make more of a profit. By the time summer ended I had earned enough money to rent my own place. I was getting tired of sleeping in my old red, rusted-out bus.

I rented a second floor one-bedroom apartment off Commonwealth Avenue in a big brownstone. I immediately painted the entire apartment in shiny black paint with iridescent pictures of animals in Day-Glow. I got my furniture from the alleys.

For fun on Friday nights I would sit on the fire escape landing outside my living room with my pellet gun and take pot shots at noisy people leaving the bar that faced my back alley. Sometimes I heard them yell out hey! or ow! They never could tell where it came from.

On any given day along the Charles River crowds of college kids would gather from the various universities in Boston. Hundreds of potential customers were sitting under trees, hanging out, playing guitar, smoking pot, dancing, laughing, and talking politics. The atmosphere was alive with ideology, "make love not war." Of course to make love, better to be stoned, and that's where I fit in.

The need to give a girl a necklace from a dirty gutter and the feeling I had when I stole from my parents were gone now. I would not ever suffer those humiliations again. I found a way to make real money and I would keep doing it.

It was the summer of 1969 and we were all making plans to go to the Woodstock Festival. Excitement was in the air. We heard Janis Joplin, Jimi Hendrix, and Bob Dylan would be performing. Everyone I knew wanted to go and was making plans, some people buying tickets in advance, others looking for rides and people to share expenses with.

I met my friends at a campground in Wellfleet on Cape Cod the Thursday before the festival. We were sitting around an open pit fire getting high and figuring out who would ride with whom. One of the girls offered me a ride in her brand new yellow jeep. She threw a small bag into the back seat and I hopped in with nothing but my stash of hash and opium. Off we went, still stoned on our 350-mile drive to upstate New York. Another group packed into a Volkswagen bus and two other cars packed with stoned-out hipsters followed them. We drove straight through the night taking turns driving. Friday morning, outside the town of Bethel, traffic was at a standstill. Half a million people were heading to the same destination. The only way we could make it to the concert grounds was by going off road, so I got in the driver's seat and drove off the highway down a dirt road. We followed the dirt fireroads for a few miles in the direction of Max Yeager's farm where the concert was being held and the trail of people who had abandoned their cars and decided to walk the rest of the way. We were going around fifty down a hill when I saw a big tree in the middle of the road. I jammed on the brakes and the jeep locked up and flipped over throwing our stoned-out selves from the jeep. When I looked up I saw the jeep was upside down and the gash on my ankle. I noticed the girl I was driving with was walking toward me. We looked at the jeep, where we were, got the hash, opium, and pipe and just left. We walked in the direction of the festival but decided to take a break in a field of tall weeds or what could have been corn for all I knew. We smoked some opium and had sex without attachment as was the ideal during the Woodstock era. Casual sex, drugs, and rock and roll were the rituals of my generation.

When we finally got to the festival we became part of the scene and lost each other. I tripped around Woodstock for two days and nights totally high on LSD, and hash. It had poured day and night turning the farm into a huge mud field. The jeans I was wearing since Thursday were caked in mud and torn, I don't know what happened to my shirt, but I still had my pipe and some hash. By Sunday afternoon, the majority of people were leaving exhausted from lack of sleep and rainy, muddy conditions. The ones who remained stuck it out to hear Jimmy Hendricks play the "Star-Spangled Banner" or, like me, were too stoned to move anyway.

The trip back was somewhat hazy. I hitched rides with people from the concert somehow getting back to my Volkswagen bus in Wellfleet where I flopped down and passed out.

When I got back to Boston, my life as a student and part-time drug dealer resumed. Carol, a girl I was dating, heard that Richie Havens was going to be performing at an outdoor music festival in Connecticut just like Woodstock. A group of friends met at my place to get ready for the trip. We sat around my apartment all night getting high. Finally I took charge herding everyone down the stairs and into the car. We were all stoned but they could barely stay awake, so I drove.

Somewhere along the highway in Connecticut I passed out. The car went off the road and down a ditch. This woke everyone up.

When the highway patrol arrived I told them I was run off the road by an eighteen-wheeler. The car was totaled. We waited for a tow truck to take the wrecked car to a garage. When the cops and tow truck driver left we proceeded to hitchhike to the festival. We arrived just in time to see Ritchie Havens sing "Here Comes the Sun."

I had now survived totaling three cars with barely a scratch. I thought, *That's odd. Maybe I'm not supposed to die in a car accident.* But it never occurred to me that I shouldn't drive while being stoned.

Carol and I had become inseparable. She wanted to move in with me. At this point in our lives we were both rebellious. The rules of society didn't work for me and I had no respect for them. I was a profiteer in the pot industry, not a consumer. I stayed hungry all the time, always on the prowl for new ways to make money. Carol did not believe in marriage and was rebelling against her parents' control over her life. So when her parents proposed we get married instead of living together, we both took that as an insult to our personal freedoms, but quickly agreed, knowing we would take their gifts and approval but not comply with the rules they were expecting in a marriage involving their daughter.

So after a while Carol and I decided to get married to just please her parents. They held a big wedding for us in Hewlett Harbor, Long Island. For me the highlight of the wedding was when this short, balding chubby man came up to me and asked what I was studying in school. I told him communications and he said softly into my ear "Pornos." Not sure that I heard him right I asked "What?" He explained he was invested in the porno film industry and it was a moneymaker. Now I was a drug dealer but there was no way I would stoop to the porno industry. My beliefs were the same as the women who protested the porno industry as degrading to women and I would not have any part of that. All of my female friends were involved in woman's lib which was a big movement of the times.

Carol and I were both products of the '60s. We did not believe in marriage and so marriage did not last long. We got a lot of gifts and bought a new Volkswagen bus with a camper top. Carol left for

Canada with a friend of mine and I went to the Florida Keys with a friend of hers. I never saw her again. Her parents had the marriage annulled and I signed a document stating I never consummated the marriage.

Back in Boston I connected with Peter, an old friend of mine from Dorchester who was going into his sophomore year at MIT. He had been dealing drugs at MIT to make extra money. After comparing notes we had decided buy hash in Amsterdam bypassing our suppliers in Boston. We had no contact there, but figured that someone at one of the legal pot and hash cafes would be able to work with us. He and I pooled our money and bought round-trip tickets to Amsterdam on Icelandic Airlines. Amsterdam's had liberal drug use policies. In Dam Square, hippies from around the world hung out and openly consumed LSD, hash, and pot. Busses left for India and Nepal for free love and drugs.

As soon as we arrived, we tripped along the red light district on LSD, ate at Chinese restaurants, and checked out all the local cafes for the best connections. We finally met a guy we thought knew what he was talking about and could deliver. This guy explained that all the hash in Amsterdam was smuggled in from Lebanon, India and Nepal. There were all kinds of varieties and quantity levels. The rarest and best hash was an opiated black hash from Nepal.

Peter and I bought a few pounds of beautiful soft Lebanese red hash with about two thousand in U.S. cash. Next we purchased ten five-pound Edam cheese wheels. We hollowed out our big round cheese wheels and filled them with hash, sealing the bottoms with the same red wax they were coated with. For effect, we wrapped the cheeses in red crate netting and made a special wax seal making them look as if they had come from the factory. We were comfortable doing this in our hotel room; it seemed perfectly normal. The next day we mailed the cheeses to my Boston address.

When we returned we unwrapped our cheeses, took out the hash, packaged, marketed it as "Red Leb," and sold it. We made so much money we thought, *Let's do this again.*

Peter wanted to go back to Amsterdam alone and spend a month or two. I would stay in Boston to receive the packages and sell the hash, sending him money to buy more. What I did not know was that Peter was not street smart. He went back to the "coffee shops" where we had met our first contact, who was nowhere to be found. These "coffee shops" sold small amounts of hash or marijuana to locals and tourists, just like going into a bar and having a drink. But that casual attitude did not extend to the purchase of large amounts of hash for export.

Peter, while looking for a new contact ended up buying two pounds of hash from a cop and spent two years in jail in Amsterdam. When that happened I did not say to myself, *Wow, lucky it wasn't me. I'd better stop now before I get caught.* No, I saw getting busted as a failure due to lack of skill. In order to progress at this promising career I had to get better at being a smuggler. I needed to put more thought into a backstory, understand the law, and evaluate the risks versus the rewards. Most importantly, I had to know what the consequences would be if I were caught. How would the rest of my life look? Did I care?

I graduated with honors from Graham Junior College in 1970. I applied for jobs at all the television stations in Boston and New York City. The field was impossible to get into. All the studio jobs were union and the unions were closed to anyone other than friends or family of a union member. I tried but could not even get a job sweeping floors at a studio. The school never mentioned that you could study hard, get a degree, and not get a job. Why the hell did I even go to college if I couldn't use my education in a career? I was baffled. Lucky for me I had an ongoing business.

FIVE

New Hampshire

had saved enough money for a down payment on a property in a remote town in New Hampshire. Two friends in the hash smuggling business had moved up there and when I visited them I loved it. Towns were connected by miles of desolate back roads. People seemed to mind their own business and there was a feeling of openness. This worked for me. As a smuggler I didn't want to attract attention and I was too well known in Boston.

I found an old farm with a barn that I converted into a small silk screen studio. I printed line drawings that were in the public domain on stained glass. Alice in Wonderland and Winnie the Pooh were two of my best sellers. I branched out into making stained glass lampshades and chess boards with mirrored glass, selling them at gift shops and craft fairs all over New England. With this small craft business I had a way to legitimize the money I was making from the hash sales. I became the sole distributor for my two friends in New Hampshire who were smuggling in hash from India and Nepal. If I needed to increase my sales to compensate for increased drug revenue I simply bought my craft products from myself and created fake receipts. Eric and John became my distributors for hash in Boston.

I researched other craft products similar to mine to get a price point. For instance, if a framed stained glass product was selling for twelve dollars in a store I knew the store paid a wholesale price of six dollars. I added up all my expenses, on a cost per unit basis and added in a profit up to a total cost of six dollars. The difference between my manufacturing costs and my sale price was my profit and taxable income. My monthly living expenses were two thousand dollars per month, so I wanted to show a legitimate income stream to cover my expenses and have a little left over. So my first year in business I claimed a taxable income of thirty-two thousand dollars. This amount of money would not raise any red flags with the IRS.

To stay under the radar, I purchased all the materials I needed— stained glass, silk screen ink, wood frames, and solder—from various hobby shops and paint stores, always paying in cash and never spending more than a thousand dollars in any one place. When I needed something expensive such as darkroom equipment, I would find out-of-state classified ads and buy it in cash from a private party.

Life was good in New Hampshire. If someone drove past my house they would hear the Rolling Stones blasting and see me in my barn with the door wide open, cutting stained glass, looking like an eccentric artist living in the woods. Eric would come up from Boston to visit. Plenty of girls I knew would come up to smoke pot and party for a night or two. I did not socialize much with the locals, but while filling my jeep up at the local gas station I did meet one man. He was filling up his red Datsun 240Z. With the gas nozzle in one hand and a can of beer in the other he looked at me with a crooked smile and introduced himself. That is how I met my good friend Lance Metcalf.

Lance's family had lived in the Lakes region of New Hampshire for generations. Lance was an inventor, as was his father before him. He owned a large beautiful farm with a farmhouse that was built in the late 1800s, but chose to live in the barn with his pet monkey. On Thanksgiving Day, 1970, we were planning our meal at his farmhouse. I went over to see him that early afternoon. He was sitting at his workbench, soldering iron in one hand, can of Budweiser in the other. He had a huge magnifying glass attached to a band around his head and his hair looked like Einstein would have if he had just woken up. On his shoulder was his pet monkey. I was delivering a batch of hash brownies for desert after our turkey dinner. I convinced Lance to take a walk with me in the snow to get some fresh air and smoke a joint. He put his monkey in his four-hundred-square-foot enclosure and locked the door. We were gone for about an hour and when we returned the monkey had gotten free, grabbed the hash brownies, and ate all of them except one. He was swinging from a chandelier over the dining room table, screeching and taunting us with the one remaining brownie in his little hand. It was such a bizarre scene. My first reaction was to laugh. Lance, on the other hand, was concerned and trying to get control of his monkey. After about fifteen minutes the monkey jumped from the chandelier onto a chair then to the ground. He looked at us, his eyes totally bloodshot and just passed out. Lance very carefully carried him to the couch and let him sleep. We got the one hash brownie and decided to eat it right then. My friends arrived carrying wooden barrels of hard cider, homemade stuffing, and pies. We were a bunch of twenty-year-olds celebrating Thanksgiving with a forty-year-old eccentric in Center Sandwich, New Hampshire. The monkey slept right through to the next day.

After dinner we sat around the fireplace and Lance told us the story about how he was once in love with this beautiful lady. He had proposed to her right in front of this fireplace. He had bought her a diamond ring and put it in a box of Cracker Jack. He handed her the box as he asked her to marry him. Without opening the box, she threw it into the fireplace and walked out. I could easily see Lance doing that. He was a recluse full of quirky ideas, one of which was his appreciation of Datsun 240Zs. He had the foresight to know they would become collector's items. So he bought three and drove one, keeping the other two stored on cement blocks in an outbuilding. That's why I loved him, he was just who he appeared to be.

I never saw Lance without a can of Budweiser in his hand. He would call me when he was too drunk to drive or just wanted to have some company. One day he called me and asked me to drive him to the bank in Moultonborough about thirty minutes away. Riding along, beer in hand, Lance was just smiling on and off for no apparent reason. We hardly talked. Lance was a man of few words as were most of the people in our town. If a stranger drove to the center of town and asked for directions he would find an old man wearing overalls and a flannel shirt sitting in a wicker rocking chair on the wooden porch of the general store. The old man would listen to the stranger's questions and simply answer yup and then continue rocking back and forth in his wicker chair.

When we arrived at the bank Lance smiled at me and walked in. When he came out he got into the car, sat down in his bucket seat, reached into his jacket pocket, and pulled out a brown envelope and handed it to me without a word.

I asked him, "What's this about? "

"Open it," he said. "Here is three thousand dollars. I know you want to expand your craft business and this is a gift for you."

I was so moved I almost cried. Looking at Lance with his raggedy clothes, unkempt hair, and beard stubble, one would never know his soul was full of warmth and kindness.

My house was in the middle of a densely forested eight-acre piece of land. The house was built in the early 1900s, constructed of wood beams with brown cedar shingles. The floorboards in my bedroom upstairs creaked and the ceiling was low. The house was heated by hot water running through old radiators. I had spent most of my life living in cities and was used to the sirens and flashing lights of police cars and ambulances. Now in the country I experienced a whole new set of sounds at night that were amplified by the complete silence. Tree limbs crackled from the weight of the first late October snow as winter set in. Owls would let out harsh hooting screams at all hours. Sometimes I would hear scratching noises on the window. The house made its own sounds as the hot water radiators let off steam or as water traveled up the pipes. The most haunting noises seemed to come from the basement—hissing and groaning, coming and going—during odd hours of the night. I spent many sleepless nights trying to identify the sounds and rationalize that nothing abnormal was going on.

One late October night, the full moon lighting the freshly fallen snow, I decided to once and for all make peace with these unpredictable sounds that kept me up all night. I dressed in my long underwear, my warmest clothes, scarf, and hat, grabbed my sleeping bag and, being a city kid, I had to have my pillow. I trudged through the snow to a tall maple tree about a hundred yards from my house. The ground was covered in about two feet of soft snow. I put my sleeping bag down, got in it, and rested my head on my pillow. My eyes were wide open just waiting for whatever was making those sounds to show themselves. I was stone sober, no pot, no booze, just me and nature. The chorus began, the hooting and crackling accompanied by the early winter wind. I could not see what was making these sounds so I thought I would close my eyes and just absorb the nighttime smells and sounds.

I imagined the crackling sound becoming hissing and screeching red-eyed demons that floated around in the wind. An Indian spirit who looked like a cigar store Indian appeared smoking a cigar, and thousands of red antlike creatures were angrily scurrying around. I decided to indulge myself with these fears and see where they would lead.

I felt movement in the forest. This was not my mind playing with me, this was real. I opened my eyes and saw the outline of a black bear and her cub walking straight for me. *What the . . . ?* I said to myself. *Aren't bears supposed to hibernate in October?* I guess this bear family hadn't eaten enough yet. My heart was racing, but my breathing slowed down and a peaceful feeling came over me like a warm golden blanket. I was looking the big bear in the eye. She was looking back at me, and the cub was just playing a few feet away behind her. I thought I saw her smile at me, so I smiled back. At that moment in my life I made peace with fear.

The irony is that when I was a little kid alone in my room in Dorchester I would summon wild animals to protect me from the human wild animals outside on the streets. Maybe this bear was my protector.

The bear kept going and walked off through the trees into the night. I sat there for a while then slowly got up grabbed my stuff and went back inside. From that moment on I slept soundly in my creaky old house.

On one of my sales trips to a gift shop in Kennebunkport, Maine, where by chance I met a buyer from Bloomingdales. She was on vacation doing some shopping and was looking at one of my stained glass pieces when the owner of the store said to her "The craftsman who made that piece is standing right here."

I showed her my catalog and explained how I photo silk-screened the images onto stained glass.

She said, "I love your work, if you can come to my office in New York with a sample of each piece, I will give you a contract for a large order."

Her demeanor was relaxed and friendly. She seemed like an honest, trustworthy person.

By that time I was making more than a hundred different products from hanging stained glass window decorations to lampshades, chessboards, and vases. I boxed up all of the silkscreened products and samples of the different colors and textures of stained glass that I had in stock and loaded up my truck and drove down to New York City.

I arrived at her upscale office at Bloomingdales and was kept waiting for hours. Observing all the activity made me uncomfortable. The office had an air of pretentiousness. The staff was fashionable and fast paced. If the illusive ladder to success were in that room, they would all be pushing and shoving each other to get to the next rung.

The woman finally showed up and she looked over each piece with her assistant by her side. Exceeding my expectations, she gave me an order for one gross of each piece and handed me a six-page contract. The contract was flagged with red stickers indicating where to sign. I glanced at the contract and after reading the first paragraph, thought I should bring it to a lawyer or have it reviewed by someone who could understand it. I decided to ignore my instincts. After all, why would a financially sound institution like Bloomingdales take advantage of a little nobody like me? My mind was already on the massive task ahead of filling the order. So I just signed the contract and left.

On the drive back to New Hampshire I was very excited about the huge order. I thought this woman must have been put into my life for a reason; it was my destiny to succeed. Many times I had looked for opportunities to get out of the drug world. I had hoped college would have landed me a job in the television industry or, if this craft business did well, I could quit selling drugs. I was smart, hardworking and creative. With the right door open I could get out of my own personal ghetto.

To fulfill this massive order I spent all the money I had in the bank to buy supplies, thinking, *This is it. If I don't succeed I will have no choice left but to be a career criminal.* I worked day and night to complete the order. While driving to New York City in a rented van filled with boxes of neatly packed In-vision Studio products, I began to worry. This buyer was very polished. She had a support staff and a huge retail store behind her and I was working alone. If things went wrong I had no leverage to collect my money. This was déjà vu, remembering the gangster in the pool hall challenging me to collect the fifty dollars he lost to me. Then I reminded myself, *Wait a minute. This buyer is not a gangster. She would never bully me.* I wanted this opportunity so badly, that any thoughts of caution or hesitation were overruled by the addict part of my brain. *Take the risk. If it doesn't work out, fuck it! Just keep on dealing drugs.*

When I arrived at Bloomingdales I was directed to the back alley loading dock, where I unpacked the van, turning over my merchandise to a warehouse worker who handed me a manifest receipt.

On the drive back to New Hampshire, I felt pretty happy. I thought in a few days, my products would sell, I'd get a check in the mail, and they would reorder. Days turned into weeks, weeks into months. No check and no phone call. When I finally got the buyer on the phone she said "Read the contract, small print, page three." I looked over the contract and on page three were there payment terms, which in essence read: if they pay within six months they take a fourteen percent discount, nine months a ten percent discount, or if the products don't sell, they don't pay at all. The vendor has ninety days to pick up the unsold merchandise or it would be discarded.

This was my fault. I had no formal business training. The pot-dealing world paid cash on delivery. My business was too small and could not afford these terms. Even if I could have afforded them, I would have never agreed if I had understood what I was signing. I took all the risk; they were covered either way—not the friendly deal I deluded myself into believing. I looked deep inside myself to find an answer as to why I couldn't accept the legitimate business rules, but my response was always the same. This is just wrong and I am tired of trying to fit in where I don't belong.

I got a few small checks from Bloomingdales over the next month or two. But I was finished with the craft business. I turned over the deed on my property to my father and left New Hampshire with just my clothes and my drug money.

Around that same time my grandfather died. While his casket was being lowered into the ground, I made a decision to become a ghost. From this point on I had no past. There would be no future. I would do what I had to do to survive. I would be invisible. I would fit into the business world when I had to and on my terms. There was no one left that I had to be responsible to. I had already separated from my parents. My bubble was long gone. There was no rabbi, mentor, or friend that I would let down if I got caught. It would be just me.

The one person who would understand my decision was Eric. He never judged my decisions. He accepted all of me, most of all my feeling that I was discarded by my family. He saw me work hard and try my best to find a place in normal society, time after time being beaten back down. Eric's family was kind and loving. Because of that he was comfortable and it showed. He was happy, went with the flow. People wanted to be around him while I had the look of the hungry one, which kept people at a distance.

After leaving New Hampshire I crashed at Eric's apartment right off Harvard Square. One night we were looking out his window and noticed a car full of girls parked outside on the street with a flat tire.

I went out and asked, "Do you need any help?"

A female version of David Bowie answered, "Yes, we do. Do you have any pot?"

I asked her, "How much do you want?"

She said, "As much as you have."

I thought, *You have no idea who you just bumped into.* She said her name was Lucy and I invited her upstairs to get high while her friends waited for a tow truck.

I opened a brown paper bag with three pounds of pot and asked her, "Is this enough?" We rolled a few joints, got high with Eric, listened to music and talked.

Lucy was thin with pale white skin. She seemed like someone who had never done any kind of work in her life. I liked her because she was kind of eccentric, different from any woman I had ever met. She was from the South but spoke with a British accent. She was a student at Wellesley College and taking classes at MIT. We exchanged phone numbers and made plans to meet at her college dorm. The next day I went to meet her at the school campus. The campus was like being on the grounds of a royal family estate with beautiful lawns, gardens, and lakes. The buildings looked like old castles, austere and reeking of history. I went to her dormitory where a very masculine-looking woman checked me in and sent a runner to get her.

Lucy came downstairs wearing a wide-brimmed straw hat, summer dress, and long white gloves. We walked down to the lake and got into an old wooden rowboat. She grabbed the oars and rowed us to the middle of the lake while I sat back and rolled a joint. We smoked the joint and fooled around a little. Her life in the Carolinas was charmed, coming from an old family of plantation owners. She had attended private boarding school in Switzerland. She told me about her coming out party, a traditional event in which debutantes were introduced to society. The purpose of it was to announce her as a potential bride to suitors whose families had the money and status to pay the price of admission to this ball. I could imagine her future, sitting under the branches of an old cypress tree dressed in a white frock, her beau dressed in a pinstriped seersucker suit, the two of them casually drinking mint juleps. Her family would have to approve the man she would marry. What went unspoken was that man would not be me. Until she was ready for marriage, she was going to experiment with men like me, enjoying the danger, the sex, and the drugs. She didn't have to say it. I knew it. She was not the first girl I had been with who had been attracted to the outlaw in me. As I got to know her she was not above getting on her knees as the price to pay for some coke.

SIX

India and Nepal

While I was staying at Eric's place in Boston I made plans to travel to India with a final destination of Kathmandu, Nepal, the source of the best hash in the world. My friends in New Hampshire who had been smuggling hash from Nepal were retiring. They had washed their money and were moving to a home on a few hundred acres in Nova Scotia. They set up a contact for me in Nepal who would meet me when I got off the plane in Katmandu.

My flight on Pan Am departed from New York, with stops in London, Frankfurt, Beirut, Karachi, Tel Aviv, and New Delhi. It was the height of airline luxury travel and Pan Am Flight 2 was known for circling the globe in a little over a day. The 747's coach section was nearly empty with about twenty passengers. My last leg would be New Delhi, a twenty-six-hour trip. The middle aisle was four seats across, so I stretched out to get some sleep. On the first stop, London, the flight crew changed. Lulu, the new stewardess, served the passengers in my section. With so few passengers, we had plenty of time to talk and flirt. She was a very attractive woman around twenty-six years old with light brown hair and green eyes. Her skin looked very soft, almost radiant. We talked for hours on end. Lulu lived on the outskirts of London. I told her about my life in Boston as a communications student and how difficult it was to get a job in my field. I told her I was going to India for adventure, that I loved traveling. She told me her life as a Pan Am stewardess was full of adventure, and about how much she loved traveling. I really liked Lulu. As a male, of course, I was always on the prowl for women. My primal drive was always to find an appealing woman, not to dominate, control, or take advantage of, but to test her, to see if she was like-minded. While almost all women were physically attractive to me, I especially liked the thin model type like the Pan Am stewardesses of the day. Lulu was no exception. Lulu would go off duty in New Delhi and the airline put the crew up at the same hotel I was staying at. We planned to meet there and go out for dinner as soon as we arrived.

When I got off the plane in New Delhi it was 114°F and pouring rain. The plane parked on the runway and the passengers disembarked on the metal staircase that had been wheeled up. We waited in the rain and humidity for our luggage as one guy handed it to the next from the belly of the plane down a ladder. While going through customs I filled out the declaration form and checked the box that said I was visiting India for business.

When I handed it to the customs officer he shook his head and said, "You need a special commerce visa to enter the country. You must take the next plane back to the U.S."

I was in a state of disbelief. It had just taken days to get here. Now I would have to turn around and go back?

The guy behind me whispered, "Do you know what baksheesh is?" He told me to give the customs guy a hundred U.S. dollars. I thought, *Shit. Here I was in India as a smuggler, a criminal, and here he was a government official, who, if he had been doing his job, would have arrested me for bribing him.* I hated people who played both sides of the law. It complicated things. But I gave it a shot and discreetly handed him $100. He took it as if it was in the normal course of his duties, erased my checkmark, and changed it to tourist. Welcome to corruption. How confusing it must be for these people. On one hand they represented law and order and on the other hand they dipped into the black market to make extra cash, putting at risk their moral standing. These people could never be trusted and there were so many of them in all kinds of disguises. This lesson repeated itself again and again, not only in my travels to foreign countries, but in the U.S. as well.

In the back seat of the taxi from the airport to the hotel, I was hot, tired, and sweaty. The driver kept turning around to ask "Do you want hash? Women?" All I wanted was a cold shower and a cold drink. The driver was infuriating. He never watched the road while cars frantically zoomed in and out of traffic. We finally arrived at the Oberoi Hotel. I was anxious to check in and get cleaned up for my date with Lulu. Wanting a tip, the bellman insisted on carrying the one small bag I had to my room. He opened the door and there in front of me was the grandest room I could ever have imagined. The floors were tan marble, the furniture exquisite. Dark red velvet curtains highlighted floor to ceiling windows with a view of the city. The room was bigger than my entire house in New Hampshire. I thanked him, gave him some rupees, and headed straight to the shower.

The marble bathtub must have been eight feet long. I turned on the cold water faucet and let the water fill the tub. After getting out of my stinky clothes I jumped into the bath. Surprise! The water was hot. Thinking the plumbing might be mixed up, I tried the hot water faucet and it was even hotter. I couldn't believe it. What's going on here? I called down to the front desk. On the other end of the phone was a voice in a proper British accent, calm and cynical. "What did you expect in New Delhi, cold water?" His tone implied that I must be an idiot. A few minutes later there was a knock on the door and in walks a parade of bellhops and maids carrying buckets of ice, which they proceeded to dump into the bath. The bell captain explained that the water tank was located on the roof of the building in direct sun, so the water was never cold. I asked for a cold glass of water, and that, too, was unobtainable. The water was unsafe to drink and the ice was made from the same water. He offered me a warm Coca-Cola and warned me not to swallow any water while in the tub. This was India, a beautiful oversize marble bathtub, but no cold water.

Lulu and I met in the lobby and decided we were too tired to go out. We ate Chinese food at the hotel restaurant and went upstairs to my room. She was wearing a black flowered skirt and black see-through top. She slowly undressed down to her sexy panties. I took off my clothes and was already fully erect. A minute later we were in bed, hungry for satisfaction after playing with each other on the plane for so long. That lasted all of fifteen minutes at which point Lulu got up, dressed, then told me she was married and had a daughter. After we had sex her attitude changed. She acted guilty, like someone afraid of being found out. Before I knew she was married, I thought we might be friends and see each other when I was traveling to Europe or if she came to the U.S., but she said no. I was sad to see her go and wished she had told me she was married before our relationship turned to intimacy. After my humiliating experience in Boston with an older married woman, I had decided to find out if a woman was married before I got involved in any way and definitely not to sleep with married women. I felt betrayed and realized I should be very careful before trusting a woman.

From India I flew to Nepal. When you are about to land in Kathmandu, the plane has to circle down to the city that sits in a valley surrounded by the Annapurna Mountain Range. It was more beautiful than any place I had ever seen. The mountains were majestic. Looking at them gave you an inner peace and sense that something more powerful than people was at play. I stayed at the Kathmandu Guest House. My room was hot and small. It had a marble floor with a hole in it for a toilet. There was no running water but a communal shower.

I met my contact Hari Gopal, K.C. there. The K.C. stood for King's Commission of the British Indian Army. Hari was a proud Gurkha, a member of the fighting men of Nepal, whose ancestors had successfully prevented Nepal from becoming part of the British Empire in the early 1800s. Gurkhas were generally short with very strong legs and known to be fierce and brave fighters. They fought with *kukris*, boomerang-shaped swords. They were known for fighting in high altitudes and had a keen ability to jump and spring from boulder to boulder. Hari loved boxing and Mohamed Ali was his hero. How crazy was that? I thought. Here I was in Nepal, which seemed centuries removed from the modern world and yet he loved Mohamed Ali. Hari and I climbed up a trail through mountainous terrain on the way to meet some local hash dealers. He told me the hash for sale in the city was low quality and cut with cow dung. The best hash was to be found in small villages where it was harvested and processed. The trail ended at the base of a mountain which looked as if time had carved out of it a plateau for this village to rest on. Hari pointed out the sentinels standing guard on the ridge tops. They were protecting the village from thieves and drug bandits. He proudly told me they were part of his tribe.

The village was made up of a cluster of small one-story run down houses. Periodically a boulder would roll down the mountainside and end up on the main village road making it impossible for a jeep to drive on. I was obviously the only white person there but I felt invisible. The villagers were sitting around talking to each other and paid no attention to me. When we met the village elder Hari did all the talking. He negotiated a price of fifty dollars per pound for about six pounds of black opiated hash. I paid in U.S. dollars. On our walk back to the city Hari carried the hash in his backpack. I did not see one policeman on the way to or from this village. Nor did I see any weapons other than a few knives. I felt safe with Hari as a partner. He was referred by good friends and his demeanor was very calm. Even though the hash trade was illegal, there was little to no enforcement on the small scale I was involved in. On a larger scale, it was known that the officials had to be paid off.

Back in Kathmandu Hari introduced me to another group of smugglers who were expert at hollowing out wooden print blocks to hide the hash in. We walked back to Katmandu to meet these guys at their shop. I was shown the old museum replica wood printing blocks with hollowed out backs. They mashed the hash into the back of the blocks, covered it with a piece of plywood, and then painted the back to look identical to wood on the front. The next day they had the packages all wrapped up in brown shipping paper and we took them to a shipping company and sent them to Eric's address in Boston.

With the shipment taken care of, Hari graciously invited me to go to his village in the mountains to meet his family and join in an annual celebration. I wanted to build a good relationship with him and politely accepted but was concerned about how he would introduce me to his family and friends. We both had to have the same story of my identity. I did not want to attract any more attention than was necessary. He told me not to worry about saying anything because no one in his village spoke English. The next day we made the three-hour walk to his home. I met his parents and sisters. The townspeople were dressed up in colorful clothes and all their faces were painted bright yellow and orange. While we were standing in the town square a bell rang and a religious looking man walked up with a goat on a leash. The goat wore a collar with a bell that clanged. The man took the bell and collar off the goat, pulled out a long knife, and slit the goat's throat. He then lifted the goat upside down so the blood would flow into a cement channel that ran through the village. The villagers dipped their hands into the blood and then rubbed the bloody hands on their faces. I just stood there and watched thinking this must be the celebration Hari was talking about. I had anticipated food and fireworks. On our way back to the city Hari explained that the ritual was their annual celebration of fertility.

With a week before my flight back to the U.S. I decided I would try out the local culture as a tourist. I would go out at night and smoke hash from a hookah at a public outdoor gazebo. The locals banged on pots and other objects all night long. Sometimes a funeral procession went by, accompanied by a lot of women wailing. It was spooky but so beautiful and ancient you just had to feel peaceful. What a different world from Boston. There was a lot of poverty, people without limbs begging, cows walking the streets, people going to the bathroom on the street just about anywhere. The smells were dusty rank. The peo-
'ple were beautiful to watch. The local Nepalese were short, well built, and had beautiful skin and hair. Sometimes a group of monks walked by dressed in orange robes with perfect posture. I noticed they were looking up at the sky, just like the old man in Boston had told me to do. At a temple called Swayambu where monkeys ran the show, one day I saw a monkey grab about a pound of black opiated hash and

run away with it with local hash dealers chasing after him.

The laws of survival were very different here. The people seemed resigned to poverty and their tolerance for pain seemed much greater than Americans'. As a smuggler I could recognize the U.S. government operatives quite easily. They all were white and did not look like the typical European or American hippie. Wearing polo shirts, khakis, and topsiders I thought of them as Yale graduates masquerading as tourists in an exotic foreign land. They would congregate at the American Pie Shop eating cheeseburgers and French fries while spying on the local foot traffic through their Ray-Bans. I was there to smuggle hash and blend in with the local people to the best of my ability, while they were there to enforce U.S. standards and laws in a Third World country. I wondered what right they had to act superior and try to enforce laws of the United States on foreign soil.

Over the next few days I developed dysentery. I could not eat anything other than raw yogurt and drink black tea. Without any medical treatment, it continued to get worse. On the plane ride back to London I was so sick I could not sit up. I asked the stewardess if I could move to first class where there was more room. She emphatically said no, that it was against regulations. The first class seats were mostly empty expect for some artwork that was buckled into a few seats. I felt the anger in me rising, thinking, *Here we go, just like in Dorchester. People with money got what they wanted. People without money were on their own.* I was too sick to make a scene so I had to lie down in the aisle and curled up into a ball. The stewardess told me to get back in my seat, which somehow I did. At Heathrow they quarantined the plane. The officials at the airport thought I might be carrying black plague and, until I was cleared by a doctor, all the passengers would be quarantined. It turned out I had vascular and amoebic dysentery and an ulcerated tongue. Since I was not contagious I somehow made it onto my flight to Boston.

I had lost about ten pounds on that trip, climbed mountainous terrain, suffered a twenty-six hour plane ride home, risked my life and freedom in a Third World country. When the packages arrived I felt like I was seeing old friends. I had left them in Nepal and here they were in Boston. I was relieved to see they had made it through customs and had been delivered safely. I unwrapped the brown paper packaging with the stamps from Nepal and looked at the ancient wood blocks. I turned the first one over and with a screw driver pried open the back to find it empty, void of hash, just museum replicas from Nepal. I pried open another and another, all empty. I was first shocked and then furious.

I was resolved to get back there and strangle those smugglers who stole the hash. I called a friend and asked him to accompany me back to Nepal as soon as we could get a flight. John was imposing at six-foot-five with bright red hair and a red beard. John had a bad temper and was prone to violence if you looked at him the wrong way.

John and I found our way through the streets of Kathmandu back to the smuggler who had packaged the hash in the wood blocks. The average height of a Nepalese man is five foot four inches and their houses and doors were scaled accordingly. John entered first, bending over to fit through the doorway of the ringleader's home. The dealer was shocked to see a red-haired giant staring at him and he recognized my face immediately. He promptly admitted stealing the hash and was quick to replace twice the amount in the form of hash oil. It was clear he had pulled the same scheme on other foreigners but we were probably the only ones who made the long trip back to confront him.

John and I had the hash oil sewn into two long leather coats and wore them through customs at London's Heathrow Airport on our way back to Boston. I had researched all the airline routes and customs habits of different international airports to find the path of least resistance. Heathrow had two lines—one if you have something to declare, the other you just walk through if you have nothing. We chose to declare nothing and walk straight through customs. But U.S. customs was very strict. It is up to each customs officer whose bags to search and who to wave forward. Arriving at Boston's Logan Airport, I walked toward the customs line with the usual negative thoughts.

This doesn't feel right. Who is the guy in sunglasses behind me? What if I get busted? When I see the customs room right in front of me, all those thoughts disappear. Now I am on—time to act the part and get through this to the street outside. My mind goes blank. My emotions turn off. One line was manned by a young customs officer with long red hair in a ponytail. This guy would know about drugs coming in from foreign countries and would probably love to bust some smugglers. A bust would look good on his work record. So I confidently walked over to the next line where an older guy who looked bored with his job was waving a traveler through as he stuffed the last bite of his donut into his mouth.

As I approached I put on my leather coat lined with hash oil. I put my suitcase on the table for inspection and said, "It is so good to be back on U.S. soil. India was interesting but you would not believe how bad the food is. You can't even drink the water without getting sick."

I continued, "When I get out of the airport I am going straight to a McDonald's to get a hamburger with fries."

Before he had time to ask me to open my bag, I had already unzipped it and pulled out some souvenirs. I showed him a few Nepalese bags and a prayer mirror. All of my dirty clothes were on top, making it unappealing for him to dig around. Even if he did there was nothing to find in my suitcase, but I wanted the suitcase, not my coat, to be the focal point of the inspection. He waved me through. As I was exiting I saw John out of the corner of my eye. Across the room a female officer was going through his bag. I pushed open the doors to the afternoon sunlight, walked over to the taxi line, and went to Eric's apartment. John arrived about thirty minutes later. The three of us then went out for food and drink in Harvard Square, telling Eric stories of our trip late into the night. The leather coats lined with hash oil hung in Eric's closet among winter coats and sporting equipment. We would deal with them in the morning. That night was a time to take a deep breath and appreciate being alive and free. John and I followed that same routine for about two years, netting a lot of cash.

All of my years of being an outsider in my family and learning how to survive by myself in the slums made me aware that I was always intensely hungry both physically and emotionally. But my full identity had not yet completely surfaced. I studied people looking for a group to fit into and realized I had to know who I was first then I could find people like me. This would be difficult since I did not follow any normal path. I was led by my sense of right and wrong as I saw it.

As a drug dealer, I was making money outside of the laws of the United States. I had to learn how much cash I could spend without becoming a blip on the radar of merchants, law enforcement, and the IRS. At the same time I learned how to tailor my appearance to blend in with the average citizen. How much should I weigh? How should I keep myself groomed? What kind of clothes to wear? What is my cover story? How should l communicate with both spoken words and body language to keep my real occupation a secret?

A drug dealer usually starts at the bottom of the pecking order. Beginning at nineteen, over a period of two years I earned around $200,000 by buying pot and reselling to end users and from hash coming from Amsterdam and Nepal.

For the first time in my life I had plenty of money—enough for basic expenses, food, clothing, rent, car, and entertainment. I had already learned how to launder small amounts of cash back in New Hampshire with my craft business. At first I paid for all my expenses in cash. Cash has a great upside since there purchases can't be tracked and you could make up any name as the purchaser. If you said you were a college student you had broad berth as to your appearance. So that was my first cover story—I was just a college kid whose parents gave him a check once a month, which I cashed and used for normal purchases and to pay bills.

That story would change as I realized I was on the path of a professional international smuggler and college student would no longer fit my needs. I was getting too well known in Boston and decided to look for a new home base. I wanted to live in a small community near the beach, a place where I could come and go without attracting attention. I looked at different coastal towns up and down the East Coast that might fit the profile. That's when I found Wrightsville Beach, North Carolina. The homes on the beach were mostly vacation rentals. A few blocks inland, you could find a simple home surrounded by trailers. The locals kept to themselves, much like what I'd experienced in New Hampshire.

I bought a two-story apartment house a few blocks from the beach for twenty thousand dollars. I rented out the first floor and lived on the second. North Carolina was good for me. I was unknown in this quiet community. The friends I made there were slow paced and very different from my friends in the Northeast. The land was flat and swampy with a lot of moss-filled trees. When you drove from town to town there was no traffic. After six o'clock at night it was dark and quiet. I never dealt any drugs there. To maintain my cover I bought pot from the local surfers even though I had plenty of my own. I could come and go without anyone noticing. This was the perfect home base for my smuggling trips to India while Eric remained in Boston to supervise the distribution.

Making so many trips to India, as many as four per year, required another kind of cover. By exporting local craft goods from villages and towns I could legitimately justify the frequent trips. I sought out small business owners who could be trusted to deliver the merchandise. Most of the traders spoke English and the ones that didn't I passed on. Putna, in the state of Bihar, was known as the most backward and corrupt state in all of India. That's where I met my business partner who arranged to export ivory chess pieces and marble plates with semi-precious stone inserts for me. When they arrived in the U.S., I sold the goods to myself or friends, made out fake receipts, and paid taxes on the profit.

On one trip to India after my work was finished I took the train to Agra to see the Taj Mahal, then on to the sacred city of Varanasi on the banks of the Ganges. In the city of Hampi I visited the Virupaksha Temple, the oldest Hindu temple in India, which was built in the seventh century C.E. I traveled around India as a businessman and tourist, taking pictures, looking at guide books, and never brought any drugs with me. I could not imagine getting busted in India as a hash consumer. I stayed away from the street drug dealers pretending to be shocked by any suggestion that I would smoke hash.

I ended up at the Palolem Beach resort in South Goa, a favorite unspoiled beach of foreign tourists and local fishermen. There I met a young American woman who was there as a member the Peace Corps or some other U.S. humanitarian outfit. After traveling for so long, it was a relief to hear American English. She told me her team had been in a small village in southern India teaching the inhabitants about birth control. Their standard way to demonstrate the use of condoms was to put them on broomsticks. With limited words in the local dialect, they would explain to the villagers that they could still have sex but by using a condom, there would be less pregnancy. The team gave hundreds of condoms to the villagers and left. Since this village was so poor and remote, having sex was the only source of pleasure these people had. Nine months later she returned for a follow-up tour to document the success of their condom distribution. To her surprise most of the woman were pregnant or had just given birth. The natives remembered her and thanked her profusely for the condoms.

When she asked if they had used the condoms they said, "Of course, look." Outside of every shack was a broomstick with multiple condoms on it. These people thought the condom-wearing broomsticks were fertility symbols and look how well they had worked.

When I was away from the U.S. for long periods of time, I missed the company of women. Hari would arrange for me to meet up with a local woman from time to time. None of them spoke any English and I did not speak whatever their native dialect was. So it would go like this. Hari would introduce me to a woman and he would leave. Somehow through sign language we would agree to go to a restaurant for dinner. After eating I would pay and leave by myself. She would silently follow me back to the hotel, into the elevator, out of the elevator, and into my hotel room. We would sit and play a charade-like game to try to get to know one another, with comical results. I would take off my clothes get into bed then she would follow. I would just lie there. I wasn't aggressive in any way and let the woman take the initiative. She would curl up next to me and put her hand on my penis and finish me off with her mouth. After about fifteen minutes she would get up to dress and leave. This same scenario played out each time. One time I thought the woman wanted to have intercourse so I got on top of her when she quickly rolled over and put my cock in her ass. I was surprised by that. This was my introduction to anal sex. I asked Hari about that. He said that was normal. The women preferred it as a means of birth control.

In the cities extreme poverty was everywhere. Some unlucky souls were born untouchables, the lowest caste, consisting of laborers, artisans, and servants who do work that is ritually unclean. Contact between untouchables, particularly the sharing of food and water is limited to avoid pollution of higher, purer individuals by lower, more unclean ones. Once born into this caste, a person has to marry someone else born into this caste in a perpetual cycle. I related to these people. I imagined I felt like them when I was growing up, only I had the illusion that I could work my way out of the inner-city poverty I was born into. In reality it was only an illusion. In fact, I was now risking my freedom to move out of poverty the only way I knew how.

While walking down a street in New Delhi, I saw a man with no legs on a crude board with recycled roller skates for wheels. He was drawing a picture of a beautiful garden on the cement sidewalk with colored chalk. People walked across his drawing as if he was invisible, but there he was, a beggar with skill as an artist. I went over to him and offered him a hundred dollars. He avoided my eyes and put his head down, motioning that I should meet him in the back alley he pointed to. He rolled over to the alley and took the money, then hurriedly pushed the ground with his hands to get his makeshift cart rolling.

When I got back to the hotel I asked a worker who knew me

from my many stays there why I would have to give beggar money in a back alley. He explained that if anyone had seen me give a beggar that much money they would have beaten him and taken it from him. Now this same worker was actually the foreman of the hotel's swimming pool, which had been under construction for at least two years. Over my various visits the visible progress I saw was the hole got a foot deeper every now and then. So I asked him why so little was being accomplished. He said he employed three shifts of workers who used small hand shovels twenty-four hours a day, every day, week after week. If he brought in heavy machinery, he could get the job done in a week, but those workers would have no work. He reminded me that India had existed for thousands of years while the U.S. was still in its infancy. Some day we would understand.

SEVEN

Colombia

On my way back from India through Boston I went to Eric's apartment to repackage hash oil and get it sold. I decided to go by myself to the Auburn Jazz Club in Harvard Square to hear some jazz. I walked into the club and sat down at a table next to an attractive girl. That was the first time I met Susan. She was sitting there having a drink while Tom Rush performed "Ladies Love Outlaws." We began drinking together, talking freely, and laughing a lot. We exchanged travel stories, mine about India and Nepal, and hers of adventures in Colombia. We had both stayed in the best hotels and compared notes on the luxuries of the Oberoi in New Delhi and Bogota's Hotel de la Opera.

We wandered out of the club, leaning on each other and kidding around through Harvard Square. We decided to go to Eric's place. He wasn't home so we just sat around and smoked some pot, getting silly stoned. The conversation turned to a movie that was the subject of controversy in 1972 called *Deep Throat*. Susan bragged that she was skilled in deep throating long before the movie came out.

I said, "Oh really, prove it." That led to the best blowjob I ever had, and being stoned as well, I thought she was magical.

By then it was about one in the morning. We were both hungry and decided to go to Faneuil Hall to the only restaurant in Boston we knew served twenty-four-hour breakfast. The place was packed with students and creatures of the night. The waitresses were known to be insulting. Maybe it was dealing with all the characters that came in or maybe it was their New England charm. Living up to reputation the waitress slammed our breakfasts down in front of us and in a rude tone asked "Anything else?" We laughed at that, still stoned. The old wooden table sat twenty-four people on long benches. We sat side by side as we ate our scrambled eggs and bacon.

Coming from nowhere, Susan said, "You are my outlaw." I was taken aback. I thought I portrayed a sense of innocence not yet worthy of being labeled anything, someone searching to find himself. Outlaw meant an unhappy ending. I wasn't convinced I was destined for that yet. Susan was a free spirit, open minded, and direct. She went to South America frequently and described the wild parties she enjoyed there, snorting coke, staying up all night, sex with Colombian drug dealers. She also told me of the pristine beaches in Colombia and Brazil. She said her friends in Colombia would love me.

I had never been to South America before and traveling with her seemed like it would be a good adventure, so we made plans to go to Bogota, meet her friends, and explore the city. Bogota was a crowded city. The cars reflected the extremes between wealth and poverty. The majority of the cars that clogged the streets were old, beat-up jalopies. The bus exhaust from low-grade diesel was suffocating. Then out of nowhere an unexpected Porsche or Mercedes would speed by. Susan was right about the Hotel de la Opera. The Colonial-era building once housed Simon Bolivar's personal guards. Now converted to a luxury hotel, the facade remained as it was since the 1500s. The interior was renovated with beautiful hardwood floors and high ceilings. The neighborhood was rich in history, with cobblestone streets and glorious old mansions.

Susan arranged to meet her friends at a club downtown. Once outside the historic district, we walked onto a main street where immediately the mood was different. The kids on the street hustled stolen watches and cameras. Every ten feet there was a beggar. It seemed that these beggars, unlike the beggars in India, had an angry look on their faces. They demanded money with the hint of violence if you turned them down. Then there were the pickpockets, street drug dealers, and emerald sellers.

Club Pescadora was full of people and loud, blasting music. Susan's friends greeted us at a private booth. They were already drunk, walking slowly, smiling. We ordered *aguardiente*, a local liquor high in alcohol content with a licorice taste. Susan was very friendly with these Colombians, getting up to dance with the girls. The guys stayed at the table to talk to me. Their English was perfect. Two of them had lived in Miami, the third in New York City. Alfredo had long, curly jet-black hair, black eyes, and a black mustache. His face was nondescript but unlike most Colombians his skin was pale white reflecting his castellano heritage. He was the smartest of the group, polite but with an edge. That night Alfredo and I hung out together. I told him of my travels to different countries hinting at the smuggling part, but leaving enough room for his imagination to fill in the rest. Since I had opened that door, he told me about his smuggling operation and his role in it.

In those days, it seemed almost everyone you met in Colombia was part of some illegal activity. Most businesses had a legitimate front and trafficked in the black market. As long as you belonged to an organization you were protected. Alfredo could trust me because he had nothing to lose. This was his country. I was on my own and at risk. Before I could trust him I needed to spend more time around him.

Susan stayed at the club to party while Alfredo offered to drive me back to the hotel. He sped down side streets in a brand new white Porsche as if he owned the city. I was along for the ride, thinking we could get into some sort of trouble when he crashed the Porsche into a parked car. We were both so drunk we just staggered away and took a taxi back to my hotel. In the hotel lobby we snorted some coke and as he was leaving he invited me to go with him to Cartagena the next morning. I asked him why and he answered "Cartagena is the Riviera of Colombia—beautiful beaches, sexy women, great seafood, and plenty of drugs." I loved that answer and thought who could turn that down?

That night Susan never came back to the hotel. She still hadn't returned by the time Alfredo came by to pick me up at eleven the next morning. I asked him what had happened to her.

"Oh," he said, "she is a crazy chick. She ended up at Gustavo's apartment." I never saw Susan again, nor got another one of her memorable blowjobs.

On the short flight from Bogota to Cartagena Alfredo slept while I looked out the plane window in a dreamlike state, maybe because I hadn't had much sleep, mostly because I was at peace with myself. Below me through a thin layer of clouds were vast areas of unpopulated countryside, tall mountains, lush green valleys, lands that looked like they had not changed since the beginning of time. As the plane made its descent miles of barren coastline appeared. I was getting excited as I focused in on the white foam of the breakwaters.

We picked up Alfredo's jeep at the airport. On the drive to his apartment, standing in the middle of two cross streets was a traffic cop. He lifted his arm toward us with his palm up, indicating he wanted us to stop. Alfredo ignored him and just kept driving right through the busy intersection.

"Didn't that cop want us to stop?" I asked.

He replied, "The cops have no guns, no cars, and no way to enforce the law, so fuck him."

We drove past a shantytown with run-down houses made of cinder blocks. The village people had dark brown skin and looked to be of African descent. They looked very relaxed—the adults were playing with the children, the men and women walked barefoot in a rhythm like a ballet in slow motion. Alfredo explained these were the indigenous peoples of the Colombian Caribbean, descendants of slaves brought from West Africa in the sixteenth century.

Alfredo owned a two-bedroom apartment in a modern ten-story building on the beach. He rolled up a joint and we sat on his balcony getting high, looking down at the beach below. I watched a tall black woman wearing a flowered wraparound dress. A bowl of fruit was balanced perfectly on her head as she walked through knee-high water. In her left hand was a transistor radio and she moved her hips in time to the music. There was a knock on the door. Alfredo had invited ten of his friends over. Alfredo was a lot like Eric—he was handsome and obviously very popular. His apartment was the place to be if you were a young, up-and-coming Colombian. Everyone was drinking and getting high. One of his friends brought a big bag of cocaine, which he chopped up and divided into huge lines on the glass coffee table. It was there for the taking, no one made a big deal about it. As the sun set we all went out to the beach, walking and talking. We stopped at a beachfront open-air restaurant and Alfredo ordered Bloody Marys and shrimp cocktails for everyone. We stayed out on the beach all night, talking continuously as people on coke do. Exhausted we lay on the sand waiting for the sunrise. This was the life here and it repeated every day as days turned into weeks.

One evening, Santiago, a friend of Alfredo's I had met in Bogota, showed up at Alfredo's apartment with a guy named Travis, an American from San Diego. We all partied late into the night and were pretty high when Travis took a camera out of his backpack and asked everyone to get together so he could take pictures. I left the room. No photos of me existed and I was not going to start here. An older man came up to Travis and took the camera away, saying only "No pictures" in broken English. The man had been there all night, standing in the background, not drinking or doing any coke. He seemed serious, not talking to anyone, just quietly observing the actions of the partiers. His reaction to the camera was a good move. This was the first sign that demonstrated that this was anything other than a group of rich kids partying and dabbling in the smuggling industry. After a few weeks of getting drunk, snorting coke, staying up all night, and crashing at Alfredo's, I had passed their initiation rites. They had a glimpse of who I might be in the pecking order of drug dealers. I had an idea of what capabilities they had in the cocaine and marijuana trade.

Alfredo and Santiago wanted to take me to see the Sinu River delta region southwest of Cartagena. They had something they wanted to propose to me in a private setting. At sunrise we got into Alfredo's jeep and the three of us drove a couple hours on the sandy beach to one of the river's mouths. The river was calm. We hired a guide to row us down the river in an old dugout canoe. The morning air was still and the chirping of birds stood out in the quiet.

Santiago told me he was a member of a family that smuggled pot and coke into Miami. He said Travis was their connection in the U.S. but that he was loose cannon and they wanted to stop working with him. Santiago gave me an overview of his business while Alfredo remained silent. He kept talking as I listened to his every word. I studied his face, the direction of his eyes. I watched his hands change position. When he was confident he sat erect. When he was hesitant, overstating his stature in the family order, he slumped over a little. After he finished talking, I began to tell him in detail about my smuggling experiences with Amsterdam, India, and Nepal. I wanted them to understand where I was in the pecking order of dealers. I explained that I trusted my distributors and, depending on the quality and quantity of drugs he was talking about, I would consider a proposal from them.

He said, "I have to check with my guys first."

The conversation then changed to women. Alfredo told me he loved American women. He liked their aggressiveness and kinkiness in bed as opposed to Colombian women who were backward and sexually naïve. I left that alone. The Colombian girls I had met were beautiful and extremely attractive in their bikinis. The main difference between the drunken parties back in Boston and the Cartagena version was that here there was a lack of sexual tension between the men and women here. The women here were playful, but in a childish kind of way, giving you the impression there was no hope of sex on the horizon. I could see why Susan was so popular here.

A few days later Santiago proposed that we try a small transaction together. He had one kilo of cocaine in Miami to be sold. It was earmarked for Travis, but he wanted to give it to me to sell. I agreed to take this on and told him I would be personally responsible for picking it up, selling it, and returning back with the money.

The next day I flew to Miami. Gustavo, my contact, picked me up at the Miami Airport. We drove to a warehouse in an industrial park near the Opa-Locka Executive Airport. Gustavo was about forty years old and had a hardened professional look about him. Observing Gustavo, it became evident to me that Santiago was only a small pawn in this game. There was no way this guy would take orders from a kid like Santiago. I doubted that Santiago even owned this coke as he had tried to make it look. So Santiago was somehow connected but not at a high level. Gustavo was in charge of this situation. He showed me around forty kilos of coke at the warehouse. As I was looking at their stash he mentioned that if this deal went well, they could supply all the coke my guys could sell. Our part would only be to go to Miami to pick it up and take it to our suppliers then return the money to him either in Miami or outside San Diego.

Gustavo weighed the coke I was taking and then hid it in the lining of a small carry-on suitcase. I made my connecting flight to Boston. John, who had accompanied me to Nepal, picked me up at the airport and we drove to his house in Amherst. I filled John in on my connection letting him know in the future he would deal with Gustavo in Miami and I would stay in Cartagena. I asked John to take Eric with him to Miami and rent a two-bedroom apartment. I did not want a record of us checking into hotels in Miami. John broke the cocaine into ounces and took off to meet his distributors. After all expenses and giving John his cut I had just made thirty thousand dollars.

Alfredo met me at the airport when I returned to Cartagena. He nodded at the customs official and the two of us breezed through the airport and got into his jeep. When we got to his apartment, I gave him the money for the coke and told him we could handle ten times that amount monthly. Alfredo confirmed what Gustavo had already told me and agreed that Gustavo would work with Eric and John.

John and Eric left for Miami and rented an apartment at the Brickel Bay Club. This was a yuppie building with a popular nightclub on the grounds. The building had tennis courts and an outdoor pool. Eric hired an interior designer to furnish the place. They bought an older model Mercedes to fit in with the rest of the apartment dwellers in the building. John rented a houseboat for me on the intercostal waterway across from the Fountainebleau Hotel in Miami Beach. We never kept drugs and money in the same place, so the drugs would be held at the apartment and the money exchanges would take place on the houseboat.

Alfredo and I sat around for a while drinking Bloody Marys and snorting a few lines. Then he started to tell me a story that sounded like a myth. He talked about a mysterious self-made Robin Hood that was the head of their family, their godfather who allegedly used the majority of the family smuggling wealth to feed peasants. Alfredo had never met this character himself but was convinced he existed, appearing unannounced without any fanfare wherever and whenever he wanted to. I thought part of this might be true, the rest was more like a romantic story. From what I had seen of human nature, people who ran companies or, in this case, smuggling operations, were greedy, self-interested characters, just like I was turning out to be. So the idea of a philanthropist drug kingpin was not very believable to me.

Alfredo helped me find a small villa to rent. If I was going to work out of Cartagena I had to separate myself from these guys, the partying, and their high-profile lifestyle. The villa I leased was on the bay, set back from the street, its entrance hidden by tropical foliage. From the street only the profile of the red tile roof could be seen. It was a beautiful place and I felt comfortable and secure there. The floors were made of rose-colored marble, the walls white plaster, and the ceilings tongue and groove wood. The master bedroom had a ceiling fan, but the rest of the house was cooled only by the breeze coming off the bay. In the back courtyard a lush green lawn with all sorts of tropical plants and trees competed for space. A hammock hung between two coconut trees near two large birdcages with blue, yellow, and green parrots. I loved my life here. I woke up around ten a.m., smoked a joint, and walked to the beach to surf, came home when the wind came up around three p.m., and relaxed in my hammock with a drink. At night I would dress up in linen suits and walk to the beach. I smoked pot during the day and had a drink or two in the evening. While I lived in Colombia I controlled my drug use, being conscious that I was in a foreign country and did not want to be out of control.

The way the business was coming along gave me adrenalin high. This was me, and this is what I did with my life. My business was expanding. I had hash from Nepal, pot from a reseller in Boston, and now cocaine from Colombia. I had a distributor in Boston, one in Northern California, and a third in Chicago. The difference now was that I did not have to put my own money at risk. The cocaine was never purchased by me. I paid for it after it was sold.

Six months later Gustavo from Miami showed up at my front door out of the blue. In his normally short way he told me he was very pleased working with my team in the U.S. We had picked up and sold more than sixty kilos in the past six months. This time Gustavo seemed a bit different. He spoke slowly and with emotion. He started to tell me about the legendary Padrino and his rise to the role as head of the family. He was convincing as his sincerity showed and I was glad to finally hear about this phantom. The Padrino had been abandoned by his mother at birth in a small village on the outskirts of Medellin. He started out in this world as a paco, a street urchin. According to Gustavo, the Padrino controlled diverse enterprises, including trading in fake emeralds, fake platinum dust, primo Santa Marta Gold marijuana, and cocaine. With absolute focus and intensity he told me the majority of the money they made went to the villagers in Colombia and Venezuela for food and clothes. What was left over was divided equally among "family members." I thought, *What bullshit, a cause-driven smuggler.* The idea was romantic and appealing, but coming from my background I was very skeptical. Why did he really come to my house? To tell me this story?

Gustavo then surprised me. He started to sing a song in a language I had never heard before. In that moment he changed from a cold, heartless robot into an ancient wise man. The song was in Chibcha, an ancient language that pre-dated the Spaniards' arrival in South America. When he stopped, he told me the Padrino and he had both come from the Muisca tribe. Their ancestral routes went back three thousand years. They were a people who did not dominate other ethnic groups or peoples. They believed natural resources could not be privatized. Woods, lakes, plateaus, rivers, and other natural resources were common goods. The peoples they helped were all connected through their language even though their ancestral roots could have been from other tribes. The real reason for Gustavo's visit was to tell me the Padrino wanted to meet me. The meeting would be at the private casino at the Hotel Caribe and I was to go there the following night at seven.

I asked Gustavo, "How will I recognize him?"

He replied, "Don't worry, he will find you."

The next evening I walked the five blocks from my apartment along the bay to the Hotel Caribe. Here I was in my early twenties in a foreign country on my way to meet a mythical man with powerful influence in government, the military, and industry. I walked alone along the sandy street in the balmy night into the unknown. My senses were heightened, my heart was racing, but I kept walking toward this destiny. Once inside the hotel lobby I became confident, forgetting all my reasons for being fearful. I walked from the lobby across a dark old ballroom to the heavy black wood door of the casino. Everyone was dressed in formal attire, the men in suits with ties, the woman in formal evening wear. I was the youngest person there and wore a white linen suit. I sat down at the black jack table, ordered a coke, and started playing. After a few minutes a small old man with a scarred face and thin, crooked nose sat down beside me. I looked straight into his eyes. They were jet black. This guy reminded me of my bubbe. The years of pain and suffering showed on his dark, wrinkled skin, but his eyes were bright and alive.

He said, "Hello, I am Fernando. I've heard a lot about you."

I just looked at him—not what I expected. He was low key, humble, and seemingly kind.

Noticing my absence of words he then said, "Let's take a walk."

We walked outside to the pool. It was now pitch black. No one was around and there were no lights along the patio. We sat down in lounge chairs facing each other. In a soft voice he asked me questions about my family and my young life. He told me about his upbringing. I felt I could be honest with him, and I believed what he told me was true. I could see it in his face and mannerisms. He and I had a lot in common. His life growing up had been much worse than mine, his struggle to survive, forming a band of brothers with other surviving street urchins, uniting under a common cause. It all made sense. He had no politics, no need for fame or glory. It was pretty simple. The family had developed their own code of honor over time. Don't steal from each other. Don't lie to each other. Don't flirt with or sleep with anyone's wife or daughter. Keep your word and, if you get caught, don't talk. Fernando offered me the opportunity to become part of the family conditional upon my acceptance of their code of honor. He told me there would be no ceremony, no initiation, just the two of us agreeing to the family code and accepting that the punishment for breaking the rules was harsh. You would literally become shark food.

This was a decision for me to make. I was not forced or threatened in any way. I could refuse without any repercussions. We both sat there in silence for a while, digesting what had just been said, I stared up at the nighttime sky, comfortable and at peace. When I looked back over to Fernando, he was gone and I could make out his figure walking away into the darkness.

A few days later Gustavo and two other guys dropped in unexpectedly as was normal for them.

Gustavo said, "Padrino has something he wants you to do for him."

I asked, "What's that?"

Gustavo did not reply. I really liked these guys but I was not a joiner. The code of honor was fine with me. I could live by their terms, but was not dedicated to their cause. Feeding hungry people was a good thing, I was all for it. If they wanted to spend their money that way, good for them. I liked being a loner. I made my own decisions. I could never be a blood member of their family, which meant on some level I would be an outsider. I would work for them and follow the rules. I never got a chance to say all that to Fernando but that's where I stood.

I told my housekeeper Carmen I would be gone for a few days and left for the airport with Gustavo and his associates. We flew over endless jungle a few hours to northern Colombia, where the plane landed on a dirt runway surrounded by dense forest and mountains. We got into a jeep and drove a few miles until we met up with what appeared to be a military convoy. Fernando got out of the lead truck, handed me two paper bags, gave me instructions, and took my place in the jeep as it headed back to the plane. You could never accuse these guys of over talking a situation. They set the operation up and plugged you in where they thought you best fit with no questions asked.

I turned my head to the right and looked out the window of an old military cargo truck straight down a thousand-foot-deep ravine. I could hear the sound of a fast-moving river at the bottom and halfway down the ravine saw the rusted-out shell of an old bus rested on its side. Our truck bounced along the road until we had to stop to move a boulder out of the way or hug the side of the mountain to let another vehicle pass us. The dirt road ahead was barely wide enough for our trucks as we wound our way up the mountain pass. We were headed to an Indian village outside El Nula, Venezuela, a few miles from the Colombian border. Behind us were twelve similar trucks carrying food and clothes to poor Indian villagers. Every time I looked down I imagined the truck rolling over and hurtling down the mountain, crashing into the rocks below and finally into the river. It was like being on the edge of a tall building with no guardrail. This was our second day of travel. Overnight we had slept in the trucks. The night sky was jet black with white and yellow sparkling stars. The expanse of the nighttime sky was limitless and humbling. After a day of driving, every moment on the edge of potential disaster, it was a relief to see the sun set and finally pull over for the night.

As we sat around the bonfire, I listened to the men I was with tell stories of their tribal history—tales of famous chiefs, warriors, and hunters that had been passed on from generation to generation. They spoke in their native Chibcha language, which I didn't understand but could sense the pride and honor they held for their ancestors. Gustavo wanted to share this ageless tribal custom with me and roughly translated the stories as they were told. I asked him why these stories had not been written down. He told me outsiders would question the accuracy and retell the stories through their own eyes. They might scoff at some of the imagery or cast judgment from a moral or religious perspective. He explained to me that the history of his tribe dated back to the beginning of civilization. The stories were to be retold with the annunciation and music from the storyteller's voice.

Tomorrow we would cross the border into Venezuela. Our cargo was a gift from my godfather. His passion for helping the poor Indians was a good deed but illegal because we would cross into Venezuela without a cargo manifest and without paying taxes. When the sun came up our caravan continued on slowly, driving about ten miles per hour as the dirt road worsened. We finally came across a remote border crossing with a lone guard standing outside a wood shack. Gustavo and I got out. I carried the bags, one with fifty thousand pesos, the other holding a twenty-two caliber silver-plated pistol in the other.

The order my godfather had given me was simple and direct: "Offer the guard fifty thousand pesos to let the caravan through." I had asked him "What if he doesn't take the bribe?" His answer was, "Shoot him in the head. He is too stupid to live."

Fernando's point of view made perfect sense even though I had never killed anyone and did not like being put in this position. Since this mission was such an important cause for my godfather, I wanted to show him my loyalty so I had agreed to take on the job. But if the border guard got stubborn and did not let us cross, I knew I would not shoot him in the head. Instead I would scare him into taking the money. The border guard had a shiny black mustache that dominated most of his lower face. His eyes were black and the structure of his face and the color of his skin told me he was an Indian. I offered him the bag with the money. He looked right into my eyes, hesitated for a moment, looked at the trucks and the men with me, and made the right choice.

We continued on for another six hours of driving. I never relaxed. The roads were treacherous, my driver has half drunk, and I had no idea what would happen when we arrived at this village. At a rocky pass, we veered off the main road into an area with lush foliage that looked totally uninhabited. As we continued down the mud path, the outline of small thatched houses appeared in the distance. We arrived at a cantina and out of nowhere a mob of about fifty people surrounded the trucks. The little children were thin with dark brown skin. Their faces were dirty and their clothing torn. The adults looked no better. I loved those kids the second I saw them and was grateful to be there and to have brought them the supplies. We unloaded the trucks, handing over the food and clothes to the village elders. I noticed a big boulder on the mountainside painted with my godfather's name. He was a hero to these people. They did not know or care about how he made the money to pay for these bare essentials or why he gave them to them, only that they were grateful for his generosity.

We left the village the next morning and on the way back to Colombia I was much more relaxed. The roads and mountains were becoming more familiar to me. I was thinking the children in that village could have been me. They were born into the lower class in the mountains with no electricity and no running water. If they had been born in the U.S., they might have grown up in Dorchester like me. The class system in South America had begun much earlier than in the U.S., beginning with the Spanish Conquistadors, so the indigenous peoples were relatively poorer. The white Spanish plunderers who came here and stole the natural resources stayed and became the ruling class. They controlled government and industry, allowing the indigenous people a piece of what was left over, the crumbs they did not want.

The convoy arrived back in Colombia at a small private airstrip in Pamplona. My godfather met us there and spoke a while to Gustavo and the other men. Then he walked over to me and stood gazing at me, peering into my soul through my eyes. We connected, sharing the same inner pain caused by hunger and fear. He was older and more mature. It seemed as if he had accepted his destiny and was comfortable with it. I, on the other hand, was looked upon by my Colombian family as a loner, filled with hunger, always hunting, never relaxed. My name in the family was El Lobo Negro, the black wolf. He was the old wolf, looking out for his pack, using wisdom as his guide. I was a young wolf, starting my own pack using survival as a guide.

As the sun came up, Alvaro, Fernando's oldest son, and I boarded an Aerostar 600 piloted by an officer from the Colombian Air Force. We were headed to a twenty-thousand-acre pot farm in the Choco region. No one talked during the two-hour flight. We flew no more than a hundred feet off the ground at a speed of three hundred mph. We landed on a dirt runway that was not visible from the air. As I got off the plane I saw a jeep was waiting for us. We drove to a farm-house, along the way passing armed peasants with old shot guns in one hand and walkie-talkies in the other.

Inside the farmhouse I was introduced to a navigation expert, a communications expert, a boat captain, and two other air force pilots. This think tank was on average about forty-five, all at least twenty years my senior. We all sat down around an old wooden kitchen table where navigation charts of the Pacific Ocean were laid out. Other men lined the room standing guard, serious-looking men armed with submachine guns.

Alvaro introduced the plan, "Because Miami is so visible as an offloading spot for drug shipments, the family wants to explore the feasibility of operating on the West Coast of the United States."

That was the reason for my presence at this strategy meeting. I would head up this operation, coordinate the shipments, determine offloading locations, hire crew members, acquire offloading boats, trucks, and communication equipment and, in my free time, try to purchase AR15s to smuggle back to Colombia. This project would take about two years to organize. The choice was mine. If I worked with them I became part of the family they would pay for everything, and I would give up my other smuggling operations. I would receive a percentage of the profits. If I worked as a subcontractor I would keep my independence but pay out of pocket for the offloading and distribution operation. But I would still have to give up my other smuggling operations to avoid any exposure to the family. The family was concerned that if a problem arose from my other ventures in India and Nepal it could filter down to them. Either way I would work for them exclusively. A part of me wanted to jump right in and get on with it. Surprisingly, I said I needed more time to think it through. Everyone nodded and the mood relaxed. The entire reason for all the tension was my presence as an unknown quantity due to the size of the operation and the possibility I might not be able to handle such a big job.

Alvaro grabbed a bottle of *aguardiente* and said, "Let's take a walk."

Night had fallen and the full moon lit the jungle pathways leading to an old barn. The haystacks piled outside made me think it was used for horses, possibly Peruvian Pasos, which were especially admired and collected by wealthy Colombians. When he opened the barn doors the moonlight revealed palates of neatly wrapped American dollars stacked from floor to ceiling. Alvaro proudly said that we were looking at one hundred million dollars and that they owned many other farms just like this. He acted as if we were looking at a prized collection of antiques. Thoughts raced through my head. *This money is out of circulation, missing from the U.S. economy. Who's looking for it? Hundreds of millions in multiple locations? This business has been going on for a long time. These guys have reach in government, military, and industry. At some point this wealth would blend into those legitimate sectors with a traceable history. Money like this has already been mainstreamed.* My mind settled down.

I looked at Alvaro nonchalantly as if I was used to seeing barns full of cash and asked, "Do you have any horses here?"

Lying on my hammock back in the villa I reflected on my life here. I had adapted well to the Caribbean lifestyle, going to the beach every morning, having lunch outdoors, going home at three p.m. when the winds came up, and relaxing in my hammock listening to the birds. Carmen made fresh fruit juices and cooked dinner every night with fresh fish and vegetables. I did miss sex, but I did not want to attract attention so I stayed by myself most of the time and rarely socialized with the Colombian men I worked with. When I was around Colombian girls it was awkward. I didn't speak fluid Spanish and culturally we were very different. They liked American clothes, music, and movies but their traditional side came out when men were involved.

A year had passed and back in the U.S., Eric was holding my money, which had grown to more than two million dollars. I had made about ten trips back and forth to Colombia. We had successfully transported and sold more than two hundred kilos of coke. I didn't need more risk. I had stopped needing that a long time ago. However, Alvaro's proposal was taking hold in my mind. This was a puzzle to be solved, a challenge with personal and financial risk. Dangerous. I liked it. I never had an attachment to money. I was not possessive of things but I enjoyed what money could buy, and success did drive me. I was obsessed with defiance. I made up my mind fully aware that any hope of a normal life was gone. This was the point of no return. I would now be committed to this family and a criminal life.

My idea of a marriage and family of my own would now change. My life would have no room in it for a woman I might want to marry. Any woman who got close to me would be a target for law enforcement. She could be approached, intimidated into providing information about my behavior, who I saw, where I went, what I did with money, how many identities I had, who forged my fake passports and travel papers, where was I vulnerable, and a host of other questions law enforcement would love to have the answers to. Even worse, if I got busted she would be humiliated publicly, asked to turn on me, and maybe be killed. I would not do that to a woman I loved, so love would have to be put on hold until I was safely out of this business, if ever.

Watching a woman walk made me smile. I love the way woman look. I always have. I would study them, the expressions in their face, the shape of their eyes, and the fullness of their lips. I never thought woman were like men only in different bodies. To me women were the opposite of men in beautifully shaped bodies. My instincts told me a woman would someday be my partner and my quest would be over. I would mate with her and together we would become a family. Understanding that love was out of the question as long as I was a criminal, I still wanted sex. I liked being quiet. I spoke only when I had to pass on information to colleagues and I did that carefully. To meet a woman and seduce her for sex was too risky. I could never talk about my real life, my real beliefs, and any woman with half a brain would run for the hills.

However there was one type of woman who seemed attracted to the part of me they knew was carefully hidden. They did not want the truth—they wanted the adrenaline rush of being with an outlaw. Lucy from Wellesley College and Susan, who introduced me to Colombia, both had that characteristic. None of those women would marry someone like me. They would take me to meet their girlfriends to show me off, play at sex for practice so when finally hunting for a husband, they would have sexual confidence. No one had to tell me that. I just knew it and frankly didn't care. Of course I could hire hookers. They would be the closest female companions I could have and they led double lives just like I did.

The sun was just coming up as I boarded a single-engine Cessna for the long, slow flight to Costa Rica. I brought two suitcases of clothes, toiletries, and my surfboard. I had no drugs on me and five thousand dollars to last me until I got to California. My pilot was one of the Colombian pilots I had met at the ranch in Choco. He was a wiry man, all about business. I was just cargo to him so the conversation for the next six hours was limited to a few grunts. Our destination was a farm on the outskirts of Playa Jaco. As the plane slowly made its way through the sky I was thinking about the tasks ahead of me. The first step in setting up the West Coast operations would be to find a low-profile safe house in Costa Rica, a place close enough to meet with my Colombian counterparts to avoid going in and out of Colombia too frequently. Arriving from Colombia sent up a red flag at U.S. customs whereas Costa Rica was not on their radar. Once that stopover was established, the next step would be to find a community in Northern California to set up operations then blend in as quietly as possible. I needed back stories to explain why I had come to these places without raising any eyebrows.

I was giving myself a headache thinking over what could go wrong, so I decided to relax my brain with a technique I had taught myself. Somewhere between India and Nepal I came to the realization that a smuggling career would eventually land me in prison. I imagined myself sitting in a prison cell with concrete floors and walls. There was a single window with black iron bars protecting the glass. I was sitting on a metal bunk that was attached to the walls with iron brackets. I imagined myself staring out the window. That's when it came to me—I had to fill my head with beautiful images and feel-good memories. I chose beautiful sunsets, dramatic vistas, ironic events, and great sex. I started taking mental snapshots so that I could bring them up when I ended up in prison. I had nothing to do on this long flight except make myself crazy with all the future unknowns, so I closed my eyes and went back to my mental slide show. I stopped on the slide I called "Huge Tits." It was the summer in Boston. I was walking down Commonwealth Avenue when I met a girl with the largest breasts I had ever seen. We walked together talking, me about photography, her about all the sexual freedom she had.

When we arrived at her apartment building I was going to ask for her name and number when she said, "I have some original Edward S. Curtis photographs. Would you like to come up and see them?"

"Sure I would," I replied, not expecting anything one way or the other. I took off my coat looking around at her apartment, a small studio with a bed taking up most of the room, and a few pictures on the wall. Silently she started to undress. Now I had great expectations for this rendezvous. Why not? Look at those breasts, Fredrick's of

Hollywood-type lingerie, the slow strip tease. She lay on the bed, spread her legs, and closed her eyes. *What!* I thought to myself, *is this?* I stripped down and got on top of her. She just lay there, as if frozen in time. I tried to stimulate her anyway I knew how—nothing. I was already inside of her so I just made believe she was a mannequin and fucked her until I came. I got dressed and left. Lesson learned—you can't judge people by their outward appearance.

The plane hit some turbulence, which brought me back to reality, and eventually on the horizon I could see the foam of breaking waves. We were headed straight down toward a hut on an open grassy field when the pilot suddenly accelerated the throttle and pulled the joystick straight back, making the nose pull up suddenly. He was buzzing the camp to let the people who were to pick me up know we were landing. He circled around and landed the plane on the grass runway.

I was furious when I exited the plane, about to smash the pilot in the face. He had scared the shit out of me. I held back my anger and took off in a jeep with two strangers. They drove me to a low-end beach motel where I had already been checked in under an assumed name. I stayed at Playa Jaco for a few days planning my strategy for the tasks ahead. The beach there was pristine the water so clean I could see fish swimming under me as I surfed. Coconut trees grew to the water's edge.

San Jose was my target destination. I needed the city's infrastructure to support my reason for being there. I went to the U.S. Embassy to request a new passport saying mine was lost. My old passport was filled with stamps from Colombia. With a new passport I could enter the U.S. without being questioned. While walking around the old part of the city I found a commercial office space for rent. It was down an alley hidden between two warehouses. The front door was solid and there were no windows facing the alley. Inside was an open space of four hundred square feet with worn out hardwood flooring. An electrical cord with a lampshade attached to it hung from the ceiling. In the back corner was a bathroom with a toilet and sink, no shower. The landlord did not ask for a lease so I didn't have to sign anything and I paid in cash month to month. I hired a taxi to take me to the hardware store where a bought tools and materials to make a bed and picked up pillows, sheets, and towels. Home, sweet home. On the outside, I was carefree. I had no drugs on me and I was invisible to any kind of scrutiny, looking like a tourist walking around enjoying the perfect weather and Costa Rican culture on a budget. On the inside I was anxious to have the groundwork completed.

My favorite hangout, the San Jose Opera House, sat in the middle of an old square. It was a miniature version of a Parisian opera house. Inside was a little café that served only tunafish finger sandwiches. I noticed a white-haired older man with a long white beard. Normally I stayed away from American tourists but he seemed different. His demeanor was relaxed, non-threatening. I introduced myself and we ended up talking for a while. Larry was from Sausalito, across the bay from San Francisco, and had traveled the world. He was in Costa Rica just hanging out. I listened to his stories for hours. Larry told me about his houseboat community in Sausalito and the culture of Marin County. I paid attention to the details. Here I am looking to find a base to operate from in Northern California and all of a sudden here is this man from San Francisco sitting right in front of me telling me all about the place. Coincidences like this had happened to me over and over again. I let them play out to my advantage. Later that evening Larry introduced me to Susan and Charlie, also from Northern California who were vacationing in Costa Rica for the summer. Over the next few months we became friends. I spent more time at their house than at my own. We smoked pot and walked around the city together. Though I told them I dealt in pot, I didn't say at what level. They wanted to get into the business themselves. They would be going back to California soon and insisted I come to their house in stay with them. They were hoping to find a place in the drug business through me.

EIGHT

Marin County

When my new passport came through I left San Jose to test out the waters in Marin County. I kept my office-apartment in San Jose while renting a room from Susan and Charlie at their home in Mill Valley. I stayed with them for about two months while I got myself organized. The distributors I worked with were also creating new covers to operate in the same county, setting up legitimate fronts.

One afternoon I was driving over to Sausalito to visit Larry when I noticed a girl hitchhiking. She looked very normal and healthy like surfer girls that hang out at the beach. I was used to hitchhiking around Boston and thought I could help a fellow hitchhiker out.

When she got in my car I asked very politely, "So what do you do?"

She replied she was a working woman, working the street. I assumed she meant she worked on the road as a street cleaner or something to that effect.

So I continued on, "Where are you going?"

She said, "Wherever you want me to."

I found this to be an odd answer. I said, "Where exactly can I drop you off?"

Angrily she said, "Are you stupid? I said I am a working woman."

Thinking she was nuts I stopped my car and told her to get out.

She muttered under her breath, "Asshole."

When I got to Larry's place, I told him about what had just happened. He said a working woman is another name for a hooker and since I stopped for her she thought I wanted to pay her for sex in the car. That was the first time I had ever heard of that—Marin County was full of surprises.

Larry lived on a houseboat docked at Gate 5 in Sausalito, a bohemian refuge with elaborate and funky houseboats built on top of old floating hulls, all different and with amazing craftsmanship and flair. This place attracted artists, musicians, and outlaws. When the sun went down it would not be uncommon to find Larry with a group of other bohemians sitting around a campfire singing and telling stories. They would be drinking whiskey from pint bottles and smoking pot. I hung out with Larry a lot and loved listening to his stories. Larry had been the first American photojournalist to visit China during the Mao regime. He directed a film called *The Moving Finger*, a jazzy indie film featuring Barry Newman and Lionel Stander. Larry also produced many documentaries for Time Warner over the years. He brought me into his circle of friends, all around his age and equally accomplished in the fields of acting and writing. His closest friend was a guy named Shel Silverstein, a well-known author, songwriter, and cartoonist. Shel had a houseboat at Gate 5 and homes in other bohemian places like Key West and Greenwich Village. Another friend, Hershel Bernardi, was a Broadway star. So there I was a drug smuggler hanging out with these older, worldly guys who were living an independent life outside of the system. They found a way to do that without breaking the law and yet were still successful. They were very curious about my travels and my thoughts on the people I had met. They understood the world I lived in and didn't judge me. They were a safe group of guys to be with. They wanted nothing from me, and I nothing from them. Whenever I was feeling alone or scared I could trust these guys and talk to them about anything.

It took almost a year to successfully set up the Pacific Coast operations. We were smuggling tons of marijuana to the Pacific Coast, offloading freighters with smaller craft to remote beachfronts north of Long Beach all the way up to Puget Sound. However, we continued to run loads of cocaine through Miami. I picked up a few kilos of coke from Gustavo in Miami to sell to Morten, a new distributor in Marin and try him out. Morten did a great job—took possession of the coke, weighed it, and paid for it within two hours. I turned the cocaine operation over to Eric to manage while I concentrated on the pot deals.

Susan and Charlie were social creatures, blending part-time drug dealing with their Wall Street careers. Friends were constantly stopping by their house to party. If they were going out to a party they would ask me if I wanted to come along. They got high almost every day. I was a loner and preferred to stay that way, so it was time for me to get my own place. I found an old cabin in San Anselmo at the end of a cul-de-sac. The cabin was secluded down a hill and beyond a long flight of old wooden stairs that wound through heavy foliage. I hired a local attorney, Robert Moran, to set up an LLC. and bought the cabin under the company's name. Moran referred me to Jim Talley, a local builder he hired to build his home. I paid him in cash and he paid all the subcontractors through his company. Moran knew there was no way to track the cash, and he had no problem with where the cash came from. At this time everything was going well—my drug business, washing money, new friends.

Robert Moran was a Stanford graduate with his own legal practice in San Francisco. He was well dressed, very articulate, and took me under his wing to teach me how to blend in with normal society, the very world I risked my life to stay out of. This attorney was the conduit between my world, the black market, and the legitimate business world. I had been around smugglers and drug dealers since I was nineteen and had no understanding of how civil and criminal law operated in the normal business world. This attorney was hired to protect me and my interests. He set up a business front for me, introduced me to high society in San Francisco, and connected me to bank board members, so it seemed like he knew what he was doing. How could all these important people do business with me unless they knew they could not be connected to dirty money. Soon I was wearing Brioni suits, driving Ferraris, flying first class, and having sex with educated wealthy women from the upper crust of San Francisco.

Robert's home was built to replicate an eighteenth-century Gothic castle on top of a hill. The dirt road to the house was intentionally left unpaved for effect. When you arrived you felt you were in a different century. Robert would invite me for dinner and it was always the same menu—filet mignons with hot mustard sauce and creamed spinach. We ate in the cavernous kitchen at an old French wood table.

Robert was as crafty and deceptive as a human being could be but I was not fully aware of his machinations until much later. I sensed it but went along with his guidance thinking he knew what to do and would not bite the hand who paid him. He had the air of an aristocrat, yet he was dealing with me, a street kid from Dorchester and career smuggler. It was obvious he had a hidden agenda but I never tried to penetrate it. After dinner we would have a cognac in his library. One evening he coyly invited me to go to his sauna in the basement. Robert pointed down a circular set of winding stone stairs and walked back to the library. As I approached I could see three naked women through the glass doors. These women were unlike any of the girls I had known. They performed like a sexual orchestra and I was the only one in the audience. This was a common occurrence at Robert's. I understood his motive for providing the women, but I could never understand their reasons for putting on the show. I thought they must be under his spell. One of the women was a concert pianist, another a ballet choreographer. Maybe they were bored with their lives and he convinced them to be sexual servants.

I liked the normal people I got to know as I lived my double life in Marin County. It was painful to deceive them every day with lies made up to conceal my illegal activities. Being back in the U.S., I was looking forward to spending time with a normal woman who spoke English. While shopping in San Francisco I met a saleswoman in a leather shop who sold me a coat. Stana had moved to San Francisco from Louisiana. I was attracted to her and decided to ask her to go out with me. I had been out of the U.S. for a long time and had not been with a woman who was not in some way involved with black marketers. This girl was definitely normal. I could tell by her demeanor that she had not been around rough people. She gave me her address and we agreed that I would pick her up and go to the movies and out for dinner that same night. While I was shopping around for a gift for Stana, I noticed a flower shop with terrariums for sale. One that particularly stood out to me had a live tarantula in it. I bought it thinking that she would really like it. I knew nothing about dating or for that matter anything about current movies. I checked the newspaper and found a movie called *I Am Curious (Yellow)*. This movie seemed to be getting a lot of attention. I also selected a seafood restaurant for dinner after the movie. I picked her up at her apartment where she lived with her mother. I presented the terrarium to her. She took it, looking at me oddly, and put it on top of the radiator. We went to the movie but did not stay because she said it was vulgar. How was I to know the movie was about nudity and sex? We went to dinner and had a good meal and I drove her home. Except for the choice in movies I thought the date was going great. When I took her home, I politely walked her to her door. She went inside, talked with her mother, then came back and told me not to call her again.

I told my friends Shel and Larry the story of my date. They said not to worry, she probably wasn't for me anyway. Right after that Larry introduced me to Samantha. She was very beautiful, with long, wild, dark blonde hair and green eyes. She was sitting at the table on Larry's boat eating a dark chocolate bar. She asked me if I wanted some. I told her only if there was hot black coffee to dip the chocolate into. She thought that amusing and it opened the door for us to start talking. We left Larry's boat and drove to my house where she stayed for two weeks. During that time she told me about being raised as a Georgetown socialite, neglected and ignored by her mother. Her father was a State Department employee who died of a heart attack at the dinner table. She was gang raped at age fourteen, and had pretty much given up on people. She was living part-time at my house and part time in a tent on Mount Tamalpais with her dogs. She could have been one of my black girlfriends from Dorchester only she was white and from a high society family. I decided to take her in and care for her. She came and went as she wanted. I bought her a car, clothes, and eventually her own house. We had an odd relationship. Sometimes she lived with me, sometimes she didn't. Sometimes she was just with me, and sometimes she wasn't. She was the kind of woman who at that point in her life that carried the term "free spirit" to a new level. I accepted her the way she was and did my best to be a good friend to her.

On my twenty-fourth birthday some friends sent over a white Bentley with six high-end call girls as a present. As they were getting out of the car I saw Samantha coming into my bedroom through the deck. She looked out the window, saw the girls, went to my closet and grabbed my sawed-off shotgun. With the shotgun sticking out the window she yelled at them "Get the fuck out of my property." I watched this show go down knowing I had just missed a great birthday present. The girls left, then Samantha left, and I ended up hanging out at Gate 5 with Larry and Shel on my birthday exchanging stories and getting high.

Eric was still in Cambridge selling drugs and working at a men's clothing store. I was having a great time in Marin County and wanted to share it with him. Eric flew out to visit. He loved California and wanted to move to Sausalito. I would have John run the business in Boston. We found a white, shingled Cape Cod-style house for Eric to rent on a hill overlooking San Francisco Bay. I bought him a baby blue Datsun 260Z. Eric being a very friendly guy, in no time built himself a network of friends both men and women who would come over to his house or go to concerts with him. He was always surrounded by people while I was always a loner. Eric respected that. He didn't force his newly-made friends on me or insist I go out when I didn't want to.

I always tried to protect Eric in the smuggling business. I gave him the jobs that had the least amount of risk and I paid him double of what the job was worth. He would count cash, load bails of marijuana onto trucks, pick me up at airports, and travel with me when I had no drugs or great amounts of money with me. I never let him meet any dangerous characters trying my best to keep him out of harm's way. My business could be treacherous. That's why it paid so well. By the time I was twenty-five my net worth topped twenty million dollars. So no matter what he did for me there would be a consequence if he were caught.

One of the friends Eric made was a guy named Raymond. He was in the music industry and had moved from London to Sausalito. They hung out a lot since Eric was a drummer and loved music.

One day at Eric's house, Raymond blurted out, "Eric has the best job in Marin County."

I said, "Really, what's that"?

He replied, "Being your best friend."

After that I kept an eye on Raymond. Eric was naive about how people perceived my wealth and my generosity toward him. A few years later Raymond was arrested selling a small amount of cocaine to an undercover agent. This type of person was the last thing I needed around me.

I watched from an emotional distance as Eric made these new friends. He stayed stoned most of the time and went to parties. He was impressed with rock stars, their agents, and producers, and became kind of a groupie supplying free drugs as a way to be accepted in their world. I loved him like a brother, but like most brothers, we were different. Eric came from a loving family with a great mom and dad. They gave him a sense of comfort and trust in people. For me, that had to be consciously developed and worked on. It did not come naturally.

Laundering money through real estate was a good way to invest money but I needed liquidity. I needed cash to pay my everyday expenses and a monthly paycheck. To accomplish this I opened a pre-Columbian jewelry store on the main street in Sausalito. I hired a recent college graduate named Christine to work there. She suspected what other business I was in but we never talked about it.

The store's walls and floors were covered in thick black carpeting with showcases built into the walls. When the lights were turned on only the showcase lit up and the gold jewelry just shined. I would go into the store once a week to check on sales and cash flow. If the sales were slow I would buy my own jewelry under fake names, hold it for a while, then put it back into inventory.

Moran, my attorney, specialized in real estate deals and knew all the ins and outs of the business. Another way to launder money, he advised, was to buy distressed properties and pay for the improvements in cash. You could buy a run-down home in a good location and funnel cash into it then eventually resell it at full value without anyone knowing where the money came from. I bought an abandoned estate on a hilltop in San Anselmo for $165,000. I hired Jim, the contractor whom I trusted and had rebuilt my first house in San Anselmo. I gave him a suitcase with $600,000 to spend on the renovation. This would give me an asset worth roughly $700,000. The house was custom-built and equipped with everything I could ever need or want. It was set on four acres, landscaped for privacy, with winding paths leading to a large swimming pool. On the ground floor, the living room was set up with a projector and six-foot screen connected to a massive McIntosh high-end stereo system with a separate billiards room off to one side. The kitchen was equipped with all the best chef's appliances and custom cabinetry. It connected to a dining room with a huge table that could seat twenty guests. The guest bedroom was in its own separate wing on the same floor. Its sliding redwood panel walls disguised a private sauna.

The entire second floor was my bedroom with big walk-in closets, marble master bath, and an eight-foot-by-four-foot custom-made Jacuzzi tub with six overhead shower nozzles. At the back of one walk-in closet was a hidden door to a closet for my shotgun and everyday spending money, small amounts of cash up to a hundred thousand dollars. I stored bulkier items in a vault at a local storage warehouse. The vault held millions in gold Krugerrands, emeralds, semi-precious stones, and pre-Columbian gold jewelry. The basement was remodeled to accommodate a hidden room where the money that was to be sent back to Colombia was kept.

Joan, my housekeeper, was an older woman who had raised a family and was now widowed. She became a housekeeper and cook in order to survive. She was from Scotland, a big woman with a strong constitution. She did not live on the property but came over to do all the food shopping, laundry, and cleaning when I asked her to. There were times when I did not want her at the house, especially during a business deal, so I would give her time off with pay. When she arrived in the morning she would check on me. She woke me up no matter what and made me eat breakfast. She was motherly yet stern. I protected her, never letting her witness any money or drugs changing hands. If anything were to happen to me she would have no knowledge of my activities. She was a good hard-working lady and should not suffer because she was my employee.

One night I wanted to visit two airline stewardesses who were on a stopover in San Francisco. I was too high to drive so I hired a limo though ordinarily I wouldn't to keep a low profile. A black Lincoln Town Car came to pick me up and drive me to the Fairmont Hotel. Larry, the driver was kind of short, slim with black hair and a neat beard. He agreed to wait for me until I was ready to go home. On the way he told me his life story. He came right out and told me he was gay which was unusual for the 1970s as gays had not yet come out of the closet. I had never met anyone who was gay before, or at least that I knew was gay. Larry told me about how being gay forced him to lead a double life. In a strange way I understood him and related to his secret life. At that point I asked him how much he made driving limos and offered him a job to drive me around for twice that amount. He agreed to take the job as long as he could pick out his uniform and could wear an official chauffeur's hat. The next day we went to an auto dealership and I let him pick out the car he liked, a dark blue four-door Lincoln. He insisted that a thin gold stripe be stenciled along the sides of the car with my company's initials. So he gave notice and a few weeks later the car showed up and so did he.

Larry kept the car at his house and would be on call any time I needed him. He did not quite approve of my wardrobe so one day he drove me into San Francisco to pick out clothes. I respected his sense of style, so I didn't fight it. We went to his favorite high-end men's boutique, Wilkes Bashford and he selected a number of expensive suits, ties, shoes, and slacks for me. When he picked me up he looked me up and down to make sure I was properly shaved and groomed. The suits and slacks were uncomfortable. I liked jeans and tee shirts. I went along with the show because I trusted his judgment as to how I should look.

My German Shepard, Ainge, was my best friend. I loved him more than I loved any human at that point in my life. I got him when he was a little puppy, maybe three months old, from a breeder in Miami on one of my countless trips there. Ainge was a real character. When he and I traveled I would not stay in a hotel that did not allow dogs and eventually I bought an RV so we could go more places together. The San Anselmo property was about four acres, all of it fenced in with chain link. So I could just let Ainge out and he could run around doing whatever he wanted.

Late one afternoon I came home to find the gate to the driveway open. My heart raced wondering what could be going on. The driveway was about a hundred yards long and led to a big courtyard in front of the house that could not be seen from the road. As I approached the courtyard, I saw four police cars parked in front of the house. Two police officers were standing at the front door. I could not believe it. I got out of my car and walked over to the cops. One of them said they received a report of someone being murdered on the property. Well, the only one home was Ainge. It turned out he had found a deer and it was screaming while he was chewing on it. "Fucking Ainge!" I had lived there quietly for two years, having parties, making drug deals, being careful not to show any illegal activity without the cops being called once and now it was my dog that attracted their attention. The cops shot the deer and took it away without any other questions.

Coming from the city and never having pets of my own I had no idea how much I would love animals. Samantha had introduced the idea of having pets into my world. In order to make her happy I went along with it. I bought an African Grey parrot named Dusty. My house was very big for one person so he had his own room. The floors were green marble and the windows were floor to ceiling looking out over San Francisco bay. Anybody would have been happy living there, but I did not have anybody so Dusty got that room. He was a funny bird. Sometimes I would come home and Ainge would be sitting inches from his cage just glaring at him. Dusty could imitate anyone's voice. He would call Ainge a couple of times in my voice and Ainge would fall for it, come running, and find Dusty instead of me.

Obviously Dusty, being a bird, had no understanding of what he was saying so I had to be careful about what he overheard. He just might repeat the wrong thing at the wrong time. Two women were spending the night after getting high for hours. We were tired and the three of us went to lie down on the bed in the room next to Dusty's. One woman said to the other, "Let me suck his dick." For the rest of the night Dusty repeated that over and over. At first we all laughed but after the tenth time they were saying "Can you shut that bird up?" For months he would randomly blurt out those words when he felt like it, embarrassing a guest or shocking the housekeeper, Joan.

Very few people ever came to the house. My chauffeur, Larry, my housekeeper, Joan, and my lawyer, Robert, were there the most often. The only other people I allowed to come over were Eric, Larry, Shel, and on one occasion, my godfather's son visiting from Colombia. From time to time I would have small parties or invite women from a carefully selected circle whom I knew I could trust. New Year's Eve was an exception and I liked to welcome in the new year with a real celebration. It is 1974. Peter Frampton, the Eagles, and Queen were topping the music charts. My ritual for this special night included serving the best cocaine, champagne, and vodka. On a beautiful Waterford crystal plate I served my guests pharmaceutical-grade cocaine called Merck. Each guest had a little gold spoon to scoop up the coke and snort it. For a first course I had ice-cold Stoly. As the night progressed, Roederer Cristal champagne was served in crystal flutes. The idea of serving food was beneath me. Who would want food when there was gourmet cocaine and the best vodka and champagne?

All my guests were in some way connected to the drug world except for my attorney, Robert. He brought two women with him that night that looked like typical Nob Hill socialites. They mingled with the other guests, polite yet restrained, as if they were attending a political event at the mayor's house. My other guests were there solely to have a good time, let their guard down, and just go crazy. There was no pretense, just a mad exchange of energy. There were probably a total of twenty people coming and going that night. The men are all dressed in their best New Year's Eve attire—black jeans with white silk shirts. No one wore tuxes or suits, except Robert. Everyone there was either in the music industry or drug dealers. The women were elegantly dressed in high heels, black stockings, and short, low-cut black cocktail dresses. As drug dealers, none of us could go out in public wearing the jewelry we owned. So when we had our get-together it was time to shine—the men with their watches and gold necklaces, the women with their diamonds and emeralds.

We all knew our lives were temporary and all we owned and our freedom could be taken away in the blink of an eye. We lived for the moment. Rock music played in the background as we engaged in the conversation of the day. I got into a heated debate over the nutritional value of cocaine versus food. I had done my research and referred back to the Incas of Peru and how they held off the Spanish Conquistadors by chewing coca leaves on Machu Picchu. I went so far as to say there was more nutritional value in a line of cocaine than in an orange. I also argued the point that sleep was a waste of time. Obviously if you did not sleep you would have more life to experience. Who could argue these points better than I? I practiced what I preached.

As the evening progressed the mood was engaging. Some people were dancing alone or with a partner. Some of the men went down the hall to play pool. The conversation at the table turned to regrets of things we had not accomplished last year.

Carol, the wife of one of my guests, Thomas, a drummer in a well-known rock band and also a distributor of fine drugs to the music industry said, "I always wanted to have sex with three guys at once." No one argued with her because we all knew she would say, "Well, if a guy wanted three women. . . ."

Thomas, being drunk and stoned asked for two volunteers to help him fulfill his wife's goal. I myself passed but Eric and another guy stepped up. Now that was camaraderie. I thought once she was sober she might regret doing this, blame Thomas, and create a rift in our future business dealings.

Just before midnight the four of them took off to the guest bedroom, bringing a bottle of champagne and invited everyone to watch the show. Truth be told, no one cared, but to go along with the spirit of her idea, we gathered around in the room while Carol orchestrated the show. This went on until midnight when we all raised our glasses and shouted Happy New Year. The four naked bodies were still entwined and stopped for a moment to join in the toast.

We shortly lost interest in that show and moved upstairs to the deck with a direct view of San Francisco and the reflection of the lights glittering on the bay. We philosophized about drugs and music until the sun came up. My guests all said their good-byes and left—or so I thought.

I went downstairs to look over the house and make sure all the drugs were put away. I checked the living room tables, the dining room table, and walked through the kitchen. Then I went into the guest bedroom and found a woman in the bathroom looking at herself in the mirror. She introduced herself as Jill. She was one of the two ladies Robert had brought. She was wearing a full-length white chiffon see-through dress. Her hair was stiffly pulled back on top of her head with every strand in place.

Jill said, "Oh, I missed my ride. Would it be okay for me to stay here?"

I asked, "Where do you live?"

She replied "Nob Hill, in the city."

I thought to myself, *She stayed behind because she wanted to find out more about me or that snake lawyer of mine wanted to plant someone close to me.* Whatever the reason, she needed to go. I had a choice of vehicles to drive her home in: a Ferrari, an Aston Martin, a Mercedes, or my motorcycle, an MV Agusta. I chose the motorcycle to blow off that perfect veneer.

Handing her a helmet, Jill said, "I won't wear that."

Fine with me. Off we went. As we crossed the Golden Gate Bridge her dress blew up around her waist. Her hair, held perfectly in place by hair spray before we left now stood straight up. We arrived at her house and drove up the circular driveway. The house looked prestigious—wrought iron gates, Ionic columns, typical old-money San Francisco. She got off the motorcycle, straightened herself out, and asked if I wanted to come in for a cup of coffee. Had I been a banker, stockbroker, or any other young, successful businessman, I would have pursued her. But I was a drug smuggler living outside the law and she would have been nothing but trouble to me. So I politely declined, and left.

Lyle and Thomas were two of my highest producers. They had great contacts in Hollywood selling large volumes of cocaine to executives in the movie industry and celebrities. As a reward for years of loyal service I invited them to go on a fishing trip in Costa Rica. Thomas couldn't make it but Lyle was very excited and couldn't wait to go. He went on about how it would be great time for the two of us to get to know each other outside of the drug business. From San Jose we flew in a private single-engine plane to a remote fishing camp on the Nicaragua River, a spot that was known for its hundred-plus pound tarpon. We landed on a sand runway where we were met by two locals who took us downriver in an old wooden dugout canoe. After several hours, we arrived at the camp set in dense jungle filled with iguanas, keel-billed toucans, caimans, crocodiles, and spider and white-faced monkeys of Barra Del Colorado. The river is also home to bull sharks which migrate from the Caribbean Sea upriver to Lake Nicaragua.

At the lodge we were given .38 revolvers and a snake anti-venom kit. This area was well known for a type of aggressive poisonous snake called a pit viper. In the mess hall we noticed four older American men. I asked the guide who they were and he said they were U.S. federal judges that came there every year. How absurd is that? Thousands of miles away from home in the middle of the jungle two smugglers take a fishing trip and end up with four federal judges as lodge buddies. We spent a week there fishing and getting to know the judges on a first-name basis. While we were talking about family life or sports, I would be thinking, *Someday I might be in front of one of them as an accused drug smuggler.* It made me sad to think I was on the opposite side of the law since I liked these guys. They were hard working, ethical people. When they asked us what we did, Lyle took the lead and said that we were in the music industry. Since Lyle really was in the music business, he had plenty of stories to tell. I was my usual quiet, distant self.

Upon my return Eric had made a friend he was anxious to introduce me to. This guy said he could provide a really good source for large amounts of pot. I worked solely for my family in Colombia and was not looking for any new partners or deals. Eric didn't know that, so he thought he was being valuable by making a new introduction. It was my general policy not to meet new people, but if I had to, it would be at their place. So when Eric asked if he could bring his new friend, over I was reluctant. But because I loved Eric and it was important for him, eventually I agreed. We arranged a time and day for the meeting.

They arrived on time in a dark blue Ferrari. Eric introduced Sven, tall, athletic, with brown hair and a narrow face. He was a professional ski racer from Colorado and had lived in Switzerland for the last few years. We talked, smoked pot, and drank vodka for a few hours getting to know one another. He asked how I had made all my money. I told him I had a chain of jewelry stores, one of which was in Sausalito, and had made a number of smart investments including buying and selling rare Ferraris. He talked openly about his connections in the drug world and the great access he had to quantities of marijuana and cocaine. I told him I had nothing to do with that world, but it did not deter his storytelling.

I suspected he might be wired and hoped to get me to talk about my smuggling enterprise. I invited him to join Eric and me in the sauna. This way he would have to take off his clothes and I could see if he was wired or not. Before getting into the sauna, I offered him a line or two of cocaine. He was reluctant, but sensed this meeting was over if he refused. Eric and I went first, snorting cocaine out of a little stash bottle. When Sven was watching Eric snort the coke, I put some crystallized LSD 25 on a mirror. It looked just like coke but was actually five times as potent and a hallucinogenic. I chopped it up with a razor and handed it to him with a rolled up hundred dollar bill. He snorted the LSD and we all prepared to go in the sauna. He started to take his clothes off and then balked about removing his cowboy boots, saying he never took them off. So in front of us he stripped naked and then put his boots back on. This could have been the LSD talking or he was simply a nut or he had a bug in his boots.

I said, "No problem," and pressed on the wall and the door sprung open revealing the sauna.

He walked into the sauna butt-naked except for his boots. Eric followed. I told them I would join them in a minute. I quickly looked through his clothes, nothing there. Eric came out of the sauna. I told him to get dressed, that something was wrong with this guy.

After about five minutes alone in the sauna Sven started weeping and crying out, "Make it stop, make it stop."

I gave him two Nembutal's, strong sleeping pills that would counteract the LSD, and he passed out. I yanked off his boots and noticed the heel on one looked different from the other. It twisted off and inside there was the bug.

We put this clown in the trunk of an old car I kept around to keep a low profile and drove him to his house. When we unlocked his front door we saw that the entire house was void of furniture, only a mattress on the floor and very few clothes in the closet. So we helped him into his house and laid him on the mattress. I never saw him again, nor did I hear anything about him. He had just disappeared from Marin County. As for the bug, I wondered just who might have been at the other end—or who was setting me up.

I understood Eric wanting me to meet Sven and how he could have been fooled. Eric knew I always gave him work that was not dangerous. In his mind he was trying to contribute to our operations. We both agreed this Sven was an undercover agent and Eric never talked about it again. The DEA and local law enforcement were offering deals to all kinds of people to get close to me and others like me. The game of cops and robbers had changed: the cops were leveraging criminals to turn on each other instead of them doing their own work and catching criminals fair and square. This was happening only in the U.S. In Colombia, we did not have this problem. In Colombia if someone tried to make a deal with the police it would be brought to the attention of the lawyers representing the drug lords and that person would never make it out of the holding cell alive. I was the only one who knew all the moving parts of the business. I was responsible for vouching for anyone I dealt with to my Colombian family. I had to be sure they were both competent and trustworthy. Anyone can make an honest mistake, but if that happened I had to be sure they could never trade what they knew for their advantage. So what and who they knew was controlled by me. The longer we trafficked in the drug trade the higher the probability of getting caught.

I had to make another trip to Cartagena with a stopover in San Jose. On this occasion I was bringing slides of navigational maps and boats that would be used in the next smuggling operation. The freighter captain in Colombia had to know what types of boats would meet him and at what latitude and longitudes. I left Costa Rica in a small single-engine Cessna from a private runway for the eight-hour flight to Cartagena International Airport. I carried the slides in my bag mixed in with slides of irrelevant maps and boats and tourist shots of beaches and palm trees. If the slides fell into the wrong hands no one would be able to discern what they were about. Using my surfer persona as cover, I brought my surfboard, some jeans, and bathing suits, along with a cheap camera.

The Cessna landed at the airport in Cartagena and taxied over to the tie-down area for small jets and other private planes. We turned off the engine and were ready to get off the plane. As I opened the door a man dressed in grey slacks, a yellow polo shirt, and black wingtip shoes walked over to me. He introduced himself in perfect English but had a Spanish name. He gestured toward his Lear jet parked across the tarmac as he explained that he and his friends were headed to Miami and had a few million in pesos they wanted to sell for U.S.

dollars. He was willing to trade at a twenty-five percent discount because they were in a hurry and did not want to bother converting their currency when they got to Miami. This was obviously yet another brilliant scheme by the DEA with the cooperation of the Colombian Departamento Administrativo de Seguridad to trap or flush out major drug smugglers. It was inconceivable to me that this was sheer coincidence. Anyone who had spent time in the drug-running world would never deal with a stranger who just walked up to you, especially on the tarmac of an airport runway in a place like Cartagena. Anyway, not to appear to be an ass or arouse suspicion by telling him to fuck off, I said sure. What dumb surfer would not want that deal? So I went over to the Lear jet, was invited in, and there sat another guy who looked just like the first guy also with a Spanish name. Pretending to be sociable, they asked some bullshit questions such as what was I doing in Cartagena? Where did I come from? Was it my first visit? and that type of probing. I told them I was a tourist surfer hoping to catch some waves and a piece of Colombian ass. They asked me how many thousands of dollars I wanted to trade. I told them I had two hundred dollars but would consider trading fifty. They looked at each other in disbelief. I was dead set honest with them— I never traveled with much cash.

As I left their plane, up drove the Colombian police in an open jeep. They handcuffed me and put me in the back of a jeep. Obviously the guys in the Lear jet were working with them but didn't have a chance to tell their clown-like partners that the sting didn't work out. These characters were just blindly carrying out their orders. The DAS agents who shoved me into the jeep were low-level police. They probably made the equivalent of about three dollars a day. These guys just did what they were told and tried to stay out of trouble. This was all part of the life of drug running. I was taken to the central police station, walked down a dank poorly lit corridor, and pushed into an empty iron cage. The DAS agent hit me in the stomach with his rifle to hurry me into the cell then closed the door and locked me in. A few hours later he came back with far less confidence, looking down at the ground, and quickly let me out. Alfredo greeted me when I passed through the corridor door.

He asked, "Are you all right?"

I thought of taking that rifle from the cop and smashing him in the mouth with it but answered, "Yeah, I'm fine. Let's go."

Alfredo drove us to the meeting with my family. Everyone had assembled at an apartment I had never been to before. Fernando sat at the head of the table surrounded by other top Mafioso family heads and a boat captain from Spain. I recognized a few faces but for the most part, because of the size of the operation, I knew almost no one beside my immediate contacts. Fernando began by laying out the logistics for the importation of fifty tons of Santa Marta Gold marijuana, the largest single shipment the family had ever engineered. It was going all the way up the coast to Seattle. This would be the only time we would all meet as a team. Each person received orders from Fernando and reported back the status of what they had accomplished so far. When it was my turn to I reported that I had lined up the offloading crew and the boats we would use. With only the necessary discussion, the meeting was over and we all left silently, set on the task ahead.

When I returned to Marin, I had a lot on my mind. The logistics of offloading fifty tons of pot required paying attention to a hundreds of details. I would have to focus on this operation and speed up my money laundering enterprises. I needed the legal money to purchase the boats and other expenses.

I loved cars and was hoping to find a way to work that into my money laundering portfolio. I located a black Aston Martin Vantage I wanted to buy in Houston, Texas. Barry Wilson represented the seller and flew to Marin County to collect the money and finalize the papers when the car was delivered. His hair was perfect. He wore khaki cotton slacks, a white button down shirt, and shiny brown loafers with no socks. He was a short man with perfect skin and soft hands, and carried himself with an arrogant confidence. My guess was he came from a wealthy family and had gone to an Ivy League college. We talked for a while and it turned out my profile of him was correct.

Barry had been in the business of buying and selling of collectible cars for some time. We were talking about all kinds of exotic cars and how I wanted to collect more when I explained to him that my money was all in cash. He saw my house and he could not help but notice the security around me. He would have to have been an idiot to not understand the level of criminality I was involved in. The men around me were all over six-foot-two, muscular and had a stern looks on their faces. I counted on the threatening appearance of those people surrounding me to keep him from lying or stealing. He explained to me he could take cash to Switzerland, buy exotic cars, no questions asked, and then ship them to the U.S. to be sold through one of my LLCs creating legal money in the bank. He showed me Polaroid pictures of about twelve collectible Ferraris he knew of for sale in Europe. There were two dark blue BB 512s, three 308 GTS convertibles, two black and one white, and one original red 365 GTS/4 Daytona Spyder. Over the next few days we worked out a budget including the purchase of the cars, his travel expenses and entertainment of clients. Then we outlined the details of legal fees for transfer of ownerships, estimated costs and timelines for transporting the cars to Switzerland and title transfers, and freight costs of moving the cars to the port in Rotterdam and loading them onto a cargo ship to the final destination of the port of Long Beach. The cars would go through customs and be trucked to the new showroom I would rent. Within a few days Barry left for Europe to purchase the cars I had selected.

Once the cars were delivered to the U.S. they could not be driven legally until they were EPA DOT certified. I decided that we would include that in the cost to the buyer and deliver the car with those certifications after the car had been sold. I rented a showroom in San Rafael on the street with all the major car dealerships. On the showroom floor I displayed the red 365 GTS/4 Daytona Spyder which Barry had purchased for in Switzerland for seventy-five thousand dollars. When a potential buyer walked by the showroom and looked through the floor to ceiling glass windows, they saw this beautiful car in front of an eight-foot-long teak desk with a computer that listed every collectible Ferrari for sale in the world. The only one who ever bought one of my cars from the showroom was another drug dealer who paid for it through one of his companies. I kept the rest of the cars, a total inventory of more than one million dollars.

Another money laundering scheme was run out of an office in downtown San Francisco. My attorney had set up and managed a securities trading firm of which I was the head. I knew nothing about stocks and made it into that office maybe three times in three years. Nevertheless, Moran was an expert at how to legalize my money and it all looked perfectly legitimate.

I talked to my parents rarely and had not seen them for five years. I don't remember why but they came to visit me once while I lived in Marin County. They stayed at my house and I gave them my bedroom to sleep in. I was totally addicted to drugs and alcohol at the time and they knew it. It was hard to miss—I never slept and was incoherent in my thoughts, which translated into disconnected conversations. I drove recklessly with them in the car. Yet not a word was said about my mental or physical state. My mother was quite taken with the wealth that surrounded me. She asked in a number of different ways if she could help me to preserve my money by taking some back with her to Boston, if not cash then art or jewelry. My father said nothing but I could tell he was worried about me. I brought them down to Gate 5 to meet Larry and Shel. Even though I introduced them as a filmmaker and a well-known writer, my mother only criticized their unorthodox lifestyles. I was worried that while my parents visited I might get arrested. I did not want them to witness what would be the end of my freedom. Fortunately, they came and left without any major event or dangerous incident. I did not want them to worry about me but at the same time my image of being worthless was reinforced in them. I was an obvious drug addict heading for a bad fall.

Robert had arranged for a bank account for me in Panama. I flew to Panama with three hundred thousand dollars in cash. The money was transported in hollowed-out stereo speakers packaged as a gift. When I arrived I hired a porter to take my luggage and the package through customs for me. I met him on the other side of the customs line after having my passport stamped. It was Saturday and my appointment with the bank was not until Monday morning. I stayed in a hotel with a casino on the ground floor right next to the lobby. With nothing to do that evening, I thought I would hang around in the casino for a while. I walked around looking at the different games and noticed a private back room. I handed the doorman a hundred dollar bill and walked into the crowded room. I saw a table with numbers on it and a guy with two cups rolling dice. The minimum bet was ten thousand dollars. So I went upstairs and got fifty thousand to play with. I was in a hurry to get back to that gaming room.

I handed the dealer ten thousand dollars. He put four dice in a cup and spilled them onto the green felt. Then he added them up. I had lost. It turned out each roll of the dice cost ten thousand dollars and you could pay to continue playing. So I went through my fifty thousand, went back upstairs, and got a hundred thousand more. I went through that and got the rest of my money. I had lost a total of three hundred thousand dollars. Now I had no money to deposit in the bank. As the dealer was counting the dice on his last throw I noticed he touched one of the dice. I grabbed his hand and next thing I knew my bag was packed and I was escorted by two Panamanian soldiers to a jeep where I was handcuffed and driven to the airport. I was on the next plane back to California.

I vowed never to gamble again. Something happened in my brain when I made that first bet. It was as if I was a different person, same body, different brain. I could not use being drunk or on drugs as an excuse, I was stone sober that weekend. A thought occurred to me that this wasn't so much about losing the money. It was about losing to the casino.

I was generous with money with friends and strangers alike. One Christmas Eve I wrapped twenty packages, each with five thousand dollars in cash, and went to the downtrodden section of San Francisco. I went there on my motorcycle with the money in a backpack. The night was cold and foggy. I gave the gift packages away to homeless people and street hookers. Some of those people followed me asking, "Who are you? Can I do anything for you? How can I pay you back?" In short, they had more integrity than any of the bankers or business people I was dealing with that had only their own self-interests in mind. My reason for doing this was I believed everyone should have a piece of heaven at least once in their lives. Maybe this money would be that piece of heaven. I wanted nothing in return. There were no strings attached, no conditions, just a stranger on a motorcycle quietly giving them a gift.

When I lived in San Anselmo it was the longest period of time I had ever stayed in one place since leaving Dorchester. I was comfortable there and considered Marin County my home. I was twenty-five years old. I owned a multimillion-dollar estate, a stable of exotic cars, and an Arab stallion. I traveled to any place in the world I wanted to for vacations, bought expensive gifts for friends, and gave them money when they needed it. With that came a familiarity of places and friends. I had to be vigilant in whom I trusted. I was pretending to be a wealthy young businessman. People were always trying to solve the mystery of who I was. It was the subject of conversation. Eric would relay gossip he overheard which speculated that I was a Boston blue blood trust fund baby. How insulting! I was proud of my Dorchester roots, but I had to keep that to myself. All kinds of people wanted to get into my inner circle. Women used sex as a way to get close to me. They were hoping for gifts, money, jewelry, or just to hang out with a man they thought was an outlaw. Men used business opportunities and social standing to try to get close to me. They were hoping I would invest money with them. So at a young age I became aware of false motives and clever disguises that normal people put on for their own personal financial gain. To protect the people I cared about like Larry, my driver or Joan, my housekeeper, I had to maintain an image that would allow them to mention me to their family and friends without raising any eyebrows. I did not want to put them in a position where they broke the law by taking money from someone they knew was a drug smuggler.

NINE

The Freighter

n the 1970s and '80s the coastline of the U.S. was the most unregulated part of our country when it came to smuggling. Any undeveloped coastline lent an opportunity to enter or exit the country without any documentation. The international shipping lanes lie for the most part three miles off shore. Where a peninsula juts out the lanes are even closer to land. So sea transport was the preferred route by smugglers because large shipments could go undetected.

Moving mountains of marijuana into the U.S. was one aspect of our operation. The other was moving millions of dollars in cash out of the U.S. One of the methods was to meet a freighter with the cash as it traveled south to Colombia. Jim, one of my guys, and I would rent a nondescript fishing boat, a fifty-two-foot Egg Harbor, at a local marina for the weekend. We would dress in brand new L.L. Bean slacks and shirts and, of course, the mandatory Top-Sider brown loafers, dark sunglasses, and caps with fishing logos. The outfits reminded me of the pretentious outfits worn by the golfers in Dorchester except for the shoes. We were the prototype of weekend fishermen working hard to look the part.

The standard procedure went like this. First we packed all the cash into suitcases and duffel bags then loaded up the truck with enough supplies for two days. We brought ice chests full of food and beer, a change of clothes, tackle boxes, and other miscellaneous gear. We put the all the gear, duffel bags, and suitcases full of cash directly into carts from the bed of our truck and wheeled them down the dock to the boat slip. While loading the boat, we talked loudly about "the one that got away."

We started the engines, cast off from the dock, and slowly headed out past the breakwater. The designated meeting place at sea was pre-arranged by latitude and longitude coordinates and we had a rough rendezvous time. The freighter traveled at about six knots and our boat was capable of twenty-plus knots.

The freighter heading south in the international shipping lanes neared the meeting point three miles off the coast of Ventura. When we recognized the freighter we pulled up alongside her. The freighter maintained her speed as to not to be caught on radar deviating outside of international shipping lanes or stopping which would have drawn immediate attention to her.

We matched its speed, about four knots at that point, while pulling up along the starboard side, which faced the open sea. The freighter's crew threw down a cargo net, which we loaded with the duffel bags and suitcases and they hoisted up the money. Now we had two days to hang out on the boat pretending to fish. I, myself, was hoping we would not catch any fish. If we did they would have to be cleaned and packed on ice. I didn't care for the flopping of fish fighting for a breath of air on the deck of the boat. I preferred smoking a joint and spacing out while listening to Lou Reed or Janis Joplin.

Even though my Marin jewelry store gave me an excuse for frequent trips to Colombia, sometimes I had to travel between the U.S. and Colombia without leaving a paper trail. Too many trips over a short period of time would send up a red flag at U.S. Customs. On one occasion when I was in Cartagena, I had to go back to Marin, pick up some cash, and be back in Colombia with it five days. I didn't want to explain that turnaround to a customs agent upon reentering the U.S. and I already had plenty of Colombian stamps on my passport. I boarded a freighter headed north from Buenaventura. I had arranged for two of my guys to meet the freighter off of Point Conception, the point closest to the U.S. within international shipping lanes. That day the swells were running ten feet high and choppy. It was impossible to tie up with the speedboat my guys had driven out to our rendezvous point. I had to get off the freighter. If I had stayed on the freighter to its destination, Customs agents at the port of entry would check the manifest and arrest me. A crewmember from the freighter threw a rope ladder over the side. I didn't want to think about what could go wrong, so I just climbed over the rail onto the first rung on the ladder. The freighter was heaving up and down and then side to side as the waves smashed into the hull. I clung onto the ladder moving with the flow of the boat. When I was about ten feet off the ocean I jumped into the water. One of the guys on my boat threw a floatation cushion into the water tied to a ten-foot rope. I had to swim fast to get away from the wake of the freighter and grab hold of the cushion. My guys pulled me in against the force of the waves and the ship's wake. My adrenaline was pumping and I was relieved just to be on the boat and to have survived.

Preparing to go ashore, I quickly changed out of my wet clothes and threw them into the ocean. I put on a pair of surf shorts and grabbed the surfboard they had brought along. As we approached the surf break in Ventura I jumped off the boat about two hundred yards from shore. I paddled over to the break where the local surfers were hanging out and picked up a conversation. They were clueless about where I had come from and I had counted on that. After telling them I usually surfed at "The Ranch" in Santa Barbara, I surfed a few waves and paddled to shore. I couldn't just leave right away as it would arouse suspicion in the tight-knit surfing crowd. So on the beach, I hung out with a group of locals for a few hours. I was tired and just wanted to get home, smoke some pot, and then sleep. Eric finally arrived to pick me up and we drove back to my house in Marin. I slept for the next twenty-four hours straight.

Two days later, after taking care of business in Marin I boarded a cargo vessel in the port of Long Beach that was headed for Barranquilla. About three miles off Choco Bay I was met by a small fishing boat that took me to shore.

Meanwhile my Colombian family was planning the biggest operation it had ever undertaken. To coordinate the successful transport of fifty tons of pot to the U.S. required the cooperation of Colombian government officials and the military. Other drug-smuggling families participated to ensure safe passage for the boats.

In Colombia, local farmers were contracted to plant a combined total of twenty thousand hectares. They would not be scrutinized since the local officials were paid off. The farmers would trim the buds by hand with scissors and put them into burlap bags. Each bag contained roughly forty pounds of marijuana. The farmers carried the burlap sacks on their backs to a barn where they were stitched closed, weighed, and stacked. The farmers had been growing marijuana for twenty years and knew the drill. They did not need to be sworn to secrecy or be intimidated. Wives and children helped with the crops. They were grateful to have a crop they got paid well for.

The farm workers moved the sacks to the river, loaded them onto old dugout canoes and rowed down the Anchicayá River to a freighter anchored in Buenaventura Bay. Steadied against the hull of the freighter, the men in the dugout canoes would put several sacks into a net that was lowered down to them. The ship's crew would haul the net up by hand to the deck and bring the sacks down to the cargo hold. The main danger of this part of the operation was the possibility of being spotted by aerial surveillance. In the late '70s the U.S. DEA and CIA regularly flew surveillance planes over areas they suspected marijuana was being grown.

The freighter would be flying under a Panamanian flag, which would arouse less suspicion than a Colombian flag. The registration numbers on a freighter are located on the main beam of the ship. That beam is located down in the hold where the marijuana would be stored. So a fake main beam number was created and attached to a beam in the ship's wheelhouse. The freighter would be traveling on international waters where the U.S. Coast Guard has no stop and seize jurisdiction.

Merely assembling this huge load of marijuana was an enormous task, but the risk was just beginning. Anything could happen on the trip to the U.S. The freighter could have mechanical problems or the Pacific Ocean could be wildly unpredictable. A ship's crewmember could be injured or inadvertently tip off the wrong person.

Over the seven years I had been working with my Colombian family, cash in the hundreds of millions of dollars had been smuggled back to Colombia. We knew by experience how much money would fit into different size containers. A million dollars would take up a hundred cubic feet. The fifty tons of pot would bring in roughly fifty million dollars wholesale when it was sold in the U.S. and our plan had to include how all that cash would be sent back to Colombia. To avoid risk, that money would not be shipped all at once and not in the same way. We would use ships going downhill to Colombia or Panama, trucks with false bottoms bringing cash to Miami then loading it onto DC-10s leaving out of Opa-Locka Executive Airport, and offshore cigarette boats.

The loaded freighter left Buenaventura Bay for the trip up the Pacific Coast. When the freighter arrived off the coast of Washington the pot would be offloaded at sea and brought down the Puget Sound by sailboats and tugboats, ultimately to be put on American soil in Sequim Bay, Washington. Then it would be transported by truck to Chicago. In advance of the freighter's arrival I rented a cabin on the waterway in Sequim, purchased a sailboat, two Boston Whalers, a tugboat and barge, and leased a fleet of trucks. The sixty-one-foot sailboat was selected because she was well known by other captains sailing Puget Sound and had won several international races. These purchases had to be made through companies that would not lead back to me.

In Sequim, I received word from Colombia that the freighter was ready to embark and that Gustavo would fly to the U.S. with the rendezvous coordinates and the freighter's estimated arrival time. It was too dangerous to communicate by phone and any direct radio communication with the ship could be intercepted. I flew to Phoenix where Gustavo met me at a Motel Six. He handed me a slip of paper and I gave him the slides of the sailboat and tugboat so the freighter's captain would recognize us.

I flew back to Seattle to meet the crew and we all left for the cabin in Sequim. We spent about a week there preparing. The sailboat was already docked in Puget Sound, as was the tug and barge. The cabin we stayed in while waiting was at the top of a fifty-foot bluff with a clear view of the sound. A steep path led down to a private dock where the Boston Whalers had been outfitted with powerful engines and portable winches. They would be used to offload from the bigger vessels to the shore. The sailboat was already docked in Puget Sound, as was the tug and barge. About two hundred yards from the cabin was a dirt back road that went straight to the water's edge. The trucks would meet us there when the sailboat arrived in the bay with its cargo. Each forty-pound bale would be hand carried to the trucks. I used multiple trucks to avoid any complications, such as if a truck broke down, got pulled over, or missed a weigh station. The trucks could carry five to ten tons safely. Each would then be driven to a farm outside of Chicago. Each bale would be opened and the pot dumped into a silo, the seeds and stems would be sorted out and the smokable pot would be repackaged into one-pound bags to be sold to wholesalers.

We had a high frequency crystal on the sailboat radio as did the captain of the freighter on his radio. He sent out a coded signal that he was approaching our rendezvous point. My crew on the sailboat left for the rendezvous point about fifty miles outside of Puget Sound to begin the hard work of offloading the marijuana from the cargo hold of the freighter to the hull of the sailboat.

Offloading pot is dangerous work. Out at sea with an average five-foot swell running the sailboat was tied to the freighter as the men lowered nets and loaded the pot into the rocking sailboat. Accidents can easily happen and your crews have to be experienced and strong. The sailboat crew loaded around eight tons of pot and sailed back through Puget Sound to the inlet. The waters of the North Pacific are frigid all year long. Even the spray hitting your body gives you a chill on the warmest of days. As the sailboat sailed into Sequim Bay that night the moon was full. The water in the bay was absolutely still. The only sound you could hear was the faint hum of the sailboat engine. The Boston Whaler tied up to the sailboat and cruised at about two knots. Anyone watching would not see the whaler and assume the sailboat was just cruising the bay. We offloaded the sailboat as quickly as possible making multiple trips. On shore the truck driver and two of my crew loaded the truck. The sailboat then went back out for the second five-ton load. When that load was brought to shore, two trucks were all packed and ready to go.

So far we had successfully offloaded around thirteen tons of pot and the trucks were en route to the farm in Illinois. We now changed tactics and would use the tugboat and barge standing by to meet the freighter and to retrieve the thirty-seven tons still on board. Twelve hours had passed and the sun was beginning to come up. Our work could only be done under the cover of night. So we had to wait all day in the cabin until dark. No one got high or fooled around at all. We ate well and stayed physically prepared for the work ahead. Very few words were spoken and not a word about the operation itself. We were all superstitious characters. Eric would not change his lucky socks and Jim would not shower or shave.

It took about three days to get the tugboat and barge en route to complete the offloading from the freighter. During this time the freighter would head farther offshore, awaiting word from us that the second phase of the operation was underway. As night fell on the third day my crew and I were in the cabin watching television when a news flash crossed the screen stating the Coast Guard had seized a freighter carrying a multi-ton load of marijuana and, along with the DEA, were towing it to the Coast Guard station in Seattle. We all looked at this in disbelief. The odds of the Coast Guard venturing out to the international shipping lanes where they had no jurisdiction were a million to one. We had selected that time of year because the seas were rough and it was always very foggy. There was no way a U.S. Coast Guard captain could legally board a vessel registered in British Virgin Islands and flying a Panamanian flag. The Coast Guard reported they spotted the freighter more than a hundred miles offshore at night without running lights and contacted the DEA.

The only conclusion we could reach was they were tipped off. I had known my crew for many years and knew it would not be one of them. The Colombian crew had never met me nor any of my workers so they could not connect us to the operation. The tug and barge came back undetected. My crews took off to different parts of the country.

I went back to Marin with Eric. The crew was supposed to scuttle the sailboat after its part in the operation was finished, but they didn't. No matter how thoroughly a boat was cleaned after carrying pot, some residue was always left over.

When DEA interrogated the captain of the freighter, they found the slides of the boats I had delivered to Gustavo. The captain was supposed to have destroyed them but said he just wanted to make sure the right boat was approaching. That picture unequivocally identified the sailboat, the sailboat led to the captain of the sailboat and Sequim, which led to the tugboat, which led to the company that bought the tugboat, which led to me.

It was only a matter of time before the DEA made all the connections. From the moment we saw the news broadcast of the seizure I knew I was going to be arrested. I had my attorney, Robert contact the legal team I would hire to defend me. The distributors I worked with all disappeared. I burned any paperwork that could have been incriminating. I was now stoned day and night, strung out on China White, completely delusional, and stayed in my house all the time. I was home in my bedroom when the phone rang.

It was a woman's voice, "The police are on the way. You better make a run for it."

I was expecting to get arrested but this call was absurd. If I made a run for it would they shoot at me? Tell the judge to hold me without bail? I took off all my clothes, put Ainge on a leash, and went outside to the courtyard. Three squad cars pulled up. The cops got out of their cars and four of them drew their weapons and aimed them at me. I was stark naked and put my hands up. One senior cop told the others to put their weapons away. This cop read me my rights.

I asked, "Could I get dressed for the ride to lock up?"

He said sure. When we got inside I asked him if he wanted a tour of my house.

We walked through the whole house and he said, "I guess crime does pay."

I replied, "Only for a short time."

I got processed and put into the local county jail. My lawyer got me out the next day pending my arraignment. I went directly to Sally Stanford's restaurant, Valhalla, in Sausalito and had a filet minion and lobster. I knew Sally. This was the first time I had gone in by myself and sat down for a meal. I usually ate there with other people or had a taxi pick up my food and deliver it to my house. My name and picture were splashed all over the local and national newspapers and television stations so there was no point in living in hiding any longer.

While I was out on bail pending my trial, I stopped all drug smuggling projects and told all the people that worked with me to scatter to places where they would not be found. There was no doubt that I was guilty and, even if by some fluke in the law I were to get off, my cover was blown and I would have to start my life over. I went through the motions of going to trial. Robert brought in a local attorney from Seattle and two high-profile attorneys, one from San Francisco and one from New York City. He also had three attorneys from his own office working on my case.

Now I had seven lawyers representing me. I paid their hourly wage as well as expenses. Of course as a smuggler all fees were paid in cash made illegally. No problem for these guys. To sum it up we all got together in San Francisco to discuss strategy for the case. I walked into a conference room with seven attorneys sitting around a solid walnut table and a buffet set up all kinds of pastries, coffee, bagels, and fruit.

As a joke I said, "What, no doughnuts?" at which point three attorneys jumped up, pen in hand, and were off to buy doughnuts of my preference. I thought to myself, *Here we go, the bloodsuckers at work. They were going to bill me a thousand dollars' worth of their time getting me doughnuts while I sat there knowing full well I was guilty and facing an eight-year prison sentence.*

At my trial my lawyers argued that the Coast Guard seized the freighter in international waters and that was illegal. The prosecutor countered that it was legal because the freighter was running at night with its lights off. The truth about how the Coast Guard found that freighter never came out. The one thing for sure was both sides were exaggerating and lying consistently and the judge listened as if he had an open mind. There was no jury trial.

Robert, scoundrel that he was, kept encouraging me to do even bigger loads while out on bail because, according to him, now that I was busted the heat was off. All of this was transparent to me, but I said nothing while feeling the pain that this guy just wanted to see me get deeper in trouble. With the exception of my housekeeper and chauffeur, Samantha, Larry, and Shel, all the other people I knew in Marin County ran to the prosecutor's office to cooperate. Even a waiter I tipped a hundred dollar bill testified about that. I watched all this empty of any feelings as if it was not me it was happening to but to someone with my name that I had become.

Outside the federal courthouse where my trial was taking place vendors were selling t-shirts with a silk-screened image of the freighter and pot logos. The prosecuting district attorney and the DEA agents testifying against me all asked me to autograph t-shirts for them. My trial lasted about six months. I knew all this to be bullshit, but why not. I was the main act in a circus. I plead guilty. The seizure was the largest of its kind and there was no way I was not going to jail. When I approached the courthouse there were pro-pot demonstrators cheering me on as if I were a celebrity. I was a criminal on my way to prison, not much to cheer about.

Eventually I was found guilty and sentenced to two five-year prison terms to be served concurrently. In those days there was no statute governing marijuana seizures of this size so the maximum I could have gotten was five years per count, very light by today's standards. I was let out on bail pending appeal .

I told my chauffeur Larry and housekeeper Joan they could leave and I would give them a year's salary. But they both refused, staying close and trying to take care of me. I was snorting a lot of heroin and smoking opium, strung out like a research monkey. One evening I was driving my car in San Rafael going the wrong way on a one-way street when a cop behind me put his siren on. I had a white paper bindle of heroin on me and threw it out the window. When I pulled over the cop asked for my license and registration.

When he saw the name on my license he said, "So you're the big pot smuggler." Then he told me to follow him to the police station. When we arrived at the police station I was put in a holding cell for about an hour. The cop who had brought me in returned holding the bindle I had thrown out of my car window. He asked me if it was mine.

I said, "No. I would like to call my attorney." I got my call and Robert came down to the police station and picked me up. I was charged with driving down a one-way street the wrong way and possession of less than one gram of heroin. Robert turned the matter over to one of the local San Francisco attorneys who was also involved in writing the appeal to the pot bust conviction. This attorney told me he could make this arrest go away for twenty thousand dollars. I didn't ask how, but gave him the cash. I had a court appearance and was on the stand in front of a judge when the DA asked me if it was my heroin.

I stood up, ripped open my shirt, popping the top four buttons, and said, "The cop framed me once he knew who I was. He was trying to make a name for himself."

I was totally out of control to the point that the judge asked me to step down. The case was dismissed.

I was nodding in and out of daily life while waiting for my appeal, knowing it would be denied. One morning I heard a truck pull up in my courtyard. I went outside to see who it was. I looked like a madman. My hair was long down to my shoulders. I was unshaven and had flea bites all over me. A big white guy with tattooed arms was at my front door with a repossession order to seize all my cars. The order was obtained by a car collector I knew. He heard I had been busted and was trying to steal my cars. I called him while the guy stood at my door. He said, "What do you care? You're going to prison anyway."

I hung up the phone and said, "Hold on, I'll get the keys," and went upstairs to my closet and got my sawed off shotgun.

I walked toward him aiming the gun at his crotch and said, "Get off my property or I will blow your dick off." As big as he was, he saw the insane look on my face. Knowing I was someone with nothing to lose, he backed away, got in his tow truck, and left.

Somehow that was a wakeup call for me. I cut down on my heroin use, snorting just enough not to detox. I decided I'd better liquidate all my assets before the IRS or marshals seized them. I put my house on the market for nine hundred thousand dollars. I moved most of my cars, keeping a dually and a dirt buggy, and my motorcycle. I asked a real estate agent who worked exclusively with drug dealers and was used to moving cash to find me a ranch in the Santa Barbara area. Time for Ainge and me to leave Marin. I told Eric of my plan but he wanted to stay in Sausalito. Our lead attorney from New York kept saying "this is a sure bang winner on appeal" and, of course, Eric believed him. I had an Arab stallion named Nabor that I gave to his trainer. She loved that horse and could never afford to own a horse of that bloodline. I gave my African Grey parrot, Dusty, to Joan. They had formed a love-hate relationship. If Joan didn't want to keep him she could sell him for more than the thousand dollars I'd paid for him now that he had a full vocabulary.

The cars at the showroom, however, were yet to be touched. So in my addict mind I reasoned I could continue with that business for a while. I contacted Barry Wilson and made plans to meet him in New York City to give him $280,000 cash for the purchase of six cars he thought would be appropriate for my dealership inventory. I took a commercial flight from San Francisco to John F. Kennedy Airport, my China White stashed in a suitcase full of cash. In the 1970s there was no airport security baggage line to go through. No one looked through carry-on luggage or checked bags.

I checked into a large suite at the Plaza Hotel. On my way to the front desk, I noticed soft classical music playing in the background. I looked around and saw all kinds of people milling about the lobby as if it was a movie set. They looked so happy and connected with each other. There were perfect-looking families, husbands in suits and wives in pastel dresses, their kids dressed as miniature versions of their parents. The rooms and hallways projected the air of old money—no fear, complete security, as if they kept a secret among themselves only people in their realm felt entitled to. They held the golden key to a world the rest of us could only see in movies or read about in books.

This made me sad. As happy and content as they were, I was a convicted drug smuggler out on bail all alone. On the outside I looked like I belonged but on the inside I felt like a fraud invading a world I was not allowed to be a part of. I went up to my room and snorted some China White and those dark feelings melted away. The heroin enabled me to focus on why I was there and forget who I had become. My body was energized by heroin, unlike most people who have the opposite reaction, while cocaine relaxed me and slowed me down. Who knows why I was different?

When I met Barry I gave him the money and off he went to the airport to make his flight to Zurich. I would stay and wait for him in New York since he would be back within two weeks. My lead attorney, Ivan Fisher, had an office in Gramercy Park, so I called him to arrange a meeting to discuss the appeal. One of his subordinate lawyers came over to the hotel. I was in a drugged-out stupor. I remember her telling me she was recently married. She seemed impressed with herself for working for this top lawyer. We talked for awhile. I signed something and somehow ended up in bed with her on top of me. I remember coming and passing out. I woke up the next morning thinking that I had a pretty low impression of myself and why would this lady want to have sex with me. There was no sign of her so I ordered room service and as I was eating breakfast I looked out the window at Central Park. Horse-drawn buggies were carrying people through the park. I thought that's what I'll do. They were parked right in front of the hotel, so I hired one and rode around Central Park and just took in the beautiful colors of the leaves, the smells coming from the hot dog carts. I loved New York City and enjoyed it with only myself for company. I thought always a visitor never at home.

I stayed in my room for a few days until I ran out of drugs. I had not slept or eaten for two days. My body was detoxing and my mind was racing, looking for a way to ease the pain. With only the clothes on my back, I jumped into a taxi and headed to Teterboro Airport. I hired a Lear jet for twenty thousand dollars to take me back to Marin County where I broke into my own house, having left my keys back in the hotel room. I went to my stash and grabbed enough drugs to last an elephant a month. I immediately went back to the airport, got on the jet, and went right to my room at the Plaza. This was one of the most desperate, self-destructive events of my life. I was advertising my insanity to anyone who cared to notice. I paid the pilots in cash. I over-tipped the hotel employees as if I had something to hide and wanted to buy their silence. In my mind, everyone who looked at me knew who and what I was, a convicted drug smuggler, an addict waiting to go to prison.

Barry returned from Europe after spending $160,000 of the $280,000 on the cars. He brought back pictures of the cars he'd pur-chased and gave me receipts that even with shipping and travel ex-penses didn't add up to the total. I asked him where the balance of the money was told me it had been confiscated at customs on his way back into the country. Customs had found the undisclosed cash in his briefcase and was holding it pending further documentation. He would have to go back to the customs office with my lawyer tomor-row to pick it up.

Barry went down to the lobby under the pretense of getting his own room at the hotel. In fact, I never heard from him again. What had actually happened at customs was that the agent inspecting his luggage discovered the eighty thousand in cash and asked Barry why he had so much. Barry, trying to avoid arrest, told him the cash didn't belong to him and gave them my name. I am sure when they entered my name into their system, sirens went off and they released him be-cause he offered to cooperate against me if any legal action was taken.

I called Ivan Fisher, told him what had happened, and we made plans for him to meet me at the Plaza the following day. I had made a slit in the carpeting in a corner of my room to stash my heroin. I was consuming it at a fast pace, never seeming to get enough. The day turned into night. I did not eat or drink anything. I just stayed in my hotel room. I don't remember how many days passed. The next thing I remember was the hotel manager breaking into my room with Ivan. Ivan had been trying to call me for the past forty-eight hours and housekeeping had reported they hadn't cleaned in two days. They thought I could be dead. Ivan wanted to call a psychiatrist friend and have me admitted to a treatment program, but I turned that down. I took a shower and got dressed. We ordered some breakfast and Ivan went about getting the money back from customs.

A few years later, a story came out in a Dallas newspaper about stolen artwork and exotic cars bought in Switzerland by Barry Wilson with drug money. The reporter who interviewed him said he had since lived in Lebanon out of fear of retribution by me. I had seen a number of people just like Barry during my years in the black market. He was from a wealthy family, college-educated with a good career. He dipped his toe in the pool of criminal enterprise but did not have the balls to jump in. He wanted to believe he was a legitimate businessman, a stand-up member of his community who just periodically kind of broke the law. Fischer retrieved the money back from customs and kept it to offset future legal fees. Of the four Ferraris Barry set out to buy, he only purchased two.

When I returned to San Anselmo, I met with the real estate agent who had listed my house for sale. He had gotten a lot of positive feedback and wanted to start showing the house to prospective buyers. He had also found a ranch just north of Santa Barbara he wanted me to take a look at. Leaving my house and letting go of the only world I had known for the past ten years, probably heading to prison to live in a metal cage tore me up. The emotional pain was so great that I curled up into ball on the floor and tensed my muscles so hard I could barely breathe. I reflected back on all the dangerous events I had survived, the multitude of characters that had been a part of my life, the love of my dog. A part of me raged on. *Get up, you're not done. Stop being a baby. Tear away from these emotions. Fuck them.* It was always "them," the oppressors, the people who wanted to keep me in my place, to have me join an army of servants and live my life under their control. That was good enough. That rage and revenge-driven energy got me up and moving. That's what justified the decisions I had made. Who were those people—my parents who left me to raise myself, teachers who let that kid get raped in middle school, Howard Ash who could kick anyone's ass, the plumber who forced me into being a sexual puppet? And the list went on. I had to make sure I was never going to be one of them.

The real estate agent wanted me to look at a 125-acre ranch property north of Santa Barbara. Larry, my chauffeur, drove me down there in my truck. On the way we stopped to pick up some methadone. For most of my life I was thin and sinewy. After being busted and becoming addicted to heroin my body turned to a loose-skinned, untoned skeleton with a roll of fat around the middle. I swallowed the pills, crawled into the truck's sleeping compartment, and slept for the entire five-hour drive.

We met the real estate agent at the guardhouse of Hollister Ranch. We drove about two miles on a paved road along the ocean until we turned down a dirt road about half a mile up a gradual hill. Halfway up the hill we pulled into the driveway of an A-framed three-bedroom cottage with a deck that looked out over the ocean. There were cows grazing in the fields, beautiful trees, and a sense of separateness from the insanity I was living in. I bought this ranch for $165,000, ironically from a judge.

Two months later I was ready to leave for the ranch. Larry would drive me one last time. I said good-bye to my housekeeper, Joan and to Dusty. When Larry dropped me off, it was just me and Ainge on the remote 125-acre ranch remotely tucked away in a valley surrounded by open space and cattle.

Hoping to get away from heroin addiction at this new house, I didn't bring any heroin or methadone with me. Within twenty-four hours of moving in I started to detox. In preparation for that I had bought six bottles of gin, thinking the alcohol would diminish the pain of detoxing. I drank the gin straight from its green bottle, but it didn't help at all. My body was hot then cold. Every joint was aching and I was miserable. I could not drive so when I ran out of food Ainge was on his own to go out and hunt. It could have been a week later when I was finally conscious I realized that he had gotten skinny and was covered in fleas. It broke my heart. He had managed to survive by eating what he killed but it was not enough. In a few days I was healthy enough to go into town and buy groceries. I bought Ainge and me each a huge filet minion. He ate his raw. In a few days he was back to his old mischievous self. My best memory of that time was sitting on the deck and Ainge came by with a four-foot-long log in his mouth. He looked so funny. It was the first time I had laughed in a long time.

Dean, a chemist from Marin I knew, came down to the ranch to visit. He made the best pharmaceutical coke I had ever seen. We were hanging out talking about old times when he said he had a new product he was working on called freebase, a smokable cocaine. He pulled out about two ounces and we smoked it from a glass pipe. It was a different kind of high, one that left you wanting more right away. After Dean left the next day I smoked all that he had left me day and night. The pipe would get clogged up with residue so I cleaned it with a nail and some pieces would fall on the carpet. I must have stayed up four or five days just smoking that stuff until I ran out. When I woke up from a long sleep I was desperate to smoke more. I got on my hands and knees and picked through the shag carpeting, finding a piece here and there. I became so obsessed that I ended up ripping up the entire carpet and beating it with a broom. Everything that came out I swept up and smoked. When that episode was over I never went near freebase or heroin again. I would stay old school, smoking pot and snorting cocaine.

Fortunately every person who came to visit brought with them large stashes of pot and coke and when they left gave me what was left over. So for about a year while waiting to go to prison I stayed up days and nights at a time snorting coke until I became delusional. On the old Indian burial ground on my ranch I thought I saw owl-shaped spirits watching and waiting for me to die so they could take my soul straight to hell. Another time I got in my dune buggy and drove to a cliff overlooking the beach, revved up the engine, and drove straight off the cliff flying about ten feet into the ocean. The cold water sobered me up a bit and I walked home, took a hot shower, lay down in my bed, and slept for two days.

I had a lot of time to think while I was alone on the ranch. I talked things over with Ainge and he was a good listener, always looking right into my eyes, sometimes smiling but always wagging his tale. He suggested I should invite one of my hooker friends to stay a few days. So I called Elizabeth, told her where I was, and asked if I could hire her for a few days. She said sure and arrived the next day with a little suitcase. We snorted coke together, got naked, and she spent a lot of time and effort trying to get me to come. She was excellent at giving head but this time it wasn't working. Finally I told her to give it up. My cock was numb from all the coke. I thanked her for trying, reassuring her it had nothing to do with her. She stayed another day walking around in sexy lingerie and preparing food for us. Before she left she asked if she could try again. She really wanted me to have a good memory of us before I went to prison. I said no thanks but that I was grateful for the many times she had visited me and taken my sexual fantasies to heart. After she left I reflected on the decision I had made years ago not to have an emotional relationship with a woman. I could count on one hand the times in my life I had a loving sexual experience with a woman. Sex to me had become blowjobs in exchange for money, gifts, or favors. Samantha was the only woman I had cared about during that time, but she was too wild to depend on. For some reason I would not have intercourse with a woman I did not care about. Blowjobs seemed less personal. I got all that intellectually, but did not understand it emotionally until years later.

Eric was still living in Sausalito and we kept in touch by phone, talking about our appeal and options. He came down one day to see the ranch and just hang out. Early that evening a helicopter landed near the house and dropped off some DEA agents and other federal enforcement characters. They barged in without knocking. I was wearing only a robe and just stood there. Eric was out walking with Ainge on the ranch. They asked if I was going to check myself into prison at the scheduled time or if they should take me right then. I made the logical argument that I should check myself in. I pointed out that my furniture, artwork, cars, and clothes were all still in place and there was no indication that I was planning a run for it. So they left. Apparently my appeal had been lost and my attorneys never notified us that we were to report for our five-year sentences to McNeil Island Federal Penitentiary in two weeks. I had not given any thought to how it would eventually all come down. Do they pick you up and deliver you or do you voluntarily just show up check in for five years? I could not imagine getting a notice in the mail saying "report to prison on September 28, bring a toothbrush and whatever else you might need during your incarceration."

Eric came back from his walk with Ainge out of breath. He had seen the helicopter and anxiously asked what it was all about. For both of us the thought of prison was unbearable. We both agreed to extend our freedom as long as possible and made a plan to leave the U.S. We had nothing left to lose. Eric, always being the responsible one, went back to Sausalito to get his affairs in order. I kept thinking about getting it over with and just going to prison but could not get my head around the idea of spending five years anywhere, let alone in a concrete cell. I made a call and arranged for two fake passports. I called Eric and told him to meet me at the Chateau Marmont in Hollywood in two days. We would go to New Orleans and then on to Costa Rica.

The saddest thing about becoming a fugitive was that I could not take my dog, Ainge with me. Luckily for me my bodyguard, Jose, who was like a brother to me took Ainge. The moment they left was one of the few times I remember when I actually cried tears. I knew Ainge would be treated with love. Jose had a wife and two children who adored Ainge. I didn't know if I would be the same without his spirit filling the deep hole in me.

Eric and I were horrible at being fugitives. We planned nothing when we decided to go to Costa Rica. Our favorite expression was "anything's better that prison." Eric came from a loving family. When he told his parents about being busted, they tried to help get him into rehab because they thought the root of the problem was drug abuse. They offered to mortgage their house to help pay attorney's fees. When I told my parents about the arrest they said they were disgraced by me and thank god the local papers in Norwood didn't make much of the story. Eric was with me from day one, and he was there now. When we got sentenced I told the district attorney that Eric was only a worker, that he knew nothing, so he got a lesser sentence.

After a few months of hanging out the beaches of Costa Rica, Eric bought a pound of pot from someone. The hotel we were staying in was raided and we were arrested. We were taken to a Costa Rican jail and put into a dark, bare cell. Within a few days a DEA agent came to visit. We explained we were just some hippie musicians tripping around Costa Rica and had bought some pot for fun. We also told him the person who sold us the pot had a barn in the mountains with tons of pot and if he got us out of prison and put us up in a hotel we would lead him there. So he agreed and off we went, two fugitives convicted of the largest pot bust in U.S. history now working with the DEA in Costa Rica on a made-up story. Well, we got drunk with this guy and when he passed out we took a cab to the airport and headed to Bolivia.

My Colombian family had strong ties with a number of Bolivian coca growers. I thought I might be able to find a safe place to live through these contacts. We arrived in La Paz and then took a connecting flight to Santa Cruz. We met with one of those contacts and were driven to a mango farm that was a kept as a safe house for fugitives and smugglers. There was a three-bedroom hacienda along with four outbuildings. The property was surrounded by dense jungle full of large red ants. Those ants could eat the skin off a human body, dead or alive, in twenty-four hours. Santa Cruz was such a harsh place that I began to take on the angry attitude of the people who lived there. Almost everyone carried a weapon, oftentimes in a paper bag. Poverty was everywhere, even more extreme than in other South American countries. The victims of that poverty were the darker skin Indians. The light-skinned castellanos, descendants of the Spanish conquerors, were the professionals, the business leaders, the policy makers. Like their ancestors, they exploited the indigenous peoples' labor and resources and only gave back what suited them, creating the extremes of wealth and poverty.

One day while walking on a dirt road in the village outside in ninety-degree dry heat, I saw a black dog with white foam on his mouth. People steered clear of this dog. He turned toward me and looked straight into me with his bloodshot eyes. Then, instead of coming toward me he put his tail down and ran the other way. It was as if he knew I was more dangerous than him.

Empty of all emotions, just a skeleton of a man, no spirit, mindless, I stayed drunk day and night while snorting cocaine. Paranoia and despair never left me, one moment thinking the feds would catch up with me and the next that if I died here, no one would ever know, no one would care. I was not feeling sorry for myself. I was convinced of that and accepted what I had become. Even though I was surrounded by people, I was truly alone. What had started out as a means of survival, selling lids of pot in the Boston Common, had turned me into a desperate fugitive running from a felony conviction. I was playing rich with drug money, always knowing I was different and an outsider with no way back in, yet acting as if I belonged to a society where most people lived a somewhat normal life. The pressure I had put on myself to have money and power above everything else was now revealing its cost. Maybe the places I had been, the experiences I had, and the people I met were a fast track to my death. I wanted to know what it felt like to not be manipulated, not to be afraid, and I thought even if it were for a short time, I could be truly free. A voice inside of me said, *Only an idiot would believe a street kid from Dorchester could live freely on equal terms with people whose birthright automatically gave them the life I had risked so much for.* That was the voice I hated. That voice created a reaction of rage that drove me to keep putting one foot in front of the other and fight all this insanity.

This was a violent time in Bolivia. Bolivia was the largest grower of coca plants in the world. The leaves were shipped to Colombia for processing into cocaine for the North American market. Being a land-locked country, Bolivia had no seaport, so all exports, legal and illegal, had to be transported by truck or plane. The truck routes were dangerous, winding mountain roads with plenty of opportunity for ambush and highjacking. A new breed of violent bandits had emerged, going after growers and smugglers.

An Interpol agent named Jacques, or at least that's what his ID said, was assigned to track foreign drug dealers in Latin America and bust them. Then he would take their dope and sell it. He had the reputation of being a murderer and a thief. The two of us did not get along. My friends in Bolivia wanted Jacques gone. One night I took a 357 magnum and hid quietly in the bushes outside his house. Even though I was drunk and coked up my senses were heightened. I thought surely this guy deserved to die. I was hoping to scare him enough that he would leave the country or provoke him into a confrontation. I knew I would not murder him and run away like a coward. I felt a gun barrel on the back of my head. When I turned around it was him. He mouthed off that he would kill me right there. However he knew the family I worked for in Colombia and if he killed me he would have no place to hide. So we agreed not to hunt each other and that was that. We never heard from him again, so I believe he left the country.

Nothing good I can say happened in Bolivia. In Santa Cruz I was arrested at a checkpoint, the officers wanted money to let me pass. I had no money on me so I was beaten and tortured. My body reacted to this pain and as if I was possessed by a demon I turned into an animal—mostly a devil wolf—and behaved insanely getting on all fours and moving my head from side to side while making guttural sounds.

Eventually my tormentors became scared or tired and let me go.

One night in La Paz, Eric and I were asleep in our hotel room when the Bolivian Special Forces broke down the door and took us to a military prison. They knew who we were and were tipped off as to our location. The U.S. Marshal Service had found out we were in the country and pressured the Bolivian government to arrest us. I was chained to my bunk most of the day and all of the night. I didn't know where Eric was as we were kept away from each other. A few weeks later a relative of my Colombian family walked into the cell. She told me I was in good standing with them, that I should keep my mouth shut and do my time in prison, but that my career with them was over because I was now too visible in the U.S.

I was told by the guards that this prison was unique in that it operated like an apartment hotel. The more money you paid the warden, the better your accommodations and amount of freedom you could have. It had a wing with two-bedroom luxury cells and another with one-bedroom average cells. This plan was available only to Colombians or Bolivians. As a fugitive from the U.S. I was offered nothing of the sort. My cell was a bare bones cement and steel cage. I had plenty of time to think about how I had arrived in this Third World prison. I was never quite sure who had tipped off the DEA and Coast Guard about the whereabouts of the freighter. I thought about who had the most to gain by my death or imprisonment. My strong suspicion was Robert Moran, my lawyer in San Francisco.

Over the ten-year period leading up to my arrest I had earned around thirty million dollars. All of this money came from transporting and selling marijuana and hashish from Nepal and Colombia. If I died or was imprisoned Moran could have the ability to steal that money. After all, it was his job to set up domestic and foreign bank accounts, stock and real estate portfolios, and cash businesses for me. He had all the connections in banks and investment houses to allow suitcases of cash to be deposited with no questions asked. A man working for him had told me of a conversation where Moran had asked "How hard would it be to kill David?" This guy responded,

"David is not just one person. If you hurt him, others will show up and brutally kill you and your family." Maybe Moran thought he could get me busted and I would never know it was him.

I almost believed his schemes to launder money would eventually translate into legitimate businesses so I could lead a normal life. I wanted that dream to come true but life had taught me many times that would never happen for me. I had tried with my stained glass company and felt like I was taken advantage of by the buyer at Bloomingdales. I had gone to college, eventually became a good student, and still could not get a job in the field I wanted. After I was arrested and Moran advised me as my lawyer to bring in an even a larger shipment of pot, I saw I was his pawn.

I had brought Moran a sample of fake platinum from Colombia to test his greed. He was all too happy to try to sell it on my behalf. He was pushing me to obtain fake emeralds, claiming he had a market for them. I was always watching him and he seemed to have an insatiable desire for money and power. If I had been an experienced, legitimate businessman, I would have fired him. But that was not an option. He knew too much. He was a dangerous man with no loyalty or compassion for others. Yet it was me sitting in this prison cell.

TEN

Prison

After four months chained up in the Bolivian prison, Eric and I were put on a plane with two U.S. marshals and flown to Miami. I sat with one marshal toward the back of the plane, Eric with another in the midsection of the plane. When we arrived we were handcuffed and taken through the airport to a van. The van transported us to FCI Miami, a federal prison where we were to be held pending our extradition to Seattle. We stayed in a two-bunk cell with a toilet and sink. In the morning a guard walked by and slipped a tray with corn flakes and milk through our cell door.

The guard wanted to strike up a conversation about our bust when Eric interrupted him, "Do you have any sugar pops?"

The guard just walked away.

I told Eric, "Well, looks like this is how we will live for the next five years or so."

We were brought before a judge for our extradition hearing.

The judge said, "The bail amount, pending extradition will be...."

A DA from Florida immediately jumped up and explained to the judge we were fugitives who had just been apprehended so there should be no bail. The judge then approved our transport to Seattle. I had no idea what would happen to us, if anyone knew we were in custody, or where we would end up. I had no control over anything at that point and it was a scary feeling.

After about six months of being moved from prison to prison, I was finally taken to Washington State. During that time I had no idea where Eric was or where I would be the next day. I ended up in what I believe was a Navy prison in Bremerton, Washington. My cell had no walls, an iron-barred cage in the middle of a room. The light bulb that hung down from the ceiling was on twenty-four hours a day. The various prosecutors and DEA agents who interrogated me wanted to work a deal with me to help them against the Colombians. They told me my life was at risk if I didn't help them. I didn't believe a word they said. As soon as their lips started to move I knew they were lying. During the next six months, they moved me to different county jails over and over again. I was given no explanation, told only what to do. This was the way the prison system controlled your life. If you had no ties, no place to rest, they could beat you down further. I was allowed to make one call to my attorney in Seattle. He was able to convince the Bureau of Prisons to move me to a prison I could do my time in.

After a year of being moved around I found myself in a level one low-security prison camp in the California desert. We lived in dormitory-style buildings with two inmates per room. There was a common bathroom and shower on each floor. My job there was landscaping. Being in a desert, that meant picking up rocks and moving them from one place to another. It was hard physical work in extreme heat or brutal cold. The good news was that the prison was on about twenty acres and the facility was bordered by a chain-link fence. In no time I figured out I could disappear at certain times during the two hours between prisoner counts. At dusk I dug a hole under the fence, crawled out, and walked about two hundred yards where friends would drop off hash and food. It was pretty tense. If I had been caught I could have gotten five years added to my sentence. I did this for a year and a half without detection. My friends on the outside who were all in the drug business were more than happy to donate hash for those of us on the inside. On one trip a friend brought two girls with him to our desert rendezvous location. The girls enthusiastically satisfied my pent up sexual needs.

Most of the guards were pretty cool. They just didn't want any trouble on their watch. So when there was pot and hash in the prison everyone got mellow. There were less fights and the general mood was pretty laid back. After several months I met with the parole board for the first time. I walked in without a shirt and nodding out from some strong pot. They asked me a few questions, which I did not answer and proclaimed I would continue my term until expiration, no early release for me. When I walked out of the hearing room other prisoners and guards were standing by to hear the news. I told them CTE, meaning "continue to expiration." The prisoners were applauding since the only ones who got any break at all were rats. Standing up to the parole board gave me credibility among the prisoners. I felt good about myself and walked over to the weight room to smoke a celebratory joint with my fellow convicts, my new family.

Frosty and Don, both bank robbers and I were assigned to the prison landscaping crew. We got up at 7:00 a.m., had breakfast, were counted, and reported to our assigned prison jobs. We would meet at the front guard tower where a guard would pick us up and drive us over to the prison staff housing where the warden and other high-ranking officials lived. There were about twelve houses with neat lawns and flower gardens. The guard would drop us off with our rakes and mowers leaving us unsupervised. Despite the hundred-degree desert heat, the duty was fairly easy and we would take our time getting the job done. On occasion, the warden's wife would come out her front door and offer us water or lemonade. She was noticeably younger than the warden. She seemed interested in Frosty and invited him in while we all sat outside drinking our lemonade. I found it odd because Frosty was not at all physically appealing, beer belly pudgy, with curly light brown hair, a pock-marked face, and a thick mustache. The warden was a tall, thin man with a well-manicured jet-black mustache, perfectly groomed hair, and clothes that were always well pressed. He did have the look of a strict, uptight control freak.

Why would this attractive woman risk time talking to Frosty and even invite him in for short spells? She could have picked any of the prisoners, so beyond being lonely, maybe she was attracted to mustaches or Frosty told her intriguing stories of his robberies. Talking to the wives of prison officials was asking for trouble. The guards and warden thought of us as animals and they did not want their wives to even acknowledge us. When you are processed into prison they tell you your body now belongs to them and it doesn't take long to understand the power they have.

For any reason the guards can put you in the hole or in a cell with a violent schizophrenic or worse. So you learn to get along. Even looking at the warden's wife could mean a transfer to a higher security prison, a longer sentence, or just being moved from prison to prison at their whim. You are woken up early morning with no prior notice, told to "roll it up," meaning get your clothes and personal items together. Then you are escorted to a prison bus where you are hand and ankle cuffed to a seat. You are not told where you are going and you have no way to notify friends or family. This prison bus could take you to a county jail overnight, then the next day to another holding facility. All the time you are in transit no one knows where you are going except the Bureau of Prisons. If they chose to, a prisoner could disappear in transfer for months or longer.

One morning Don and I reported to work, but no Frosty. Our guard told us we would no longer be working at the staff compound. Instead were to pick up rocks, put them in a wheel barrel, push the wheel barrel through the sand several hundred feet across the prison yard, and dump them in a pile. This was pointless work made up to induce us to tell them where Frosty went. Frosty hadn't said a word about what he had planned so we had no idea where he might be. That afternoon another inmate told us the warden's wife helped Frosty escape and left with him. The next day when the warden made his rounds with the captain and some guards, the heckling began. "Hey, warden, your wife sucks good cock!" "Your wife likes it up the ass and so do you." The warden tolerated this verbal abuse because he couldn't tell who out of the crowd was yelling out these comments. But he knew it was the talk of the prison and that he was the focal point of the ridicule. It was probably the snickers and sideways looks from his peers, the guards, that sent him over the edge. He was transferred to another facility and later we heard he cracked up and ended up in a psychiatric hospital. To this day, no one's ever heard a word about Frosty or the warden's wife. For all we knew, they could be living together in Mexico and be grandparents by now.

About halfway through my prison sentence I was woken up at 5:00 a.m. and told to "roll it up." The prison captain suspected I was smuggling in drugs but couldn't prove it. He transferred me to a level four prison called Terminal Island off Long Beach, California. This prison's population was made up of Mexican mafia, Black Guerrillas, Arian Brotherhood, and other prison gangs. The group I fit into was made up of smugglers. The prisoners at Terminal Island knew I was coming there before I did. A file of each prisoner's history is kept in the warden's office, including the details about the crime committed and sentencing report. The file is sent ahead to the receiving prison and the warden's clerk, who is almost always an inmate, reads all the details and spreads the word about the incoming prisoners. So when I arrived I had a greeting committee of other smugglers waiting for me. After being processed I was put into the main population, given a cell assignment, and prison clothes.

Another guy who had been on the transfer bus was visibly shaken by being admitted into prison. He was in the cell next to me and at night after we were counted and the cell doors clanged shut he would start sobbing. He was a middle-aged guy with a family. He missed them. He missed being a part of his kid's life and was sure his wife would not be there when he got out. He was full of shame for the crime he committed. I had no one waiting for me when I got out. There was no life outside of prison that I missed. I had one visitor who saw me once a month. She was a colleague in the drug business. She brought me news of friends in the business, food, and helped co-ordinate smuggling drugs into prison for my personal use. My parents visited once during a vacation they took to California. When I saw them enter the visiting room I realized I was so disconnected from them that they seemed like strangers to me, just two people I had known from my past who were visiting me out of curiosity. We had very little to say to each other. My father seemed distant and my mother in a quiet sort of pain. After they left, I felt relieved that I could go back to doing my time with no emotional scene to remember them by.

One day during an exercise break I was standing in the yard when some guards walked by and one of them bent over and picked up a small bindle of heroin off the ground. There were about ten inmates in the vicinity but the guard was sure it was mine. No one would admit to owning it, so the guard took me to the hole. After about a week in isolation in my metal cage, the prison captain came to see me and asked who I got the heroin from, the truth being it was not mine. But there was no point in arguing that. In prison you are guilty if the guards say you are. So out of frustration I told him "From your wife, after she blew me." That did not sit well, so I stayed in the hole another thirty days but I didn't mind because I was stoned every day. With top security and only a slot in the door for passing meals through, it would seem pretty impossible to smuggle anything into the hole. But the prison plumbing crew, who were all inmates figured out a way. They would put valium in partially blown-up rubber balloons in the pipes and the little pill-filled bubbles would float up daily in my toilet bowl. The valium got me through solitary. I was hardened and shut down emotionally. When I got out of the hole, I stayed by myself or with my group. No one bothered me and I minded my own business.

On my second meeting with the parole board they called me incorrigible after reading my file, but who cared? I would never receive early parole anyway. The thirty-seven tons of pot was a huge bust and I was not on track for release for good behavior. When I left my parole hearing the inmates in the hall outside were all waiting to hear what had happened. I told them, just like the first time "CTE," continue to expiration, once again confirming I was a stand-up guy.

Some inmates did not belong in prison at all and were defenseless against many of the aggressive prisoners. I met a man in his seventies who was in for refusing to pay his taxes. He had worked for the railroad his entire life and had always paid his taxes. When his wife got cancer, he went through his entire savings, paying for what his insurance didn't cover and became broke. Out of frustration he told the IRS he refused to file tax returns and they locked him up. We looked out for this guy to make sure no one took advantage of him.

Another sad case was a sixty-four-year-old Italian man who was in for eight years for unarmed bank robbery. He spoke very little English. When his son came to visit, he told me his father was a drunk and had walked into a bank and handed the teller a note on the back of his own deposit slip which said "hand over your money." The teller called the cops and he got arrested for attempted bank robbery, a felony punished in the federal courts. If he had had the money for a decent attorney he probably would have gotten sentenced to an alcohol treatment program and probation. Then there were a lot of lousy criminals, first offenders who had driving across state lines with a pound of pot or a few ounces of coke. They made up a good part of the prison population.

The most disliked group was the white-collar criminals. There was something distinctly dishonest about them. They were educated and had respected positions in society yet they betrayed their own kind for personal profit. When the guards weren't looking those guys got punched in the face, or tripped, or had their cigarettes and commissary goods stolen from them. The sex offenders and rapists were put in separate prisons. By past experience the prison officials learned they did not last long in the general population. However, plenty of gay men who played the female's role were available for sex if that was your thing. One had a crush on me and would leave notes for a rendezvous under my pillow. I never met up with him, but was concerned he might take rejection the wrong way and stab me in my sleep or during a shower.

The Italian organized crime inmates were a closely-knit group. They associated with the union guys. Most of the younger men like me were smuggling drugs into prison, but these guys were smuggling in all their favorite Italian delicacies. I was invited a number of times to eat with the Anthony and Giorgio when their families visited and to their cells where they stashed away their breads, cheeses, and salamis.

Jim Whittier arrived around the same time I did. He was a former green beret who upon being discharged from the military found his wife in bed with another guy. He shot them both to death and was serving a life sentence. Everything about him was controlled and focused, the way he lifted weights, the way he walked, his eyes. I heard him shouting in the yard late one afternoon. Someone had stolen his new sneakers and he wanted them back. He was standing out in the middle of the yard alone, so I went out to stand next to him. I did this only because he was my friend. The idea of getting stabbed or thrown into the hole over a pair of sneakers seemed stupid to me. Three men walked up, one of them carrying his sneakers. Once again I heard the same words I had heard as a kid in the pool hall: "If you want them, take them." Jim walked toward the man holding his sneakers, telling me to stay back. He quickly punched the thief in the throat with such force the guy fell on the ground grasping for breath. By now half the prison population was watching. The other two said "Hey, it's cool," as they slowly walked backwards. Jim sat down and put on his sneakers and calmly walked away. Those three guys had to be idiots to challenge Jim. Jim was already serving a life sentence with no possibility of parole. If he had killed one of them, as he would say "What are they going to do, put me in prison?" That was his leverage.

Ed, one of the union guys, was getting close to his release date so he applied for a furlough weekend to go home and see his wife. Being a cagey old guy with a younger wife he thought he would surprise her. When he walked into his house his wife was bent over the couch getting humped by the postman. As Ed told it, he gave the postman a hundred dollar bill, thanked him saying, "Better you than me." Hopefully the postman moved to another state because Ed was well connected and definitely not someone to insult. When he got discharged I heard from one of our Italian friends that he got rid of his wife, however that should be interpreted.

While I was in prison I thought a lot about my life and the decisions I had made that got me locked up. I knew the way I lived could not last forever. I had hit too many brick walls trying to fit in. I was a Type A personality with the need to succeed in whatever I did. I could not reconcile spending my days without a purpose. No one but me was responsible for being there. Smuggling was a chapter in my life that had closed and a big part of me was glad it was over. No one has a happy outcome from dealing or abusing drugs or being part of that world. So when I received news that my attorney Robert Moran had committed suicide I was not surprised. Here was a man with a great education and a successful law practice as a criminal defense attorney, but he wanted to have more and it killed him. Friends from Marin met with similar tragedy. Susan, the woman from Mill Valley I met in Costa Rica and Mark, a doctor who had taken care of me at times, had become addicted to shooting heroin. They had gone downhill fast and had probably gotten into debt. They were found dead from an overdose of adrenaline in a seedy motel in Miami. These three people had one thing in common. They were all from decent backgrounds with professional careers and had a lot to lose, and they played in the smuggling world on different levels but nonetheless wanted it all. They wanted acceptance as high achievers in the legal world and when the sun went down to be reckless as players in the drug world. I was glad I was in prison when they all died, as I am sure there would be some suspicion that I was involved. At the same time I was sad to think those lives ended so prematurely and so pointlessly. These people had taken their own lives. Everyone has a breaking point and when you are addicted to drugs like these people it is impossible to look past what seems like a series of unsurmountable problems.

By the time I got out, I had served every day of my five-year sentence. By today's standards, the sentence was light. In the late seventies, a thirty-seven-ton-pot bust was inconceivable and the penalty was the same as for a fifty-pound bust. My two five-year sentences were served concurrently with special parole, meaning that if I violated any condition of my parole, committed even a minor offense, I would go back for eight years. When I left prison I thought incarceration had had no effect on me, that prison had just been a place to pass time. Even if the Bureau of Prisons had a program for learning a skill or trade, I didn't believe it would help because I thought no one would hire an ex con.

Freedom to choose was always a big deal to me. It drives almost everything I do. That was taken away by being imprisoned. Prison controls where your body goes but your mind can take you any-where. At night I would go to my mental slide show of my erotic sex-ual experiences or great sunrises, sunsets, or Ainge's face when he had a log in his mouth. On my way out I was encouraged by the prison counselor to clean toilets or pick up dog shit since that appeared to be my true calling.

ELEVEN

Freedom

Upon release, I was assigned a parole officer. At our first meeting he gave me instructions to call a number every day at 5:00 p.m., an automated system that gave the parolees a random time to report for drug testing so they couldn't prepare in advance. One of the conditions of my parole was that I not drink any alcohol or consume any drugs. I understood these conditions and the consequences if I did not adhere to those rules. When I left his office I had no intention of violating my parole. I had already lost my freedom in prison and did not want to go back.

My old crew from Marin got together and put on a party for me as a free man. The party featured coke, pot, booze, and about twelve hookers in of lingerie. Splendid. I did not miss a beat, got right back to where I was. The resolve to not drink and not use drugs went right out the window. By the time I got out of prison all my houses and cars had been seized and most of my cash was gone. However, I did have more than a hundred thousand in cash and gold stashed away in the U.S. and more in Colombia.

I moved into a guesthouse on an estate in Santa Barbara with a woman I had known in my smuggling days. Nancy had two young sons whom I liked very much. They were handsome, athletic, and very energetic. The sons had different fathers. One father had been an artist in Marin County who was murdered, the other a record producer and drug dealer who, after years of fighting heroin abuse, killed himself. Nancy owned a lingerie store in Santa Barbara. When I stopped by, her girls would model thongs for me in the back room while we snorted coke and drank champagne. This was me on parole. I was supposed to be looking for a job and staying sober.

Although I could no longer work for my Colombian family as a smuggler, they said I would be taken care of and could work in a low-profile capacity that would not involve the direct handling of drugs or money. After a few months of partying with my Marin friends, I was missing the excitement of my past smuggling days. One part of me knew that I was on parole and wanted to stay on the straight and narrow, but another part just didn't care. I was contacted by a member of my Colombian family who lived in California that he had set up a meeting for an operation that could use my expertise in logistics. Rodrigo, an Air Force pilot from Colombia was loosely associated with my Colombian family and his group was planning to land a DC-10 on a dry lakebed in the California desert with a full load of pot. I had experience with this kind of operation, so they asked if I would work out the logistics for this operation.

Rodrigo and I met at the Montecito Inn. I checked in a few days in advance and waited for him. During that time I stayed drunk and coked out. There had been a trail of women in and out of my room and sitting in a chair in the corner was a blow-up plastic doll of a woman with her mouth open. I was out of my mind when he knocked on the door. I opened it wearing a pair of boxer shorts and a t-shirt. We both started drinking whiskey and snorting coke. I called a hooker I knew to come over and join the party and as he showed me maps and discussed different geographic areas to land and offload the plane. He had her bent over a table, her panties down around her ankles, I looked at the absurdity of this scene and in a moment of clarity it dawned on me that this show was over for me.

I turned down the DC-10 project. I knew in my heart that way of life was over. Yet I had no idea what to do. The hopelessness of my life took me to a dark side of myself. I continued to stay high day and night. That way I did not have to feel anything.

One Friday my parole officer called me in. He said, "You have given me six dirty drug tests."

I told him, "I knew they were dirty. I have been high every day since I got out."

He and I had talked a lot about my life. When I told him stories of my childhood he would look at me and appeared sad. I was very sincere with him about my frustration of not knowing how to fit in to mainstream society. He said he thought I was a good guy with potential to do good things. He dealt specifically with parolees who had special terms attached to their parole and just once he wanted to have someone succeed. He gave me an ultimatum: get into a drug treatment program by Monday or return to prison for eight more years.

That Friday night I checked into a hotel room with a few ounces of coke and four hookers. We partied for two days. The girls were trying hard to please me but I had not slept and was totally coked out. As much as I had sex with them and regardless of what techniques were tried I could get no satisfaction. By Monday morning they didn't know what to do with me and couldn't just leave me alone in the hotel room. Two of them packed me up, put me in their car, and drove me to a treatment program in L.A. I had no idea what a treatment program was or what I would be doing there. But they knew if I did not check in I was off to prison so they insisted I admit myself.

I brought my briefcase containing cash and coke. A doctor checked me and asked me how I felt. I told him I felt like a jet plane flying high in the sky with no particular place to go and no way to land. A counselor came into the room to search me and my belongings. He flipped when he opened my briefcase. He threw the coke in the toilet and put the cash in a safe with my watch. Next thing I knew I was in bed and given a valium. I must have slept straight through till the next day. A psychiatric aide woke me up, gave me a schedule, and assigned a doctor and therapist to me. My first appointment would be in one hour with the therapist. While giving the therapist my family history, I remembered that my parole officer had to know that I had checked in and asked the therapist to call him. He said they had already notified him. I must have mentioned my reason for checking in during my detoxing delirium.

My memories of the treatment program are pretty good. There were some bad moments, but overall it was a start for me. Our day was structured. In group therapy sessions we were encouraged to bare our souls about events in our lives that could have led to such self-destruction. There were about twenty patients in the program at a time, of all kinds and from all walks of life—men, women, black, white, policemen, accountants, musicians.

The only things we all had in common were that we were all over eighteen and had abused drugs and alcohol to the point that we were in a psychiatric hospital. At first in group therapy sessions I was guarded. I had very little to say. As time went by I became more comfortable and shared what I felt sincerely and honestly. I didn't judge anyone. I listened to their stories and hoped their lives would be better when they returned to society. I was the only one who was on parole and had been in prison. Some had families who loved them. Some had families that were straight out of a horror story. I had never held a real job and most of these people had at least functioned in the normal world at some point in their lives. This was a disconnect for me. I was going to have to start from ground zero while they were picking up the pieces of their lives to salvage what was left.

I met with my assigned therapist three times a week for an hour. At our first meeting, the therapist and I left the office together. As we walked down the corridor he put his arm around my shoulder as if to befriend me. I reacted violently, kicking his feet out from under him and he fell to the ground. I kneeled on top of him ready to hit him. Though he didn't struggle to get up and didn't fight back he reminded me that my parole officer would not approve of this kind of behavior. During our next session I explained my reaction to the therapist. I did not like being touched by men and told him that it was not to happen again. I didn't know what was behind the reaction, but it was something that had stayed with me since Dorchester. He told me now that I was sober my emotions would be heightened and that it was a good time to be vulnerable and talk about the traumatic experiences in my life.

My therapist wanted to call my mother and father because he said family involvement was an important part of therapy. I told him that it would be a waste of time. I had not talked to my parents since they visited me in prison two years ago, the last conversation being about how I disgraced them by being in prison. Nevertheless he did call and my mother answered the phone. He explained to her that I was in a hospital for drug and alcohol addiction. She told him in no uncertain terms that I was not an addict or alcoholic and she wanted no part of this nonsense. When he hung up the phone, he told me not to talk to them during treatment, that they were a sure trigger for me to relapse and a setup for emotional pain. That was no problem—I had gone on for years at a time without them, creating more and more distance between us.

Every night the patients went to twelve-step meetings together. I did my best. Here was a room full of people just like me who were making sense to me. I listened to the speakers, the people with years of sobriety, talk about their lives. They spoke about their experiences as alcoholics and addicts and their lives as sober members of society. A lot of these people had taken paths similar to mine, some more extreme, some less. They all shared a common cause, to stop the pain and have a good life.

In the hospital, other patients all seemed to have horrific stories from their childhoods. Those deep wounds were not readily discussed at the twelve-step meetings. They came out in group therapy. One twenty-year-old girl had been turned on to heroin at age twelve by her father who then had different forms of sex with her and offered her to his friends as a party favor. One might assume she came from a poor family but the opposite was true. Her family was very wealthy and her father was a diplomat. Another girl in a similar circumstance was raised by a famous Hollywood producer and grew up around bizarre sex parties and drug use her whole life.

The saddest case was a young gay man who was very smart and handsome. His family, especially his father, would not love him because he was gay, so he turned to cocaine. He left the program against medical advice and went to his parents' house, into their bathroom, filled the bathtub, got in, and slit his wrists. After he died we were called into group and asked to remember him in silent prayer.

After being in treatment for two months I was having trouble putting memories into words. As the memories surfaced, raw emotions would turn into instant rage. My therapist brought in a psychologist who specialized in hypnotherapy. He asked me to close my eyes and imagine taking an elevator down to the darkest place in my mind. In a few minutes, my mind traveled there. All of a sudden I felt a pain knotted up in my body and I blacked out. When I came to, I was back in my room with my therapist sitting there. He told me I had slithered out of my chair to the floor and curled around like a snake, hissing. Then I had lunged at the hypnotherapist grabbing his neck. It took two orderlies to pull me off him. After that, they took me to my room and I slept for twenty-four hours straight. My therapist told me it probably had been too soon for me to go down to that dark place and that we would continue on our cognitive therapy path.

When my parole officer came by to check up on me, he was pleased with my staying sober and out of trouble. But I was still confined to a hospital and he worried about what would happen when I got out. When he asked me about how I thought I would do on the outside, I told him in all earnestness one day at a time I would go to meetings, get a job, and continue my mandatory drug testing. He was still doubtful and was inclined to sending me back to prison. I told him that was okay. I would bring my big book of AA and organize meetings in prison and stay sober while helping other people.

Well, he let me stay in the treatment program, but told me I needed to be confined there for another sixty days, not just the usual thirty. Since I was there for such a long time, I got to know all the hospital staff. I liked them and talked to them about staying sober and the conditions of my parole and asked them about their own families. Most of the staff were recovering addicts and they told me about sober parties and concerts. Knowing my past experiences with drugs and alcohol and my ability to talk to people and understand their situations, they thought I would be a good counselor. I was offered a job by the medical director working on the adolescent unit with teenagers who were admitted for drug abuse problems. This would be my first real job and I was very excited about going to work and to help young people who might have gone through some of what I did. At thirty-three years old it felt like my life was just beginning. This would be the first time in my life that I was forced to relate to others, to be in a job routine. I had no real training in dealing with these kids other than life on the street. Even though I was used to earning millions of dollars a year, my self-destructive behavior humbled me and I had realized in treatment I'd rather earn the $6.50 per hour than go back to using and possible death.

To think it through, I used the analogy of the addictive mind to someone who was exiled to Mars, a faraway planet that had no connection to the behavior of normal people on Earth. The treatment program was the first leg of the long journey back to Earth. I found that accepting life on life's terms as opposed to my terms was the only way to adapt to being an Earthling. Hearing the good news from other Martians who had made the journey successfully and that it could be found all over the world in twelve-step meetings was reassuring. These former Martians were more than willing to help provide guidance and support to get a daily reprieve from going back to Mars.

I don't think I was always a Martian even though I always felt separate from family and community. Becoming an addict definitely brought me there. When I arrived on Mars, I was immediately accepted and became a full-fledged Martian. Other Martians were more than willing to support every aspect of my bad behavior to make sure I would stay there and be a part of their community. Mars has its own rules: The Martian Commandments, the Civil Code of Mars. In order to live on Mars I had to exhibit high levels of self-interest. I was judged by my ability to do what felt good all the time. Everyone else was there solely for my amusement and pleasure. On Mars, it was insisted on that I stay in an altered state. I had my choice of alcohol, cocaine, heroin, prescription pills, or any combination I craved. These substances would be made available simply by following the Martian moral code. By the time I had landed on Mars, I had already lied to, stolen from, and deceived enough Earthlings to propel me to this special planet and earned the right to abuse any substance I wanted. The Martian code is simple: steal to get what you want, lie to defend or misdirect attacks on your behavior, be arrogant enough to dismiss any doubts about your lack of character, and hunt any prey that serves your self-interest. The longer you stay with us, the less likely you will return to Earth. The more you get away with, the closer we get to you. I learned expressions like "Live everyday as if it's your last." "What's in it for me?" "You can never have enough of a destructive habit" and of course, our favorite, "Fuck it."

We have casinos that let you win and win, but as the hours go by you lose it all and embrace your feelings of depression. You judge yourself as a degenerate loser, overwhelmed with guilt. We love this because within a few hours, those feelings are replaced with the pre-programmed thoughts of "Let's do that again only this time I will win." Of course our citizens never win in the end. We know the addict only cares about recreating the miserable feelings they get from losing. Yes, they are programmed to destroy themselves—these are the Earthlings that live on Mars.

We have all kinds of food here. Everyone has the chance opportunity to eat as much as they can to the point of nausea. They are encouraged to eat in secret. They hide like rats in a wall, gnawing away at their food. To lie is our first commandment, so when asked about their eating habits, they lie with great imagination and conviction. We even have mirrors that lie so when our fatsos look at themselves they see a model-perfect imagine.

We must give credit where credit it is due. These Earthlings voyaged here with the support of their families, friends, bosses, and communities. They unwittingly bought the ticket to our paradise and did not even know it. How beautiful is that! Our Earthlings grew up believing they were worthless, unloved, inadequate, judged, and ridiculed. All this was successfully absorbed into their personalities before they were old enough to even know what was happening. Without understanding any of these emotions, they slowly but surely drowned themselves in self-destructive behavior. As Martians, we know all the shame, hurt, and horror they experience at an early age get mixed together in their subconscious, creating a beast lying dormant. These weaklings try to control the beast and act like they are normal well-adjusted citizens of Earth. But we know better. It is only a matter of time before they can't stand it and look for more ways to dull that pain.

I felt encouraged that I had begun the long journey back to Earth. The treatment program was just the beginning of my attempt to leave Mars. I met three other guys through the twelve-step meetings. They were also newly sober and trying to making their way to a new life. We thought we could all be supportive to each other, so we rented a three-bedroom house in Burbank. I went to twelve-step meetings every day. These complete strangers became the family I had been looking for, a family whose code I believed in, and people I could trust. They accepted me regardless of my past. I could go into these meetings and talk about my innermost feelings, my weaknesses, and it bonded me to them. I was not afraid of being rejected for telling the truth about my feelings. This would be a new life for me and I only had to focus on one day at a time. Being sober was a new experience for me. It meant no more running from life but participating with everyone else. I had been living my own code for so long that this new way of thinking and living was not going to be easy. I had depended on drugs and alcohol for so long, they had become my best friends. Now I was saying good-bye to them.

Going to the supermarket scared me since the moment you walked in, there stood a full-sized cardboard cutout of a woman holding a Johnny Walker bottle. Behind her was an aisle of all kinds of alcohol, from beer to wine to hard liquor, right there staring me in the face. Everything I did was like I was doing it for the first time. Driving a car gave me anxiety. In a restaurant choosing a meal took me twenty minutes. As all newly sober people typically do, I talked to anyone who was polite enough to ask how I was you doing. I blabbed on and on about myself until they fell asleep or walked away.

Yet I was good as a counselor for young people. I shared with them a truncated version of my life and an enthusiastic picture of being sober. Most of these kids were ages twelve through eighteen. Their parents had committed them to this psychiatric hospital because they felt they could not control their kids. In almost every case, the parents were sicker than the kids. Most of these parents, for different reasons, had left their children to parent themselves. With my upbringing I had an easy time relating to the kids. Some of them acted out by using drugs and alcohol, others by stealing cars, getting in fistfights, and other kinds of trouble resulting in being expelled from school. None of them were hardcore psychiatric cases but they all had behavioral problems. They stayed committed in the hospital's care for long periods of time, sometimes nine or ten months, some until they reached the age of eighteen. A number of these kids emancipated themselves, meaning they legally separated from their parents. They felt so unloved and unwanted that nothing could induce them to be a part of their families. Many kids came from wealthy families. Some of those parents committed their children when school let out so they could have the summer off without them. These parents did not want the trouble of parenting to interfere with their adult fun.

During the time I had this job my life was routine and comfortably predictable. I woke up, took a shower, ate breakfast, went to work, came home, and had dinner. Then I would go to a twelve-step meeting, after which I would go to coffee shops with other members of the fellowship to share stories and bond. This went on for about two years. During this time I noticed that while I made $6.50 an hour, the businessman who started this treatment program drove a Ferrari, had several other cars, a ranch in Malibu, and a stable of horses. On some level it registered that what I earned as a staff member compared to the management seemed way off balance. But I saved that thought for another day.

During my first two years without using drugs or alcohol as a crutch my emotions were raw and all over the place. I got angry very quickly. The smallest thing that did not go my way enraged me. When I was driving if someone passed me I thought *Fuck you, moron* and had to keep myself from running them off the road. I was overly sensitive to what I perceived people thought of me just by the look on their faces. I had very little sense of what was normal. Though I had my own code of ethics in the drug world, I had put it out of my mind since I was trying to overcome all the bad things that had come of it. I didn't trust myself to know how to behave in what was called normal society. What, in fact, was happening was that the very society I hated, the one I risked my freedom and life to not have to live in, was the one I had to learn to cope with. I had to develop a new code I could live by without sacrificing the freedom that was so important to me. I was working a nine-to-five job, attending daily meetings like a good soldier, and was staying drug-free. So a part of me did accept a new code with a blind trust, and a part of me watched and waited for all this to blow up so I could return to my old self and way of life.

Ellen and I met at a twelve-step meeting and afterwards we would go out for coffee with a group of friends. She seemed to like me but I wondered why any woman would want to be with me at this point in my life, especially someone who had heard me talk about my past openly in meetings. What kind of woman could she be? She had been sober three years more than me and had her own sordid past. Sex for me was now different. While I was dealing, I had made the decision not to be involved with a woman romantically during the time I was a criminal. The lies I would have to tell, the secrets to keep, and the danger I would put her in, were not fair for someone who loved me. But now that I was an ordinary person, I had no reason not to. I had been on the receiving end of many blowjobs but had no real idea how to please a woman sexually. Ellen was good at directing me in how to please her. I thought this must be what all women want. I couldn't have been more wrong. I was very consistent and dependable about my sexual timetable; she was all over the place. What seemed like a good time of day to have sex one day was the wrong the next. I couldn't understand her unpredictability. At this point in my life I could only relate to women sexually. I had been shut down emotionally for so long that it was hard for me talk about my feelings. I was loyal and generous, I listened to her talk, and I spent time with her doing what she wanted. That was my way of giving. I even learned how to please her in bed.

I finally found out that she was trading blowjobs for prescription pills from a well-known M.D. who specialized in addiction. She was also screwing a famous musician at the same time she was pretending to be loyal to me. I felt betrayed. I did not medicate these feelings but talked about them in meetings, ultimately realizing I should not be in a relationship at this time . Betrayal of all I was trying to accomplish was enough to make me want to get drunk. I hurt all over and stayed in my room for two days in a state of confusion. Here I thought I could trust the people in our group to follow the principles. The blanket trust that everyone was telling the truth was broken. That rekindled the fire of my dark side, now looking for reasons why all these people were just like everyone else I could not trust.

In twelve-step meetings you are asked to live by spiritual principles. In theory that sounds great, but for me and my reality, you don't survive that way. Unlike a lot of people I met in twelve-step meetings I was different. I had been estranged from mainstream society since I was eighteen I had nothing to return to. While I admired the people who obtained long-term sobriety I still felt separate from them, not fitting in. That's when my old self showed up saying *Fuck all this bullshit. Go back to Colombia and live on the money stashed down there.* I related to my Colombian friends and family. They were not complicated. What you saw was what you got. When we were together they let their guard down and spoke freely and truthfully with emotion. Here in the normal world, even in twelve-step programs, people were careful about what they said about themselves. Only the image of whom they thought they should be showed up. It was frustrating, difficult, confusing, and different. There was a pecking order among groups of friends. People with more money got more attention. One woman told me I would be judged by my watch and shoes.

It would be easier to be back with my old peer group of smugglers than to go through this experience of trying to fit in here. My hatred for this kind of society hadn't changed since the time I was little boy walking the streets in Dorchester. I began to realize the problem was me, that even though I was not using drugs or drinking, I still felt alone and empty and that's why I separated myself out. I had to give this society a chance. I also thought about many other things I had never thought about before. Those first two years also showed me that I could really feel good about myself, too. I had moments when I felt successful. I was learning how to live within the boundaries that our society finds acceptable. My favorite Earthling expression was "Life is not fair. You don't have to like it. You just have to do it on life's terms." I knew I had a long road ahead of me but I did not have to get there within any timeline. My old drug dealing friend told me I could never stay sober, He said "People don't change." They didn't know me before I was a drug dealer. I was just a gentle kid then not wanting to get hurt. I was determined to change my character and find out how to do that.. On this path I was always questioning whether I could make it through and kept asking myself what life would be like if I went back to my old ways. This conflict was driving me insane.

Driving home from work one night I saw a teenage girl standing in the road. I stopped my car to ask if she was all right. Her hair was all disheveled, her shirt was torn and her legs looked bruised.

She said in a very childlike voice, "I hope I get to keep the baby this time."

I realized she was mentally slow, so I gently asked her if I could give her a ride. While driving she told me she had been raped before and had gotten pregnant. When the baby was born it was taken away from her and she was sad about that. Before I stopped to pick her up she had been in an all-night laundry washing her clothes when a group of men walked in and raped her. When they were done with her they brought her out to the street and told her to wait there and that's where I found her. This beautiful, sad creature entered my life purely by coincidence. My reaction to her story was outrage. I wanted to find these men and return the favor. But now my new code had other rules. I drove her to the Huntington Beach police station and helped her explain what had happened. They called a social worker whom I stayed to meet. I gave her my name and phone number and offered to help in any way I could. It turned out the Huntington Beach Community Health Center was setting up a helpline for teenagers on drugs, so I volunteered to train their peer counselors. That girl left an impression—she was pure of heart. Not a vindictive, selfish thought ran through her mind. Meeting her helped restore me to sanity.

I had tremendous empathy for the pain of others. I could almost feel their pain in my own body. Any act of kindness moved me to almost crying. I don't cry, my body just doesn't, and so almost crying was the equivalent for me. I learned not to cry tears back when I was in Dorchester. When a sad emotion hit my stomach it would work its way up my throat and that's where I stopped it. After a while I think my body just automatically stopped shedding tears.

Toward the beginning of my second year of sobriety, I was released from parole and free to travel. There was a twelve-step convention in Laughlin, Nevada. It was my first convention and I was very excited to go there with friends I had met in meetings. The convention was held in a casino hotel. As I checked in I saw a line of people waiting to play this huge slot machine right next to the check in desk. The woman playing the machine was wearing an AA nametag as did the people in line waiting to play. The machine had a large ball on the end of the handle you pulled down on to make the wheels of cherries and lemons spin around. Someone called the woman's name as she was pulling down the lever and when she looked up she hit herself in the head with the ball. She did not miss a beat and kept putting money in the machine and pulling down the lever. When she struck herself in the head and just kept on playing I was shocked. What was this? I looked at this AA group, the woman, and the long line of people waiting to play that machine and thought could we gamble even though we were sober? I knew we could not drink or use drugs, but gambling as an addiction was something I had never thought of. I found it odd that the convention was in a casino hotel but who was I to judge?

The hotel was on the Colorado River and my plan was to water ski during the day and go to the meetings which were scheduled at night. I had no thoughts of gambling. But sure enough after dinner I meandered down to the casino and found a twenty-five cent Double Down video poker machine and put in five dollars. If you won the first hand you could double your winnings if you drew the high card on the next round. You could double down again and quadruple the amount and keep going till you lost it all. So that first night I did not go to any meetings. I played at that machine until two in the morning. I was too tired to go water skiing the next day and went to an ATM to drain my account of the $120 I had left to my name. I spent all day Sunday in the casino. I never made it to a single meeting or went waterskiing. I felt like I was out of control when I was playing. After I lost it all and went upstairs, it took me about an hour to settle down. I was uncomfortable about those feelings, but I wasn't taking drugs or alcohol. So when I left the next day, I just put it out of my mind. In those days there were no casinos in L.A. so you had to travel to Nevada to gamble. When I got back to Burbank with no place to gamble, the idea of it just disappeared and I carried on with my sobriety, job, and life.

Word about my reputation as a good counselor spread and I was offered a job in a new hospital program in Orange County, California, an hour away from Burbank. If I took this job I would have to move, meet new friends, and work with new people. The job involved marketing and community outreach for the drug and alcohol treatment program in a medical-surgical hospital. I knew nothing about marketing for a hospital or for a treatment program. My experience was in marketing marijuana and cocaine. For years I sold drugs without thought to what taking drugs did to some people. Now my work was to get addicts off drugs. In a strange way it seemed like life was giving me a chance to undo some of the damage I had caused. The job seemed challenging and I would be my own boss most of the time, reporting to the hospital administrator only once a month. I went to the library and read about the history of advertising, the different types of marketing, and how to budget a marketing program. The money was much better than my $6.50 an hour Burbank job so I decided to take it.

I found a room for rent in a small ranch-style home three blocks from the beach. The house was owned by a recently divorced fifty-year-old psychologist. He interviewed me for the room and I got it. I liked him. He was very different from any friends I had in the past. He had gone to college, had been married for fifteen years, had three kids, and a successful career. The house was a fifteen-minute drive from the hospital. This would be the first time that I had lived alone since I became sober.

The hospital had a wing set up for drug and alcohol treatment with sixteen beds for adults and sixteen for adolescents. As the marketing director my salary was three thousand dollars a month plus bonuses, depending on the occupancy rate of the hospital. Bonuses based on occupancy were a regular practice in the hospital industry even though it seemed to put pressure on me. My success was not judged by the outcome of treatment, but on the volume of patients. I had never done anything like this and had no way to judge right and wrong in the legal world. I just assumed the company that hired me would not create a payday scenario based on questionable ethics. I was offered the job because I was a good public speaker and because of my past being so extreme that people took an interest in me. In a way I was a kind of celebrity as a former record-setting pot smuggler and now a transformed business executive promoting good mental health. That does not mean the company executives liked me, it only that meant they could use my life experiences to make their company money.

I continually educated myself on how to develop successful ad campaigns. Every day after work I would go to the library and take notes on how to buy radio time, television time, and newspaper and print media advertising, as well as how to develop an overall marketing plan with a budget. My supervisor, a woman close to the owner of the company who was clearly hired for her looks, had no idea how marketing worked. She was very pleased with my work, supportive of my efforts, and never challenged me about my ideas. I was part of a team of twelve marketing people, one or two per facility. At our monthly meetings at expensive restaurants my marketing plan always seemed to be the main subject of conversation.

Part of my job was to be the community outreach coordinator where I visited schools and spoke to different groups of parents whose teens had drug problems and to the teens themselves. One time I was invited by the Santa Ana school board to one of their middle schools. I looked around the room at thirty little faces. These kids were in continuation school, taken out of the mainstream population for dealing drugs, stealing, or fighting. The common theme for these kids was that they all came from poverty. The poverty created broken homes, drug addicted parents, with one or both parents in prison. These kids connected with each other and formed their own families, much the same as Fernando did in Colombia. Everyone wants a sense of belonging to something. These kids were born into their lives. They did not choose the dirty streets, drunken parents, or anger and hostility that surrounded them. Just to get them to come to school was a miracle.

The school's principal had heard about me and was hoping I would have an impact on some of these youngsters. I told the kids the truth about my past, that I had grown up in a poor neighborhood, and about being out on the streets. I described what it was like to be a drug dealer, be arrested and spend four years in prison, and how addiction to drugs and alcohol made me make bad decisions in my life. I went on to tell about what my life was like now and that I found a way to live being off drugs. They really tuned in and asked me questions about the Colombian drug trade, expensive cars, and the bloodiest fight I had seen in prison. They could see my drug dealing as their future, only unlike me, they thought they would die before getting caught. I told them they were already caught, that none of them should pursue a criminal profession, because they were lousy criminals.

I told them, "You're sitting here in continuation class because before even turning fourteen, you're already on your way to juvenile hall."

By their responses I sensed certain innocence in them, a dark innocence. One boy told me about his father who was a gang member and now in prison for murder. This kid was proud of his father. Another kid told me about how his gang controlled certain street corners and his disdain for the white people who drove through the neighborhood looking for hookers and drugs. As I listened to what they had to say, I saw myself in them, the anger and distrust of authority, how the people who were supposed to take care of them had let them down. It became truly clear how desperate and sad most of their lives would end up.

I tried to turn the conversation to a positive tone, so I asked, "Who wants to tell about the best day in their lives?"

A fourteen-year-old Mexican girl shyly raised her hand. She had jet-black frizzy hair, brown skin with dark eyes. Her lips were covered with thick, bright red lipstick. Smiling, she said the best day of her life was when twelve boys gang-banged her, one after the other. I had heard and experienced just about everything during my years in my former life, but this was unimaginable.

So I asked, "Why that day?"

She looked at me as if this was a stupid question and said I should know the answer.

"On that day I finally had a family. I felt needed and wanted."

The other kids in the room all looked at her with understanding smiles.

I drew comparisons in my mind of my life, Fernando's life, and their lives. One advantage I had was to be born white. Growing up I

166

noticed the degree of a person's social acceptance was determined by the color of their skin. The darker the skin, the more a person was treated like an outsider. I had two parents, neither of whom had gone to prison or been drug addicts. Fernando had no parents while growing up. These kids had parents but one or both could be addicted to drugs or in prison. What we all had in common was being raised in violent neighborhoods, parenting ourselves, and poverty. What these kids had that I did not was that they had found other kids like themselves and formed gangs with a common cause and helped protect each other. These gangs or groups provided a feeling of being wanted and loved. They also provided a code to live by.

I never joined a gang. I was a loner. I developed my own code to fit my needs. What Fernando did that I did not was to take most of the wealth he earned from the black market and use it to help the poorest of people from his tribe. He lived a middle class life but could have lived any life large amounts of money could buy. I became a drug addict, learning about money from a greedy, sick lawyer who taught me how to trade my wealth for personal pleasure, buying houses, cars, and businesses. I gave money away and helped friends, but it was nothing compared to what I could have done if my parents and teachers had pointed me in the right direction early on. I let myself down. I used my illegal money for selfish reasons when I could have been courageous and noble, sacrificing my own self-interest for the interest of kids like this. Time and time again I heard the same kind of sad messages—absent parents, physical abuse, sexual abuse, food deprivation, and loneliness.

I was also invited to speak around the country to parent groups, a totally different kind of audience. In the 1990s, drug use among teenagers, especially the use of marijuana, grew rampant and by 2000, it had reached a crisis around the U.S. Various communities wanted to know about prevention and options for private or publicly-funded treatment for their youth. I was asked to speak on the subject in Toledo, Ohio, at an elite private club, whose members were civic leaders, politicians, lawyers, doctors, and socialites. The Toledo Club opened in 1889 in an historic building in the center of the city where members paid a premium for every convenience. They could dine, get a shoe shine, haircut, and connect with their cronies.

After spending more than a hundred hours of due diligence on my own time and at my own expense, I authored a plan to present viable low-cost residential treatment that included underprivileged youth. The plan would utilize empty HUD housing and employ drug counselors who made eight dollars and fifty cents per hour in lieu of therapists who made seventy-five dollars per hour. The plan included creation of support groups for young people that promoted a teenager's healthy lifestyle. My fee was two thousand dollars for the one-hour presentation. I did not want to waste my time just giving a narrative on the problem. I wanted to give them a plan they could put into action and take some steps toward solving the problem. If this model was implemented, studied for a year, and proved successful, I thought we might be able to let it grow nationwide. It could provide a good model for state, federal, and local agencies working together.

Dressed in my dark blue suit, white shirt, and red tie, I was escorted to the podium in the front of the Red Room. I looked out at my audience and studied them before beginning my talk. They were a conservative-looking, well-dressed middle-aged group of around sixty men and women. They sat at elegant dining tables chatting while being served by white-gloved black waiters. I set up my presentation materials on an easel. The club director introduced me as the president of Focus Healthcare and a recovering addict and alcoholic. I proceeded with the speech, giving important facts and figures on success rates and why it was so important to help all underprivileged and privileged youths with drug or alcohol problems. Half an hour into the talk I noticed the waiters were serving Bloody Marys to the audience. This set me back. I realized all this work I had done was only of entertainment value to them. The audience was only paying lip service to the cause while they lunched and socialized.

I politely wrapped up my speech and was walking out when a woman approached me and said, "Thank you. Your approach for the poor is admirable. However, I have a daughter with a problem who is eighteen. Could you recommend the best program in the country for her?"

I replied, "Call the Betty Ford Center."

As time went on I started to feel a sense of acceptance in my professional world. I continued to speak at different organizations and made new contacts. I had a natural ability to connect to addicts and alcoholics, and I saw myself in them and did my best to help them find a starting point to change their lives. I could go into the worst neighborhoods or to a corporate human resources office and talk to a person in emotional pain. Oftentimes people had no idea their lives could be better. Although I was no longer on parole I kept in touch with my parole officer who encouraged me to apply for a presidential pardon. He even sent me parolees who were having trouble meeting the terms of their parole. None of those guys made it. They all ended up violating their parole and going back to prison.

My social life was doing just fine. I had found other meetings that I liked and had met a group of former addicts to be friends with. I was saving money in the bank as opposed to burying it in my backyard and the money was in my name as opposed to shell companies and offshore trusts. I worked out a budget for myself and paid all my bills on time. I was keeping my body in good shape. I went surfing when the waves were good, worked out in a gym lifting weights five days a week, and gave up red meat. I attended four meetings a week and sponsored two or three men.

My relationship with Ellen was over even though she called periodically and had stopped down to visit once in a while. She had told me she liked to have a man in her back pocket in case her current boyfriend didn't work out. So I guess I was the one person she kept in her back pocket but that was in her mind only. When the time comes that I am through with someone I am really through—the door closes and there is no way back in. After we broke up, Ellen told me that one reason we did not work out was because when she went to the well it was empty. She was referring to my emotional self. That may have been true from her point of view. For me, we did not work out because she had the need to try out every man she was attracted to while at the same time pretending to be loyal to me.

My work in the hospital field was broadening into an executive position with expertise in business development. The hospital industry is made up of operating companies and property management companies both under the same corporate ownership. I worked for the operating company and was asked to develop a formal marketing plan. In a short period of time, my hospital became the most profitable hospital in the group. I received good bonuses, more than I thought I would. I learned fast about hospital operating companies and their relationship to property holding companies. I listened to the hospital president and began to understand hospital management. My reputation grew and the top executives who owned and managed a total of fifty-five hospitals went out of their way to meet me. In fact, my hospital was doing so well that the parent company that owned it wanted to open three more units in their other hospitals with me as the V.P. of marketing or to hire me as an outside contractor.

All of this was new to me, so I hired a major law firm in Santa Monica to review the contract I was offered as an independent contractor. The attorney assigned to me was a health care specialist. He told me the contract was standard and widely used in the hospital industry, but that it contained a gray area. Those words did not escape my attention. I asked numerous times what gray area meant. He explained that under current law it was legal for hospitals to offer incentives to professionals who referred clients to them. Hospitals could give out free office space, vacations, tickets to events, and contracts for a per patient day fee so they could keep their beds filled. The attorney said to go ahead and sign the contract but to watch for legislation that later could make it illegal to be paid per patient day. Now I was familiar with how the black market operated and had spent most of my business life in that industry before getting sober, but I did not know there was a gray area in legally conducted business. It seemed to me that the gray area was the time before legislation caught up with a business practice that had yet to be scrutinized for any possible improprieties. I was trying to make a living in the legal world. I had given my word to my parole officer that not only would I would stay sober but I would not break the law. Yet here was an area of law that was not clear. I learned there were two kinds of law, civil and criminal, and the distinction between them. Apparently if convicted of a civil crime, the individual or corporation would pay a monetary fine but not risk imprisonment as in a criminal conviction. So I wondered what qualified as a real crime in this new world of business.

To be my own boss as an independent contractor was a great opportunity. Although I had some apprehensions about how the business was structured, I put my heart into the fact that my work helping addicts would be successful and, at the same time bring me a lot more money. I could tailor the programs as I saw fit and get real results. So I put together the best medical professionals I could find along with drug and alcohol counselors and created an inpatient treatment program. Working with a prominent psychiatrist, I created a program, which I named A.A.C.I. to treat patients who on the outside were addicts and alcoholics, but after going through detox exhibited other diagnosable psychiatric problems. The roots of their addiction could be found in manic depression or bipolar disorders. The hospital company would absorb all the staffing and marketing costs so I had no risk. I was free to really help the people I wanted to and the results were exciting. I felt good. After three years of operation my units were the most profitable units in their system. The company proposed that I lease units in their hospital for a performance-based contract.

The program I created involved a referral network of therapists, doctors, corporate human resource directors, and community agencies. I selected them because they were the best in the business and understood my approach for treatment. When the opportunity to open my own program came about, these people were loyal to me and they referred patients to the new venture, which really helped make it succeed. Later on I developed a strategy to combine the referrals I got from existing sources with patients from a nationwide marketing campaign. This was not a new idea. Competing hospitals were doing the same thing only my team worked harder and focused more on helping every caller regardless of whether they had insurance. The callers with no ability to pay for treatment were given the helpline to community agencies, Alcoholics Anonymous, Narcotics Anonymous, Cocaine Anonymous, or, in some cases, outpatient therapists. When we had the space, I gave free beds to people who were absolutely in need. It was a gift and in my mind it was the right thing to do. So here I had a company that was helping people, was a service to the community, and at the same time was extremely profitable. I was proud of this formula. I encouraged the doctors and treatment staff to be advocates for the patients—not the hospital, not the insurance companies—but to be front and center for the patients.

We eventually got seventy thousand calls a month from people who were seeking help on their voyage from Mars to Earth. Of those callers, less than half of one percent had the financial means to pay for treatment. This was a problem that needed to be solved. So I hired a software company to set up a tracking mechanism, which along with the phone system data gave me a picture of where our calls came from and the demographics of that area. I then compared that information to census data. The outcome of this ongoing study determined where we would spend our marketing dollars. We wanted to be able to help everyone that called on some level by referring them somewhere if they could not afford treatment at our hospital. Needless to say, that was a huge problem that still exists today. Treatment for drug and alcohol abuse could be available for anyone that needed it, but our money goes toward fighting a war on drugs, fighting growers and drug wholesalers. As a former professional in the dealing of illegal drugs I knew the reason for the success of that business was the demand in the market. If the demand wasn't there the supply of illegal drugs would dry up.

I was personally invested as a former Martian to make sure my fellow travelers received the best, most thorough treatment we could give them. I hired only fellow former Martians who had been clean at least one year to work with me and paid them twice the market rate. The employees who worked for me were all characters in their own rights. My longest-term employee was Margi. Her painful past included prostitution. Tony had been a Mafia soldier and had given up alcohol after serving an eight-year prison term. Mervin was black, a professional football player who got addicted to pain pills after his career ended with a traumatic injury. Greg was a minor league baseball player whose career ended with an injury to his shoulder. He found his comfort in alcohol. Linda was a gay woman conflicted with her sexual identity and had developed a love affair with cocaine and prescription pills. The one thing we all had in common was our voyage from Mars to Earth and our desire to remain here.

Paying the employees more meant me making less, but they deserved to make more. I was making plenty of money so it was no sacrifice for me. I had learned in the smuggling business you had to pay people well to begin to expect loyalty.

I moved back to Burbank to be closer to my friends that I made when I came back to Earth. I bought a house with legally earned money. I bought furniture for the house and a used car, all totally legit. The commute to work was an hour each way and I worked seven days a week. I loved my life. Yet in the back of my mind there was that nagging feeling that this would all be taken away.

Part of my job was to attend hospital business conferences. It was at one of these business conferences that I met Claudia. She was sitting at a table with three other people, one of whom I knew. I heard her voice through the noise in the room and was immediately drawn to it. She was telling a joke that was somewhat out of place for the conservative nature of the conferences. I looked over to see who owned that voice. There sat a beautiful woman with black hair and dark eyes. She had a very Italian-looking face. When she stood up she was the perfect height, her body thin and well-toned. Her legs were long and beautifully sculpted. I was taken with her. She held herself with confidence and an attitude of indifference.

I did not go over to introduce myself as I thought a woman like her would not take someone with my past seriously. She reminded me of sophisticated women like the San Francisco socialite at my New Year's Eve party. They jumped into my life for short periods of time and then went back to their normal lives. I was all right with that in the past. I got plenty of sex with no commitment. I wanted to get to know her but would wait and observe her from a distance.

That night at a dance I got a chance to talk to Claudia. I walked up to her and said, " I'm David. I've been watching you and feel compelled to get to know you better."

She introduced herself and told me that before the employee assistance job she had now, she had worked with Down syndrome children at a community health clinic. Because of her sense of humor, irreverence for the establishment, and strong connection to the emotionally wounded, I decided to let my guard down and tell her about my past. If she rejected me, I would know right away.

Claudia and I got on well and took a walk, talking for hours. She seemed to have an inner pain she was wrestling with and, feeling like a kindred spirit, I was drawn to find out more about her. We spent all of our free time together during the three-day conference. It turned out we lived close to each other. At the end of the conference, we exchanged phone numbers and went our ways. When I got back to work I called her and we made plans to meet at my hospital so I could give her a tour of the facility. When she arrived at the reception desk she was in a business suit. Most of the woman I knew, even those in the health care business, had a look that was sexier. But I didn't care. I was so happy to see her the moment I saw her, I rushed over, and picked her up, and spun her around like I had just found a long-lost friend. She did not say anything about that but later when we were walking alone she told me it was not an appropriate business greeting. After the tour we went out to lunch and talked. I could have talked to her forever but we both had to get back to work. Afterward I walked her to her car and asked for her phone number. I took a chance and kissed her.

I called her that night and we made plans to meet the next evening at my favorite diner that I loved for its baked apples. Claudia told me about her family. She explained that her mother was married at a young age to a good man, not necessarily the man she was in love with but a man who worked hard and would be a good husband and father. Her mother already was involved with another man she was passionate about whom she saw throughout the marriage and Claudia was actually his child. The father who raised her probably knew about the affair but still loved her mother and was a kind and loving father to her. He raised Claudia as his own never once showing animosity that he was not her biological father.

Claudia was very close to her mother and had taken care of her during a long fight with cancer. The sadness of her loss was in her eyes. She told me about how she had driven home every weekend to New Jersey from Washington, D.C., to be with her mother. When her mother became very sick and was hospitalized, she stayed at her side full time. The treatments her mother underwent were was so painful she would cry out. It reminded me of my bubble when she was in the hospital. Claudia was with her mom when she passed away. I could feel her pain and but wanted to understand how such a bond between a mother and child developed. When the mother of a friend died I would always ask, "Did you love her?" I did not want to presume just because someone was a mother they deserved to be loved. With my mother a deep hole was left in me where that relationship should have been.

Claudia had been abused by men at a young age both sexually and emotionally. I asked her if she would have liked to have killed them. I have never had to face such a situation, but I believe if I was fighting off a man who was raping a woman I could kill him. She said she could not murder anyone. I was learning Claudia's moral code and it was very different than mine. I had learned to make decisions based on survival. Her sense of morality had come from the security of a loving family. In the back of my mind I thought Claudia was the first woman I had ever met that I wanted to marry. I knew she would be a great mother and a good partner for me. I admired her independence she knew how to stand on her own two feet. She had her own career, owned her own house, and paid her own bills. This was not a woman who wanted to be kept.

At this time I was dating two other girls but it was only for companionship. I somehow had the idea that to be in a relationship, you did not have to be emotionally attached. So when I met these girls I told them from the beginning, "Listen, this is only about sex. I don't want marriage or a relationship. I just want to have a good time." They agreed so I felt perfectly fine that I was being honest with them. Being honest does not always ensure a happy outcome. They could have said no thanks, in which case I would have been seeing no one. When Claudia asked me who else I was dating at the time, I told her about the two other girls but explained that they were not emotional attachments, that they were only for sex. She disapproved and said I was selling myself short. I didn't really know what she was talking about but I thought her message was that she would not take me seriously unless I ended those relationships. I trusted her judgment.

We dated for a few months going mostly to the same old diner in Burbank, ordering baked apples and talking for hours. We did not have sex for a while and I respected that. I liked hanging out with her. Oddly to me it was more important than sex.

We went on a few weekend trips to Laughlin. Some days we rented a houseboat and just cruised around on the lake, swimming and lying in the sun. At night we would go to the casino where I introduced her to my favorite poker machines. She would play for an hour or two and go back up to the hotel room, once again displaying a sense of normalcy, unlike me. I played until I ran out of money. One night I gambled so late I left Claudia alone in the hotel room all night. I had missed out on sex for gambling. Claudia was furious with me, but I talked my way out of it with some story or another. I did not even notice the time when I was in front of the slot machines. If someone sat next to me and tried to start a friendly conversation I snubbed them. I had given up smuggling, drugs, and alcohol.

This gambling seemed like the only vice left for me to enjoy.

On a trip to Maui we had our first fight. We were driving in a rented jeep up a mountain road when I pulled over onto a muddy embankment. I knew of a twenty-foot-high hidden waterfall that spilled over into a pool of water deep enough to swim in. To get to this waterfall you had to hike along a rugged half-mile trail. I hadn't noticed that Claudia was wearing a white dress and white sandals. I headed toward the trail and she followed hesitantly. When we got to the end of the pavement she took a few steps in the mud and rocks and stopped dead in her tracks, "I'm not going."

How could she miss such an opportunity? I thought. She then went on about how stupid I was not to notice what she was wearing. I couldn't believe it. So we argued about it for a while. She won and we went back to the condo. She explained that she was not an adventurer and the idea of hiking to a hidden jungle waterfall was about as attractive as having sex on a bed of nails. I got it and made a mental note not to plan any surprise side trips that included hiking through a jungle. We got over that argument and had a good time the rest of the trip.

We continued to see each other several nights a week and every weekend. I invited her over to my house in Burbank for dinner. I thought a roast turkey would be a special meal and it was one of the few things I knew how to cook. When I served it she asked what else we were having. Vegetables? Bread? I had not thought of that so we just ate the turkey. Claudia was beginning to see how little I knew about regular living. She took it as a challenge to polish a diamond in the rough. The next time I invited her over I gave more thought to foods that might impress her. I bought the food from the deli, an assortment of fruits with bright colors, papayas and strawberries, and for the main course, chicken curry. She complemented me on this dinner. I could tell by the way she ate the food she was enjoying more than just the taste. She knew I was making an effort to please her.

We talked every day and saw each other as often as we could. After six months of knowing each other we agreed to move in together to see if we were compatible enough to get married. Claudia rented out her house and moved into mine in Burbank. I loved her company and listened intently to her talking about normal decision-making and acceptable behavior. We could have been friends when we were eight years old. I was very honest with her about sex. I told her what I liked and how often I liked it.

Claudia responded, "You have met your match." It seemed to contradict her overall attitude toward men and sex so I felt I was special.

Claudia talked to me about having a moral compass and she believed in honesty and personal integrity. Although she had had her hardships and tragedies, she did not act out against society. She maintained her principles. To match her moral standards would be impossible but I made every effort to trust in her judgment. There was no doubt in my mind that I loved her and her influence would be good for me. Left to my own devices I had was driven toward extreme risk-taking that resulted in self-destructive consequences.

We were married that May in 1989 and decided to have a baby right away since I was thirty-nine and she was just a year younger. The attempt to make a baby became like a pleasurable task. We saved our money and decided to go to Cozumel for our honeymoon, a beautiful island with tall palm trees, warm water, and great food. We went to the beaches, ate at the local restaurants, and worked at making a baby at night.

One day while snorkeling a barracuda came up to us. Before I could motion to Claudia to get out of there, she had already swum off to the floating wooden raft, leaving me to deal with the barracuda. Luckily the barracuda just swam away.

When I caught up with her on the raft, I said, "What was that? You split and just left me there?"

She said with a smile, "That's right."

To me it was funny. I loved that a fish had scared her. It was like a part of her was still a little girl. On the other hand, I thought of it as a crack in the wall of her moral code. My code was never to leave anyone behind. Here she was looking out only for herself. I made a note of that in my mind, not a big deal but something to watch for in the future. It was the perfect honeymoon, full of laughter and relaxation and, by the time we got home Claudia was pregnant.

Beyond my day-to-day life with Claudia I struggled emotionally to find a place to fit in with the rest of my world. I acted like the other men in my peer group but I did not like them. They seemed to relate with each other, enjoyed the country club lifestyle, and talked about golf. They were comfortable with their wealth while I felt like an outsider. I observed the normal patterns of behavior—how to be polite, how to choose your words so as not to offend people, and to be neutral on any political or religious issue. I was very opinionated but kept my thoughts to myself if they seemed too far outside the scope of what everyone else was thinking. I did not break any civil or criminal laws. I had no thoughts of taking any kind of drug or drinking. But I made no male friends. I had to control my aggressive nature and try to find common topics of conversation like football or the stock market in order to fit in with other guys.

Claudia's pregnancy was uneventful and we were both looking forward to the birth of our first child. The day Claudia went into labor and we headed for the hospital she said she was sorry if this turned out to be false labor. That statement caught my attention. She was going to give birth and her thoughts were on being considerate to me. I could not believe she said that. She was doing everything; all I did was inject some sperm. I was surprised when someone was kind or considerate, so much so that it moved me. The least I could do was go to the hospital with her even if it were a hundred times until she delivered. I was with her all the way. This was real and she would deliver our son in no time.

Claudia said she did not want any drugs during her delivery, but as the contractions got stronger, she quickly changed her mind and demanded an epidural. Since I was known in the hospital industry the anesthesiologist cornered me and asked if he could get a job at one of the hospitals I worked for.

I said, "Hey, could you pay attention to my wife?"

After she got the epidural Claudia was ordering everyone in the delivery room around saying things like "Move that mirror over here. Doctor, you stand over there." The delivery went well and out came our son. I was overcome with emotion. Look at my wife—she was so beautiful and she grew a baby inside of her. Her blood supplied life to this little creature that was our son. I was overcome with emotion. Now that he was born and in the world, he would need his mother for food, love, and comfort. As a new father I was not sure what my role would be. I knew at that moment I had made the right choice in finding a woman who would be a mother for our child.

We took our son home from the hospital. We were sitting on the back porch with him still in his car seat when I said, "Well, what do we do now?"

We looked at each other and realized we had no idea of how to take care of an infant. But as nature would have it my wife never took her eyes off of our son. In a few days I had to go back to work. I helped out as much as I could but during those early years it was all her. This had to be. Claudia had the maternal instinct and I could do nothing but look on with respect. I saw what a mother does to bond with her child. I never had those feelings of attachment with my mother. Being a mother came naturally to Claudia, but this was the first time I got to be a part of this deep love.

My life now became the three of us. Claudia was now completely focused on our son. She had resigned from her job a few days before she delivered. I went to work with baby spit on my shirt. I had no set schedule so I could stay home and help out doing whatever was needed or come home early. After Adam's birth Claudia changed sexually. That seemed reasonable after giving birth and staying up all night with our son. I did not take it personally. After all, that phase could not last that long.

A few years later we moved to a three-thousand-square-foot Mediterranean-style home with a half-acre of manicured lawns and a pool in Southern California. My business was doing great and Claudia and I were in love with our son. Except for when I was at work, the three of us were inseparable. Claudia now had the son she had always wanted. It was as if her destiny had been fulfilled. But her affection toward me changed. When I would watch her while she was getting dressed or cooking in the kitchen I would be overwhelmed with the desire to hold her. But she would elbow me and push me aside saying all affection from me was intended to end up in sex and she wasn't interested. I became distant. Each of those rejections started to add up to the feeling of being an outsider in my own family. I started to think she was reliving her mother's attitude toward her husband. Her mother had not been in love with her husband and had sex only when absolutely necessary. Her mother had saved the romantic, passionate sex for her lover. Was this what Claudia was doing? I know Claudia respected me for my ability to provide for my family, but was she getting sex somewhere else? I didn't think so. She was moral and honest. Did that mean the woman I fell in love with had just used me to have a baby? Having sex with my wife was the only way I felt accepted and loved. When I was rejected I felt alone and my quiet darkness took over. On the outside I would be void of emotion but on the inside the beast was being fed.

As the years went by, I saved a lot of money, all legally earned. People around me had all kinds of suggestions on what to do with it. I was distrustful of these people so I might have agreed with them, but a part of me just could not accept anyone else's ideas. If the money had been illegally earned cash I would have known the rules, but this was money in the bank for anyone to know about. We decided to buy a second home as in investment. We bought an empty beachfront lot, hired the architect, builder, and interior designer and built our own home. I thought putting money into beachfront property was better than keeping it in the bank. Socially I tried to make friends with people that were not in twelve-step programs. I wanted to be a part of our community but was always conscious of my past. I sorted out the men I liked and decided to try to get closer to them.

One man in particular I had known for three years. We got along well at dinners and shared a similar sense of humor. I decided to tell him a truth about my past, thinking that was the only way he would ever get to know who I really was beyond the veneer of the Orange County social sphere. Will and I were sitting at a Starbucks when out of my mouth came the story of how I was busted for trafficking a large amount of pot when I was twenty-eight years old. He listened without commenting. By the look on his face he seemed shocked and uncomfortable. We finished our coffees and walked out together in silence. Before parting, I started to tell him about an opportunity I was thinking about as a paid board member of a public company. That's when Will said "I wouldn't do that if I were you, not with your past." I knew at that moment I had lost him and he would never look at me in the same way. I felt an instant pain in my gut, a pain that I knew all too well. Our potential long-term friendship would dwindle and the attempt to get closer to a human being was cut off.

My family and I did everything together. Claudia and I did not take vacations or even go to a restaurant without Adam while he was an infant. So we stayed home together loving and taking care of him. When Adam was around three years old Claudia and I decided we should take our core employees on a team-building weekend and, lo and behold, we decided to go to the Mirage Hotel in Las Vegas. The first night there I was going downstairs to meet everyone for dinner and on my left I saw a group of video poker fifty- and hundred-dollar slots. I was in a hurry but what the hell, I had five hundred dollars in cash in my pocket. So I walked over to the closest machine and put in the maximum amount which was three hundred and the machine dealt a royal straight flush, paying out a hundred thousand dollars. How ironic was that? At that point in my life I did not need a hundred thousand dollars but I had just won it. Well, a technician came over to make sure the machine was not malfunctioning, the cashier checked my ID, and about an hour later handed me a check. I had told the casino hostess I wanted a check because I wanted to leave with my winnings.

She said, "We don't worry about that. You all come back and lose."

That weekend I went back to high stakes video poker room as often as possible. I noticed within twenty minutes of sitting at the machine I hated everyone else playing. I was hoping they would lose and leave. I did not want to eat or talk to anyone. My brain was taken over by the adrenaline of gambling and I became an antisocial degenerate. I left that weekend having won more than $110,000. So, of course I had to find ways to get back to casinos to keep that going. Every family trip I planned was to a resort with a casino—vacations in the Bahamas, Lake Tahoe, or Las Vegas. Eventually I played only $100 and $500-dollar slot machines that had payouts in the hundreds of thousands of dollars. I never enjoyed myself. I was never happy because no matter how hard I tried to figure out the slot machines, studied or thought I could beat them, I could never really figure out a winning pattern. I was mesmerized and out of control. Most of the time I left owing the casinos money. I always told the casino hosts and employees I was a recovering alcoholic so please don't offer me free drinks. I had $150,000 credit lines at two casinos and $100,000 at another. I very seldom left the casino without owing some of the money I drew down from my credit line. I was the perfect mark for an industry designed to take advantage of people prone to addictive behavior.

My wife got the news from her doctor that she might have ovarian cancer. A cancer specialist was called in to operate to remove and biopsy a cyst. Claudia was worried she would not live to see our son, then two years old, grow into a man. The time leading up to her surgery was emotional for all of us. After Adam and I dropped Claudia off at the hospital, I took Adam home and waited for any news. We sat together on my bed and I told him, "Mom will be all right. She loves you very much and soon we will go get her and bring her home."

While I was telling him this, my voice was cracking and my eyes got watery. Inside I was terrified of losing her but had to put on a brave face. I had thoughts of the two of us alone without her. Those thoughts were unbearable. As a man who had been threatened at gunpoint, tortured in a foreign prison, and had risked my life, I was more worried about my wife and our family than I had ever been worried about myself. Late that afternoon we went back to the hospital to pick Claudia up. When we walked into her room, she gave me a high five, grinning and obviously on pain medication. However, I took this as a positive sign and felt a little relief. We met with the doctor and found out that they had removed both ovaries, but no cancer. My wife was smarter than I was about practical matters in life. She seemed to agree with their decision to perform such a radical procedure so I went along with it and kept my mouth shut. For a benign cyst, I thought the complete removal of both ovaries was way too aggressive. Later we found out later this surgery put my Claudia into menopause at a very early age. That was going to be hard for her physically and emotionally. On my end I had no idea what to expect.

Most of the married men with children in our social circles or at work had sex outside their marriages. In Southern California there was actually an escort service that for a monthly fee would send a woman out twice a week to go wherever you wanted and do whatever you wanted. I knew a number of guys who used this service. But my code would never allow me to do that. Being married meant I would have sex only with my wife. Claudia became less and less interested in sex. I figured we could work it out over time, but it became a wedge in our marriage. Somewhere along the way I got the idea that when you got married you could have sex whenever you wanted it. I even fantasized that a wife might surprise you at the door in exotic lingerie and parade around to please your eyes. I knew that a wife showing her sexual side would be mostly an act to please her husband, but I thought that's what wives did. I was raised never knowing what it felt like to be loved. Having sex with my wife gave me the security I needed to be assured I was still loved.

I loved my wife's independent spirit. She had strong beliefs about men and women being equal and often thought that women were better qualified to make decisions than men. I respected those beliefs and understood from her past why she had them. On the other hand, she never missed an opportunity to berate men as a breed and her distaste for their body parts. Eventually I figured out what drove Claudia. What she wanted most from me the most was financial security.

Money was as important to my wife as sex was to me. Having been deprived of money in my childhood, I became a criminal and risked my freedom and life to get it. I did not love money or the things money bought you. I had plenty of it while living in Marin, at one time close to thirty million dollars. I just did not know what to do with it. Lack of money had caused me great pain as a child. Now with more than I needed, once again it was just a way to buy things.

My attachment was to my wife and family. I never related our family's survival to money. Claudia's aversion to sex was equal to my distaste for money. After her surgery she had no sex drive. She was glad that sex would now not have to be an issue in her life. Before we were married I told her in detail of my sexual needs. But it would be unfair of me to expect our sex life to be the same after her surgery. It was not her fault that she had gotten sick. We would have to agree on some formula where my needs would be met by her. We were far too young to just give up our sex life with each other. We went to a psychologist for counseling. He told Claudia she should "service me" twice a week and told me I should give her more control over our money. Neither of those things happened and in our own ways we grew distant from each other.

TWELVE

Beaten Up

n 1996, while the beach house was being built, the hospital company I was contracted with was sued by Zente, a giant in the insurance industry who alleged the hospital company I was contracted with had fraudulent billing practices. At first I was not involved because the insurance company investigators could find no wrongdoing on my part. But after about a year my name was added as a defendant. My lawyers assured me I would prevail. I had no idea what I would be in for.

The lawyer for the insurance company who took my deposition was a round man. He wore the same dark blue suit and bright white shirt every day. When he took his jacket off large, saggy male breasts were revealed. His walk was more of a waddle, his hands soft and pudgy. To me he was an embarrassment to the male gender. My lawyer told me to answer his questions with a simple yes or no, which was impossible because all of his questions were opened ended. If I answered them at all, they would require needed an explanation or qualification.

He asked me questions going back to my childhood, about my career in smuggling, my time in prison. He tried to connect with me by saying as a kid he almost got into in a fight once when a bully tried to take his golf clubs. He showed me a document their investigator had obtained. Alan Leavitt, a former hospital administrator who had been fired for incompetence, reported that one day after work he was walking to his car when a black SUV with tinted windows drove by him slowly. The window opened and a rough-looking character told him, "Don't mess with Victorson." I couldn't believe what I was hearing. I knew Alan had made that up. There was no possible way anything close to that would happen. It was clear that the insurance company was going to attack my past and create any possible fiction to discredit me and win a settlement in court.

My attorney in Santa Monica California who handled my health care contracts and day to day business matters brought in an attorney who specialized in health care litigation from within his firm and an outside legal expert who was politically connected. Now these guys made an average of four hundred dollars per hour. So now I am in a conference room surrounded by four attorneys costing me twelve hundred dollars per hour. The scenario reminded me exactly of when I was represented for the marijuana bust. A table in the conference room was again set up with all the amenities of a meeting with a CEO, the same coffee, bottled water, pastries, and fruit.

I had brought along a friend who was sitting next to me and whispered to him, "Watch this."

Addressing the group I asked, "What, no doughnuts?" at which point two lawyers immediately jumped up and asked what kind I wanted.

This time I said, "Just sit down and get to work." I did not need another eight hundred dollar box of doughnuts. These guys got paid whether I won or lost, and the more time-consuming and complicated they could make the case, the better for them. I probably would have been better off just representing myself, telling the truth, and dealing with the results. Half of those lawyers smoked pot, snorted cocaine, hired hookers, and were half-drunk most of the time. But they were accepted by the community because they represented the law. Of course, not all lawyers are the same and there must be some who love the law, believe in it, and who have achieved great things. I just never met one.

The civil litigation deposition was a fixed game that would be won by whomever had the most money and hence leverage. Since I was being sued personally, I had to pay the lawyers out of my own bank account. If I were to receive a judgment against me, I would be severally liable and it would bankrupt me. The other listed defendants were corporations that would not suffer personal loss. Those corporations were owned by parent companies who paid their legal fees and whatever damages came along. After the first few days of being deposed my old thinking was returning. I should make this lawyer suffer personally. I only had to make a phone call. But I wouldn't do that. It was not the code I was living by now. Because of these investigations my past came back and the depositions were leaked to the media. CNN did a negative story on me as did a number of nationally syndicated newspapers. I was characterized as being immediately guilty because of my past.

The hospital company I worked with assured me they would help out as since the lawsuit was primarily about their actions and they did not intend to settle. Behind my back they settled with the insurance company and closed the hospitals, leaving me as the only defendant left in the case. Now, I knew I had done nothing wrong and settling this lawsuit cast the appearance of guilt on me, so I kept fighting to clear my name. I took a stand against injustice the same way I had in neighborhood fights back in Dorchester: "Don't quit until you win or are too weak to fight anymore." This insurance company had attacked me and neither of us was going to get out of this without one of us dying or not being able to fight anymore. The feeling of a being bullied was overwhelming and I had no idea how to deal with that frustration. But these were moral principles. Wouldn't I have been better off just to settle and move on? These emotions were so powerful in me that the more I got hurt, the tougher I had to be. One person fighting a huge insurance company with stockholders and many lawyers was obviously not a fair match. My decision-making regressed to that of a street fighter instead of a shrewd businessman.

The worst part of the fight was that I was so consumed with winning that I jeopardized my family's financial security. I was running out of money. I used credit lines from casinos to pay my lawyers. I could have settled the lawsuit at its beginning and walked away a rich man, but I was so sure I was doing the right thing I fought them. For two years I was the last man standing. I was defenseless against such power. Money was the only thing at issue, not honor or who was in the right. It blinded me to what would normally have been a common sense business decision.

Money was flowing out to the contractors finishing our beach house, to pay lawyers, mortgage payments, as well as making payroll for my employees. I paid my staff out of family savings even though the hospitals were closed and we made no money. The staff maintained the phone lines while I tried to find new hospitals to contract with. All of the people who called in were referred to local community agencies or given choices of three different hospitals within their local area. For the first time since I joined the legal world, more money was going out than is coming in. I ended up having to pay Zente two million dollars and had to sell our beach house to get the money. My friends and family didn't know. Secretly I turned to gambling and casino credit lines hoping to fend off creditors and maintain our family's level of comfort without them knowing about the massive debt. Life became brutal. I carried this burden alone. I felt like I was on my way back to Mars.

This went on for at least six months. My expenditures on business and personal expenses amounted to more than a hundred thousand dollars a month. All the money I had saved was gone. I had changed back to a Martian without drugs and alcohol to ease the pain. I was so stuck in my dark self I could not summon the courage to tell Claudia how deep in debt I was. I had acted for so long like nothing was wrong that I could not find a way to the light. This trip to Mars was sponsored by my own self-will. I brought the shame and failure upon myself. I was not trained to see the moves that played out on the legal chessboard. I was a naïve Earthling acting like a god who was infallible. Inside I held onto a pain that would not let me show any weakness or vulnerability to the world. I acknowledged my inner pain but could not bring myself to share it with perhaps the only person I ever met whom I could trust. I never gave Claudia the chance to be with me or against me. I was terrified to find out what her allegiance would be. It was not as if I had cleverly hidden money from my family so I could run away and live another life. Those thoughts never crossed my mind. I was not hiding money for myself. I was hiding the shame that I brought on myself and my family.

I kept working at recreating the business and, at the same time, sneaking off to gamble in the high stakes rooms at casinos in Las Vegas and Lake Tahoe. I was hundreds of thousands in debt. I thought about the night I had hit the hundred thousand dollar jackpot in the video poker slots and how I felt when I won. It seemed like an instant antidote to the pain caused by all the debt.

With my new addiction came different consequences. Gambling is a legal addiction much like cigarettes and liquor. The gamblers in the high stakes rooms did not dress or behave like drug or alcohol addicts. I did not connect gambling to my program of recovery. I was not taking a mind-altering substance. So I thought even though I hated to lose money, if I could last long enough, at some point I would have a big win in the millions of dollars.

After the lawsuit was settled and the hospitals I had contracted with were sold, I tried to find new business partners. I traveled to hospitals in Fort Wayne and Dallas hoping to secure management contracts. We desperately needed new sources of income.

Mark, my CFO, set up a meeting with a hospital group in Riverside, California. I was looking for a hospital unit to open our treatment program in and admit our patients to. This hospital became the first new partnership we had been offered since the lawsuit. This hospital was owned by a group of venture capitalists based in Tennessee, which included a doctor as chief of staff.

Breht, their head negotiator, was a short, thin guy with a pot belly. He always had a Southern country club golf tan and wore expensive yet casual clothes. He began the meeting by saying in a thick Southern accent that if we showed we could be successful with this one hospital, they would put up the capital to expand our business with joint acquisition of new hospitals. Breht could make a statement like that for the simple purpose of motivating me to work hard for them. He could, in fact, not have the means to fulfill his offer or its intent. It was clear to me that in the legal world when money was involved, the character of people changed from one of community to one of greed.

Breht took me with him to Dallas with three other executives for a meeting with a company that managed a real estate investment trust. I was told to wear a polo shirt under my suit jacket. Breht explained that people that who wore white button down shirts and a tie were beneath people who wore polo shirts. When I heard this I thought to myself who thinks like this? But instead of saying anything I just looked at him as if this was a perfectly normal conversation. The meeting went well. Two of the three investors wanted in. The third investor was concerned about my criminal past and opted out.

The downside to the deal was clear. I do all the work, give them my client base, then they could recreate what I had done without me, making it more profitable for them. I was so broke I ignored my gut instinct and put caution aside. We signed a contract giving them sixty-seven percent of the new company and thirty-three percent for me. When I first joined normal society my life was very simple. But as I got more involved in the legal aspects of business, I became skeptical. The hospital company I was previously contracted with had told me they would never settle the lawsuit and they did behind my back. They had also said they would pay my legal fees and they did not. The lawyers I hired told me I would not have to pay Zente, but I did.

From what I had observed and felt in the aftermath of the Zente suit, one possible result with these guys would be the bullshit civil court torture that I had just gone through. No wonder people with more money manipulated, lied, and stole each other's humanity. During the lawsuit I felt the same as if I had been betrayed by my family but couldn't define where to place the anger. These fat fucks had no fear of retribution. They only sat on their asses, dressed in suits, and let a judge decide how much money who should pay whom. For these executives it was just another day at the office. My mind jumped to why this group of hospitals owners would be different than the last. What had to change was me.

Unlike what I did with my former partners, I did not show Breht my marketing formula. I kept the investors away from my employees and sat back, reserving my judgment, and waited to see what actions he took to honor his contract. I arranged to have an office for my CFO at the Riverside hospital. My CFO then reported back to me on the internal relationships Breht had with the medical director of the hospital and their administrator.

Breht's arrogance was difficult to deal with and he was always late with any payments, but eventually performed. My company did a good job increasing revenue at the hospital in Riverside. So after we had proven ourselves, the investors decided to commit more funds. I flew with Breht and another person from his group to Ohio, where they bought their first hospital that my company would operate. He was very aggressive in his approach to business. Breht carried a laptop and portable printer with him everywhere. When the deal went through he already had the purchase agreement on his computer. He walked in to the administrator's office, printed out the offer, signed it, and walked out.

The investors kept their business model to themselves. The brick and mortar hospitals they bought were owned by a land holding LLC and they were the only members of the corporation. My company would assume all the operating duties and lease the hospitals from the LLC. We would manage the hospital, pay salaries, do the marketing, manage all the outside contractors such as food service and building maintenance, and hire and fire the medical staff. The investors held a sixty-seven percent stake in my company and a hundred percent stake in the land holding company.

As president of the operating company I was responsible for reporting to the board. After one year, the operating company was showing a profit. So instead of paying a dividend to themselves as owners of the operating company, their land holding company, one hundred percent owned by the investors, would raise our lease payment. At that point the owners would go to the bank to refinance the hospital based on increased lease revenues. They would keep the money pulled out of the refinance tax-free. This made it impossible for the operating company to ever show much of a profit.

The investors bought a total of four hospitals. I would do a preliminary due diligence on each hospital and, after I gave it my approval, Breht would move in and make the purchase. Then my team would visit the hospital, transition the employees, and take over the operations. This went on successfully for a few years. During that time I never became an insider with Breht and his group. There were too many personality differences. I traveled around the country with my CFO, visiting with the hospital employees, eating in the hospital cafeterias, and staying in two-star hotels. When Breht visited a hospital he traveled in a private plane, took a limo to the facility, spent less than an hour there, didn't talk to anyone, and left. He had no concern about the people working there, only the condition of the building itself. I had raised myself and was disassociated from my family while they came from upper class families with whom they still had strong ties. They had attended private schools and I had gone to inner-city public schools. Most of all, they expected to be treated like American royalty; I was looking for a level playing field. They had a "good old boys" attitude about women, meaning you marry one to breed with and you have others for sex and eye candy, never having those two worlds collide. I married one woman to be a wife, mother, and anything I needed from a woman I would get from her. Claudia, my wife, was the human resource director for our call center and fifty percent owner of my company. She walked into one board meeting with me and Breht told her to go shopping while the men got down to business. That did not go over big with her and I heard about it for the next ten years.

On one conference call Breht wanted to invite me and my "mistress" to a resort island in South Carolina for a few days of partying with their group, and in case I didn't understand, wives were not invited. I myself did not drink or take drugs. I had no mistress. These guys had religion. They were outspoken about their Adventist backgrounds and the charity work they did on behalf of their church. How did that add up? The contradiction in character gave me an uneasy feeling, I wondered if I did have a mistress, what would she look like? An image popped into my head of a buxom woman with blonde hair dressed in white lingerie, garter belt, stockings, and red high heels. Wait a minute—that was a postcard I saw somewhere. That thought came and went. One woman was plenty for me.

One day Breht called and told me fly up to San Jose to meet him. They were consolidating and moving all their investments back to Tennessee. They wanted to offer me a high-paying job as part of a think tank that would oversee the management of their asset portfolio. They also wanted to buy out my percentage of the hospital company.

I made a decent salary working for these guys with occasional bonuses. I was still hundreds of thousands of dollars in debt to lawyers, paying back casino credit lines, and making late property tax payments. In the meantime, the IRS was claiming I owed them more than three million dollars from gambling winnings. I had a red flag on my back. They thought I had duped them out of hundreds of thousands of tax dollars during my pot-smuggling days. That statute of limitations had expired while I was in prison. So why not go after me even though I had filed and paid everything since? The casinos sent me a win-loss statement every year. It listed my winnings less my losses. Most of the time there were only losses, but if I showed any gains, I paid taxes on them. The IRS decided not to accept this form generated by the casinos and went after me for all my winnings regardless of how much I had lost. One way or another they were going to get the tax money from my drug smuggling days. I was powerless against them and tax court would have cost thousands. Now that I showed large amounts of income again the red flag initiated audits every three years. If I sold my interest in the company it could be a way for me to get back on my feet financially. By this time I owed the casinos so much money I could not go back to them to try to win some money. I was so much in debt and had lied about it for so long that I turned my addictive mind on to the problem of untangling this huge mess I had gotten myself into.

This buyout deal came hard and fast. Breht had a plane on standby and wanted me to go to Tennessee with them at that moment. We could go over the details and sign the contracts during the flight. I knew there was no way my wife would agree to moving to Tennessee. I decided to sell my interest for three million dollars with the caveat that if the company sold for more than we expected I would receive my share of the difference. We made a verbal agreement and shook hands on it. I flew back home after the meeting and told Claudia what had happened. She seemed glad we were not going to have to be around the Tennessee hive much longer.

The next day I went into the office and told my employees about the buyout. They had a million questions, mostly about their own survival. Would their jobs be open in Tennessee? What about health benefits, vacation time, and salaries? I let them know that all those questions would be answered in the upcoming weeks. I pulled aside the people who had been with me the longest and told them I would take twenty-five percent of what I was paid and divide it up equally among them. I was under no obligation legally to do any such thing, but I felt they deserved it.

My heart sank. I knew this was the end of an era for me. This company was like a child to me. I had given birth to it in Burbank, parented it through its problem adolescent years, and now it was grown up and I was selling it. I thought, *Is this betrayal? Wait a minute, it's only a business, it's not human. Humans depend on this company to feed their families. Could I trust these guys to do the right thing? Absolutely not.*

This little company, my company, the company I had built from the ground up had a history. The people who worked for me at the call center had been with me for more than ten years. Our children had grown up together. Our annual Christmas party hosted seventy to eighty people. Every Sunday we would get together at my beach house. The kids would play on the beach while the adults would prepare food together. These people were part of my family and now I felt like I was selling them out.

I was tired of the pressure, tired of meeting investor expectations based solely on profits. Breht had unlimited energy when it came to squeezing every cent out of this company and delaying payment of our bills as long as possible. I was tangled up with them. If I didn't sell my percentage they would move the company anyway, replace me, and I would receive yearly dividends based on their accounting. That could mean I got nothing or at the very best what they thought I was worth. They would run the company without me and control the profits and losses. In my gut I knew this would end up in court with more lawyers. I wanted to be done with all of that. I was still in a lot of debt and this was the only way out. I made a verbal contract to sell my shares to them for three million dollars in exchange for all the intellectual property I had developed for marketing and the treatment program. Our computers would be included in the sale and be moved to Tennessee as soon as I received the first payment.

Clear deal—they pay me three million in installments, I handle the move of the offices to Tennessee. After the first payment of five hundred thousand dollars and all the property was transferred to them, they stopped paying me. My debts continued to grow and I was forced to sue them for the balance. They knew their pockets were deeper than mine. The suit dragged on for two years and I was forced to settle for less than half. During that period I had no income and a lot of money going out. I was not surprised at how this situation unfolded. I had learned since getting sober and joining the legitimate business world that the goal of the game was to win at any cost and to protect and insulate yourself through attorneys. But camaraderie, morality, and any other concern for human decency were not in the equation. This reality was hard to accept, but for the fact that money is what drives business. Money turns good people into monsters. The monster wears a great disguise.

This would never have happened in my dealings with the Colombians. They honored their words with blood and expected the same from me. Breht and his group would be chum for sharks to feed on if they tried any of these snake-like tactics in my former life. I could not help but feel the rage of injustice, another bully, a clever little man who was skilled at outmaneuvering me so he could end up with the most. One of the most important lessons I learned while working with my Colombian family was to always let people know where they stood. When I was nicknamed Black Wolf, my godfather told me "When someone wants to ride on the wolf's back, he should always be told it is up to the wolf when and if he can get off." Breht had not been honest with me from the outset. His intention was to maneuver me into taking the least amount of money. Not paying off the deal was dishonest knowing I was at a disadvantage to collect on the deal.

The $1.5 million I did collect cost me $150,000 in legal fees. The payments for the balance were spread out over a two-year period, which kept me afloat but was not enough to pay off all my debts. My family was able to continue our lifestyle in Southern California but with no sense of security about the future and with the uncertainty of the $3 million debt to the IRS looming I was completely overwhelmed. The only time I had any peace was when I coached my son's soccer team.

THIRTEEN

Soccer Coach

My son, Adam, loved soccer from the age of seven. His first coach was always late for practice and when he finally did arrive he just threw a few balls on the field and told the kids to play. Adam's team lost every game that year and the boys were all disappointed. I had played basketball in Dorchester on a street team, in high school, and in college. I liked sports and being with the kids. I thought I would give coaching a try. I had no idea what coaching a team of ten-year-old boys would be like. I sat them down on the pitch beside the goal and asked the boys to give their names and tell something about themselves. In front of me were my son and three other white kids who went to his private school and four other white kids and six Hispanic kids who all went to public school. The white kids were outgoing and talked freely about themselves and why they were there. The Hispanic kids were shy. They gave their names but were not willing to go beyond that.

I asked, "Who here wants to go to college?" All the white kids raised their hands. That was a profound moment for me. I got it. The white kids had families and communities that were steering them toward a future. The Hispanic kids were on their own. At that moment I realized that for me this was no longer just about soccer, it was personal.

I had built teams before. I had put together a top-notch smuggling team and a hardworking, creative hospital management team. Now with a soccer team I could apply the same principles. From those experiences I knew the most important part of team building was to connect the members emotionally, for them to see themselves as a band of brothers with a common purpose. In soccer each position requires a certain set of skills. I wanted to work with the desire and ability of each kid to teach them the skills they needed to be great at that position. Strategy, understanding your opponent, and how to win would determine the success or failure of the team.

I took on being a coach the same way I looked at any commitment. As a husband, father, or businessman I never thought *My God, this is taking up too much time and I am spending money instead of making it.* However, my wife, Claudia, was irritated that I had extended myself to kids and their families who were complete strangers, with no expectation of earning money. At that point Claudia did not know about my gambling, only that I planned on selling the company and had no job or business prospects lined up after that. She thought I put too much effort into being a coach and not enough effort into running my company or, later on, into finding a new career. I never took on anything thinking of the end result. I loved the process, the creative part of figuring out how to put a project or team of people together with a common purpose.

The team practiced year-round. When the fields were closed we got together to run or played in an indoor arena. Sometimes I would take them to my office to watch videos of prior games. I let them tell me how they could have played better. Our practices included conditioning, team building, and individual skill development. The boys became friends and, as the years passed, more and more players tried out for the team. We won our division and took home a lot of trophies.

One game that stands out was against our archrival Mission Viejo, coached by a guy named Chan. We were playing them for a division championship on our home field. A lot of parents and fans turned out for that game, the last of the regular season. That week a major firestorm broke out in Southern California. The fire was about five miles from us but the sky was bright red and grey smoke hung in the air. Soot had collected on the field and the officials had a serious discussion about whether to play the game at all. Some of the parents were worried about the air quality. The league officials and the refs decided the game should be played.

The teams were well matched and both sides were playing well. Going into the last five minutes we were tied at one to one. One of our forwards, Max, received a pass about ten feet from the goal and hammered in a goal. Everyone sitting on our sideline was ecstatic. Chan's team put on the pressure, trying to even the game with less than a minute left. Their star striker was two feet from our goal and took a shot, hitting the ball hard. It was impossible to see what happened from the sideline since players from each team blocked the view. Finally the ball was in sight heading toward an unprotected part of our goal when my son, our goalie, dove toward the ball and caught it between his legs. Game over. We finished in first place. I was proud of my team and happy for my son. He had the experience of being a hero, yet he was humble and acted like it was just his job.

The end result of all the practice and coaching could be seen by watching the game. What went unseen was the care that went into helping the kids grow emotionally and become a valued part of the team. I was not their parents. It was not my job to feed or clothe them, but when they were in my care it was my job to counsel them. When I heard one of the boys call out, "Hey coach," I was honored.

I loved these boys, their little faces from the first day of practice, the confidence in the white kids and the bewilderment in the Hispanic kids. It had taken time and consistency to get them to trust me. For the Hispanic kids this was it, all they had. The white kids had planned vacations, new cleats, perfectly organized backpacks, and freshly washed socks. The Hispanic kids were on their own, or at least felt that way. Slowly they would understand they had two hours a day, three times a week to be in a place where they could be safe, carefree, and enjoy being outdoors running and kicking a ball and horsing around with their teammates. I brought a case of water and fruit snacks to every practice. I liked all the boys but I particularly identified with the poor kids. I knew life to be a giant, and they did too. I knew that without some guidance that giant would eat you up and you would walk through life in disgrace. I did not want that for these guys and I would do what I could to change a script that had been written for them before they were born.

Some of those boys had parts of them that reminded me of myself as I was growing up. I knew from the look in their eyes that they were defensive and skeptical that anyone would do something for them without wanting something in return. Like me, they observed the behavior of anyone whose size or demeanor appeared to be threatening. They were hypersensitive to any inconsistency or sign of upcoming abandonment or disregard for a commitment made to them, especially Armando. He came to our team in its second year. He was a shy kid. He was also the star forward of the entire league. He had insane speed and an instinct to score goals. His father had been killed in El Salvador and his mother had smuggled him and his sister into the U.S. She then married a Mexican man and had two daughters. Armando's family was loving. They were good, hardworking people. Like other families on our team, they lived with the constant threat of being deported at any time.

One day while driving Armando home from practice I asked him, "What would you like to do? Any thoughts on your future?"

He said, "Coach, I want to be a doctor." I was taken aback. I had no idea those thoughts ran through his head. I explained to him that to be a doctor you had to be a good student, especially in math and science. He told me he was a straight "A" student. The next day, with his parents' permission, I went to his school and talked to the school counselor. She told me Armando was an excellent student and that the school was not set up to teach a kid with his advanced understanding of math. I thought to myself *Someone should take an interest in this kid and help him out. I guess that would be me.* My son attended a private school with excellent college prep courses. So I went to my son's school and asked about entrance requirements and scholarships and told them about Armando. This was a first for them. This private school cost thirty-two thousand dollars a year and they had no scholarship program, but they did have an entrance exam. They agreed that Armando could take the exam and we would discuss the finances later.

The day of the exam I picked Armando and his parents up and we toured the campus. The school sat on about ten perfectly manicured acres with athletics fields, and a stadium. The architecture was Spanish—white stucco with red tile roofs. This environment was a shocker to Armando's parents as it would have been my parents coming out of Dorchester. This was a place where the rich got trained to be richer and the poor were kept out or did the landscaping. Armando passed the entrance exam with ease. I approached the fathers of the other white kids on the team about raising the money to get Armando enrolled. We all chipped in something and I found a corporate sponsor to pay the difference.

Some of the PTA members were angry with me for introducing Armando to the school. One parent explained that they paid good money for this school to give their kids an edge in getting into a better college and higher paying career.

They actually said, "Why should poor kids have the same advantage as our kids? We are paying for this opportunity."

So I asked, "Are you saying you don't want a level playing field? You want your kid to have an advantage? Isn't being born into a wealthy family enough?"

This kind of thinking by the parents who did not want Armando there was what had enraged me most of my life, the entitled attitude, the classist hierarchy. Who in the hell did these people think they were? Like the royals of Europe, did God speak to them and tell them "You are better than everyone else. Create a lower class. Rule them as you would a farm animal?"

Arturo was our leading goal scorer. He was so into the flow of the game that many times when he could have scored, he would pass the ball, giving another player the opportunity to score. To him the execution of team play was more exciting than individual glory. He practiced all the time and always had a ball at his feet wherever he was. He could score with either foot and would surprise everyone with new dribbling skills he taught himself. His little brother, Jose, was our team mascot. He would shag balls and wait until practice was over to ask the older kids if he could play with them. Jose also had the foulest of mouths saying things like he enjoyed fucking everyone's girlfriend. Jose was a street-smart wise guy.

Arturo had a good dad and mom. His dad was a skilled carpenter and his mom cleaned houses. They were in the U.S. illegally even though their children were born here. So the entire family lived in fear of the parents being deported.

Arturo called me one night and said, "Coach, I won't be at the game tomorrow. My house was raided and my parents are gone. I have to take care of my little brother and sister."

I asked him, "Do you need any help? What can I do?"

He replied, "My uncle will pick us up tomorrow and we will stay with him."

This was a good kid. He worked hard, did nothing wrong, but now his parents were gone and he did not know where they were. I didn't hear from him for a few days and was worried, as were the rest of the team. Finally he called to let me know he was all right and would be living with a relative until his parents smuggled themselves back into the U.S. His uncle lived twenty minutes away and brought Arturo to practices and to school until his parents finally returned.

Chris was tall for his age. His mother was from Brazil and his father from Mexico. He had great speed and a bad attitude. He had been kicked off other teams for getting into fistfights with other players and referees. He had no home life. I never met his parents during the four years our team was together. He slept on the floor under a stairwell. He was on his own and became involved with gang kids. Chris walked with a swagger, an attitude that was easy to read. He was such an outstanding player that after we won a highly competitive tournament, the coach from the other team spoke of him at the awards ceremony, saying "He plays like a man." If you were respectful to him he melted and would do anything for you. At one tournament we stayed in a nice hotel and Chris had his own bed and chair. Around game time we were all at the bus waiting to drive to the tournament and Chris was missing. It turned out he didn't want to leave the hotel room. I reminded him we would be back for another night and the room would be there waiting for him when we got back from the games.

Before games I would drive through gang-infested neighborhoods to find Chris and bring him to the game. He tried to push me away by acting like he didn't care, but I had been him and I knew he just needed the reassurance that he really did care. Eventually he became part of the team. He got himself to practices and, after graduating from high school, he went to Mexico to play for a professional team.

My son, Adam, had trained with various goalie coaches over the years, which gave him an edge for this position. He became friends with the Hispanic kids. He would go over to their houses, hang out with their families, and would also invite them over to our house. He never showed a "better than" attitude and became a man of character. Although he attended an expensive private school, he never acted like he was better than the poorer kids. When he was fifteen, one of his coaches, Mike, put him through a grueling two-hour nonstop goalie training program in ninety-degree heat. Mike shot ball after ball at him, some high, some low, which he would dive for to catch or block. He never complained or asked for a break. Adam took on the challenge and reached down deep to push himself.

After the session was over, the coach told me, "Your son handled that like a college goalie."

A goalie can be the hero or the dog of a game. He carries the heavy burden of ultimate responsibility for letting a ball get passed him into the goal, while another player's mistake can be shared by nine other field players. If the team lost it would be blamed on the goalie. If the team won maybe the goalie would get some of the hoorays, but never as many as the field players. This position taught leadership and built character. When my son played for his high school team, he brought the fans to their feet on a number of occasions by stopping shots either from the field or in penalty situations. He showed me the two most important qualities a young man can have, courage and humility. This meant to me he knew he was loved and wanted. He knew his mother and father would be his anchors and no matter whatever life had in store for him, he had a family. My father had never been involved in any of my sports teams and never went to see me play. I would have loved it if we had walked to the field together with baseball gloves and a ball, or to the basketball courts. He was different than me. I knew nothing about soccer, but because it was an opportunity to be a part of my son's life, I learned about the sport and cherished every moment with him, even watching him from the sidelines. When we drove home together after a game, seeing him beside me made me feel like a whole person.

Brad, one of the white kids from public school, was one of my favorite kids. He was a handsome, funny, talented athlete. However, he had a number of broken bones during two off-seasons, which limited his ability to play. His dad understood the level of commitment I had to these boys and was always warm and friendly with me. This was a man who had a past that was the polar opposite of mine. He graduated from UCLA and became a dentist. He was as handsome as a movie star and soft spoken. I cared deeply for him and when he passed away after a two-year fight with cancer. It was heartbreaking. Of all the people I had met in my life, this was one person who should have lived to be a hundred years old.

I didn't think most of the white kids needed help in the same way the Hispanic kids did. They were dedicated to the team and never looked down to the Hispanic kids. The boys all got along well as soccer players. The Hispanic families would invite the entire team to family birthday parties with Mexican food and piñatas and the white kids would invite the team to parties at their houses and to other events. One season after winning our league championship, one of the dads who owned a restaurant invited the whole team for dinner. All the boys ordered the same thing, steak and lobster.

David was a born athlete. Whatever the sport, he excelled. He worked hard at practice, was polite, and helpful. His family were legal immigrants from Mexico. His dad stocked grocery shelves on the graveyard shift while his mom cleaned houses. A new private school had opened in our town, a Catholic school. The tuition was a lot less than the school that Adam and Armando were going to. This school was promoting their athletic program in the community. They had built a large sports complex with fields and a swimming pool, two indoor gyms, and a beautiful track. Our team was well known in the community for being highly skilled and winning many tournaments. One day at practice I was out on the field when the school's soccer coach stopped by. He had a particular interest in three of my players. As we talked I explained to him these kids came from poor families and they had no way of paying for a private school. I also explained that we had gotten Armando into a private school based on his entrance exam scores. The coach said that it was against California Interscholastic Federation policy to draft players but that he could leave their names at the admission office and it would aid their chances of getting in on full scholarships. Why not try it and see what happens? It would be good for the boys. He was particularly interested in drafting David, Chris, and Arturo. I spoke with them about this offer, letting them know this would be a good thing for them. This school had an interest not only in them playing soccer, but good academics that would help them get into college.

Submitting their names presented another moral dilemma. On one hand it would be a great opportunity for these boys. The scripts written for them before they were even born were not bright and rosy. This could change their lives giving them a chance to see how the other half lived. They would be going to school with upper class kids, making friends with them, going to their houses, and making future contacts for jobs and moneymaking opportunities. Attending this school would almost guarantee they would continue their educations. On the other hand, drafting players was against the law. Club coaches were not allowed to assist high school coaches in soliciting athletes.

I explained all this to the boys and their parents, except for Chris's parents who were never were around. Chris said no, he didn't care for the opportunity. David and Arturo were all for it. They went over to the school and applied for admission. Just like the coach had said, they were accepted on full scholarship. A foundation would pay for their tuition and meals. The classrooms were wired for Wi-Fi, so every student had to have a laptop. I organized the parents and we raised the money for a laptop for each of the boys. The only thing left was the cost of the school uniforms to be purchased from the school store. The woman running the store told me the students wore their uniforms for only one year then bought new ones. So they had used uniforms for sale at a deep discount. David and Arturo's parents insisted on paying for the uniforms. Now three of my players were on track to go to college. This would not have been possible without the help of wealthy people who donated money. My life had been spent hating people who had more than I thought they needed, but here I was proved wrong. The kindness of these people changed my attitude. I no longer lumped all wealthy people together. There were some who were decent.

Fernando was the youngest player on the team. He was smaller than the other boys and got knocked down a lot. He also had great foot skills. He was a natural playmaker, never selfish, and put one hundred percent into his training. He was a handsome kid with red hair and light brown skin with freckles. He did his best to hang out with the other boys but the pecking order was clear. Whenever he got knocked off the ball and ended up on the ground the other players would just look at him as if to say he'd better get up and not complain. He was my fourth player to go to private school. Fernando was very smart and hardworking academically. He passed the entrance exam and joined Adam and Armando at their school.

These were my core players. I was their coach from the time they were twelve years old to about sixteen. I would meet the boys on the practice field three days a week. At three p.m. I would change out of my business clothes into my coaching clothes at my office. I would take off my wingtip shoes and put on soccer cleats. I would hang up my white shirt and tie and put on a jersey with my name and title "Head Coach" on the back. I could shed the pressures of work and finance for a few hours and just be a man on a field with two goals and fourteen players. When I arrived at the field my mind was free of all anxiety. I would not have to think about moving people around on the chessboard of business or moving money around to cover debt, pay bills, and earn more. The kids had no expectations from me other than meeting my commitment to be there on time. They did what they were told during practice in an orderly and disciplined way. There was never a fistfight or any sign of physical violence. In all the years I had coached them and in all the games we had played, we never once had an instance of a fight breaking out.

This championship game would determine which team would advance in ranking for the next year. Both sidelines were full of spectators, including competing coaches from other teams and a local news reporter. The team we were to play was from Laguna Niguel and made up of mostly big white kids from wealthy families. Each family on that team paid a registration fee of two thousand dollars. Most of my players had received scholarships to play on the team and the parents volunteered to help out with the snacks and field preparation. The players and coaches were tense. The outcome of this game would determine which team moved up in the brackets the next year. With fifteen minutes left in the game we were ahead three to one when the largest white player from the other team punched my smallest Hispanic player, Beto, in the mouth because Beto had taken the ball away from him. Coming to Beto's defense one of my boys, Armando, punched that kid in the face. The kid struck back at Armando. Then two other players on our team started punching the opposing player until he fell down and then they started kicking him while he was still on the ground. My guys took off their jerseys so the refs would not be able to identify them by their player number. A few of the parents from the other team rushed onto the field yelling and pushing my kids. Finally the referees stopped the game. The ref awarded the victory to the other team stating we had forfeited the game because of the fight.

I had to watch this unfold from the sideline as the coaches were not allowed on the field without the ref's permission. Looking back at my Dorchester roots and all the fights I had been in, a part of me was not surprised that my guys had stepped right in and punished the kid who started the fight. Another part of me knew that street justice did not play out well in the suburbs. My guys had acted in a savage way and it was wrong. They felt if one of them was attacked they had to protect him. They knew this from their experiences growing up in the ghetto. They did not experience the comfort of depending on the police to sort out violence. During the four years I had coached them they were trained to get on one knee on the field if a fight broke out or a player was hurt. All of the pent-up restraint against what they perceived as injustice just exploded at the point when Beto was hit. The part of me that was now living within the guidelines of a normal community knew the fight would be the end of our team. It made me sick to my stomach.

When the fight broke out I knew my kids were reacting to race and size. A white kid had just hit our little brother who was smaller and Hispanic. These kids did not trust the white refs to deal with the situation so they took matters into their own hands. I knew that feeling all too well. I had felt it my whole life. Two of the fathers from the other team came walking over in an aggressive manner and demanded, "Why don't you control your kids?" I told them it was their kid who started the fight and to go fuck themselves. The referees were supposed to stop that fights before they got out of hand. I was a D-licensed coach and had been a referee for my son's league before coaching this team, so I knew the type well. Usually they were the non-athletic version of the male species, kind of accountant by day, authority figure by night. The official referee uniform was a yellow-collared shirt with black stripes, tight short black shorts, high black socks, and black shoes. When I had worn this uniform I felt a little like I was part of an uptight group of comedians. For this game there were three referees total, two for the sidelines and one for the center of the field. The center ref had a limp, so for the most part he oversaw the game from the middle of the field. When the fight broke out near the goal, he was nowhere near to see who had started it. By the time he made it down there all he could see was my guys kicking the big white kid.

Our team was suspended from the league pending investigation and I was cited for failure to control them. The future of our team would be decided by three governing boards. That meant I had to put together a case for my boys and myself as to why we should be allowed to stay together as a team. How ironic. I had been to criminal court, sentenced to prison, dragged through civil court, ordered to pay two million dollars to Zente, and now to soccer court. Based on my win-loss record in all these legal proceedings I was not optimistic. This team's spirit was just like mine. It had a caring heart and a strong will with a great deal of difficulty accepting that they had been wronged. Why they should they trust in some authority to correct the wrong on their behalf?

Two weeks later the club's governing board convened. I brought the three players who had been involved in the fight at the board's request. They questioned us one at a time. After deliberating, my boys received a three-month suspension. I was given a slap on the wrist. The next governing board to review the fight was the county league, made up of twelve officials from the league, other coaches, referees, and administrators.

After listening to my version of what happened, they came back with the verdict, "Other teams in the league have been involved in fights. Referees have been attacked after games. We need to send a message to coaches and players that fights will no longer be tolerated."

The team was to be disbanded and no more than six of my players could be on any one team in the future. I myself was given a polite reprimand and encouraged to rebuild the team with new players. I knew and cared deeply for each boy on my team. I could not pick six and drop the others. That would be the end of the team and my coaching career. There was no punishment for the kid who started the fight, no punishment for the coach of the other team whose parents ran out on the field. Well, just like other times in my life I had built a great team from nothing, had many victories, made great friends, but somehow did not play by the rules and now it was gone.

I treasured those practice times. It was a place for me to forget the pressures of running a business, the feeling that my only value to my family and the community I lived in would be measured by my net worth. The dads of the white kids were good guys. When I had asked for help in getting gear for the poor kids they chipped in. Tournaments were expensive. We needed money for rent hotel rooms, have transportation, and food. As a team we all helped and got the job done.

From the time I had started coaching them we had a party at the end of the season for the team and their parents. At this event I would give a presentation with the best pictures and videos made that year. When I got up to make my speech about the boys, how they had grown, how they had matured as young men and, most importantly, how they had taken care of each other, I would be emotional, fighting back tears. I was overwhelmed with gratitude that I could be accepted as part of their lives. The parents knew how invested I was in their kids and always had looks of appreciation. Of all the chapters in my life the only one more precious to me was the birth of my son Adam.

Now there would be no more team. It felt like the ending of innocent chapter in my life. I had dedicated myself without condition to the individual outcome of the boys that made up that team. Now it would be up to them how they took what they had learned and moved forward. A part of me died. It was over and I had to let go. There was no blame, no revenge to be had. I would fold up my coach's jacket and put it away. On weekends when I drove by the fields and other teams were playing, I would feel a pain of loneliness.

FOURTEEN

Settlement

t took me two years to sue and recover the balance of the judgment on the Focus Healthcare sale. Here I had been embroiled again in a civil law suit. Between the time I signed the contract to sell my share in the company and their last payment to me, they had already resold the company for ninety-six million dollars. They had agreed to pay me only three million, far less than my thirty-three percent. The sale had taken place without my knowledge and with a buyer I had introduced them to. By buying me out before the sale, I would be left out of the negotiations. They netted twenty-two million more and a percentage of that money would have gone to me. This was done in secret. I only found out about the sale through my CFO who read about it in an industry magazine. I was proud to have built that company and have it grow to a point where it was worth such a large amount of money. I did that right. What I did wrong was misjudge the character of the people I had partnered with. I knew I was an outsider but I had no idea they were so greedy that after a huge upside to their investment they would take advantage of me. I was in a constant state of frustration. It seemed like I could do nothing right.

With one dollar and eleven cents left in my bank account, I flew to Tennessee for an arbitration meeting with a judge to collect the balance due me. The lawsuit had drained me of all my funds. I was living on credit and could not let my former partners know how broke I was. Their counterclaim stated that I had misrepresented the profitability of the company and that it was worth a lot less than the

CFO had projected. Hence they did not owe me the three million dollars. Breht alleged I had our CFOs alter our books by making our collectible income look stronger than it actually was. The hospital industry is based on an accrual accounting system. Hospitals' books show projected income instead of collected income because insurance companies never pay one hundred percent of a bill and what they pay out is based on how long they can deny payment. They can stall with doctor reviews, make endless requests for clarifications of billing codes, or just pay out a ridiculously low amount. The hospital writes off the unpaid portion as bad debt. Breht alleged I gave instructions to our CFOs to alter our books by making our collectible income look stronger than it actually was. To tell someone to alter these figures to show greater profit would not only require a sophisticated knowledge of accounting, which I did not have, but it would also be illegal, not something I would have dreamt of doing.

After hearing from both sides, the judge almost fell out of his chair in disbelief. These guys had a stable of accountants who were academically trained and been in the hospital business for many years. Besides being majority owners of my company they also owned and operated fifty-four nursing homes. I, on the other hand, had an associate's degree in communications, spent four years in prison, and was a recovering addict. I relied on our hospital controllers and accountants to provide my CFO the proper financials to consolidate and present them to me and the board on a quarterly basis.

The judge explained that no jury would believe that I had outfoxed them and urged them to settle and not waste the court's time. We agreed on a settlement of one third of the original contracted amount. I felt forced to agree. I was in no position to pay more attorney's fees and go to court. Even though they signed the arbitration contract, they stretched out the payments to me over one year. That killed me financially.

I went to my office every day at eight a.m. and worked until ten p.m. I was trying to build another company through contacts I had made over the years. Sometimes I was so tired and depressed I would lie on my couch and doze off. A dream would play in my head, one that had recurred since I was twelve years old. I am on a platform at a train station. I feel ageless. I can't see myself but I know it is me. I am lying on my back and I can't get up. I sense the presence of bodies walking around me. They are all adults, knowing where they are going and on their way there. Lying there helpless, I feel all my emotions centered in my stomach where a huge boa constrictor is strangling them. I don't say anything. I don't ask for help. I use my soul to transmit pictures of my internal suffering to the passersby. I try to connect with them using all my psychic energy. I can sense they feel me, but the faceless men and woman continue to walk by. I reach my hands straight out above my body so they can touch me and pull me up, but they continue to pass as if I am not there. I look for a railing or something to anchor myself to so I can pull myself up, but nothing is there. I can't move, paralyzed like a bug lying on its back. I feel desperate that I will die like this. I look up to be sky, to see its colors and the depths of the atmosphere, but the steel overhang completely blocks my view. I wake up feeling broken. I hated all the people on the platform. I could trust no one.

I reflected back to the time when I was making good money as president of Focus Healthcare. I was known as an upstanding and generous person. I met Ken Norton, former heavyweight champion of the world, at a gym and we became friends. One day he came to my office and told me his story. He was driving home from a fundraiser at the Biltmore Hotel in Los Angeles, when his sports car went off an overpass and plunged fifty feet. He was hospitalized for four weeks, his vocal chords were shattered, and the right side of his body was paralyzed. As a result of this accident and poor money management by his manager he was left with very little money. He needed eleven thousand dollars to help get him on his feet. He offered to let me keep his championship ring as collateral. I refused the ring but gave him the money and told him that he did not have to pay me back. It was clear to me that what he needed then more than money was faith, to know that all people were not takers. Nevertheless, Ken showed up every month with a thousand dollars and eventually paid every cent back. When he came to my office I would smile to myself and was happy to spend time with him.

What had been my somewhat normal life was now a nightmare. I had mortgage payments, school tuition, a housekeeper and other monthly bills to pay. The life my family had gotten used to was impossible to maintain. I did not have the heart to tell my wife and son the truth about our finances. I had failed. I had been beaten in the Zente lawsuit, been outmaneuvered by hospital venture capitalists, and strung out on gambling.

I was reminded time and again that I did not belong in this Earth-based moral structure, yet I did not want to go back to the alien principles of Mars. I had to find a life and a code that was mine alone. Since agreeing not to break the law I had created a legitimate business to support my family. I had learned that in business you start out with a product. It has to be a great product that you are proud to take to market. You sacrifice all your time and effort to develop the product, first in theory then in reality. At a certain point if your product is successful in the marketplace then you need capital to produce and market it. That is the point where attention is focused on maximizing profit and not the quality of the product itself. That is where I had failed. It was impossible for me to play that game. I had grown up in the black market world where product development was equally as important, but there were no games played when profits were distributed. The rules were black and white and the consequences for breaking them were clear. You kept your word. There was no need for contracts or lawyers. If you thought you could outmaneuver someone it was called stealing and you could end up dead. No one went running to a court for justice. I knew I couldn't be in that world but somehow I would have to find a way to exist in this one.

After the sale of Focus Healthcare, my next venture was a radio show. I had met a comic celebrity and his producer while in Las Vegas and we became friends. I thought it might be a good idea to do a radio show based on what happens in Vegas and the casino gambler lifestyle.

I went about organizing the business structure for the four partners who would back the show. One partner was an agent for radio talent with contacts in the radio industry. We created the format for the show, brought in a second talent, contracted with three major West Coast radio stations, and I brought in the advertising dollars to pay the expenses. The show was very funny and the advertisers were happy with the response from the listeners. With the show's initial success, we wanted to take it into national syndication where the real money was. At the time, the radio industry was shrinking and our timing was off so we had no takers. After a year the show ended when the main celebrity was offered his own showroom in Las Vegas. It was a lucrative and sustaining opportunity for him. There were no hard feelings, I was happy for him. We had had a lot of fun made some money.

After the radio show I put together a team of mortgage and banking professionals to develop a niche lending program for ex-pats who were flocking to Costa Rica to buy homes. I had assembled a network of real estate agents in Costa Rica and sent two employees to live in Costa Rica to open offices and get the program up and running. I went to New York City to meet with the main lender. The meeting at UBS Bank went well and everything was ready to launch. The mortgage industry collapsed the next month at the beginning of the 2008 sub-prime mortgage crisis and all that effort, time, and money went out the window.

I still had my office building in San Juan Capistrano where I kept an office and went to work there every day. I planned on leveraging my business contacts and putting together deals. For my first project I was able to put the right people together to finance an oil and gas exploration company. For my efforts I made eighty thousand dollars over a period of one year, barely enough to keep up with all the bills. I was working twelve to fourteen hours a day, spending thousands of dollars on rent, phone bills, travel, and legal fees. During the next two years I put together an iron ore export deal, a gold bullion sales deal, a compressed block technology project, an export deal for boxhaul, and an asset portfolio.

None of these projects made any money, all for different reasons. I did the research, wrote the proposals, and spent countless hours with the principals. But on one deal after another, one side or the other would fall apart. It was certainly not for lack of effort on my part. I would say the main reason none of those deals made money was the people involved. I trusted them to have expertise in what they professed to know or come up with the money they said they could supply. In my old world this would not have been tolerated. These kinds of people would simply be killed for putting other people at risk. The one thing they all had in common was their lack of unwillingness to take responsibility for the failures.

The most recent project I worked on started in September of 2011 and involved reviving a gold mine first built in 1867. For more than a year, I researched the well-documented history of the mine, the conditions that forced its closing, and the rationale behind reopening it. I drew from people I had known for more than ten years and, unlike the earlier ventures, I could testify to their expertise. I put together a twenty-two-page offering to raise the capital to pay for all the land, equipment, and personnel costs. I had the project approved by an underwriter, hired a law firm and an accounting firm. Three potential investors showed an interest but none of them followed through with the needed capital.

I kept my friends and family up to date on each of these projects. I lied to my wife every day about our finances. I made up a story that I had put money into an offshore bank account and came up with fake account numbers, the name of a fake banker, and emails I sent myself from that bank. When Claudia came into the living room and sat next to me I could feel my blood pressure going up. I tried my best to be optimistic about the future but my lies were catching up to me. My wife confronted me about the ridiculousness of the stories I was telling. I finally had to tell her we had nothing and were deep in debt. I felt more guilt and shame at that point than anyone should ever have to bear in a lifetime. I knew this day would come. I thought I could recuperate before anyone found out. I did not have the courage to confront the truth on my own. No, I had to get caught.

The debts going back to the Zente lawsuit were still weighing on me. My other bills including the IRS amounted to more than four million dollars and were all in arrears. My son was a senior in high school and about to go off to college. On one occasion, in my wealthier days, his best friend's father had approached me for a loan. He had inherited a large trust from his parents and was in the middle of building a new house and taking over the family business. Before the trust was settled, he was desperate for money, having overspent on the new house. Finally when the trust came through, he was hit with a huge inheritance tax and the estate was essentially worthless. So I lent him $289,000, agreeing never to tell his wife.

I never pressed him to repay the money, but when I was in real need, I asked him for it. He denied ever having a loan agreement with me even though his financial advisor was the one who had drafted it. All calls from my lawyer were ignored and the debt went unpaid. I never spoke to him again. When I realized he was not going to honor his debt all sorts of vindictive thoughts ran through my head. But in the end I realized our sons' friendship was more important than money.

Out of the blue my sister called me up from Boston and wanted to come out to California for Adams graduation. Without getting into the details I told her I had financial problems. My sister offered to help and lent me money to pay for Adam's last semester in high school and some extra money for bills. During the conversation she said my parents had some savings and thought they might be willing to help with Adam's college tuition. I was deeply moved by her act of kindness and asked her why she wanted to help me.

She said, "What did you expect? You are my only brother."

Before I called my parents I went over in my mind what I should say to them. My feelings about them as parents were mixed. When I was a child I had asked them for money to go to the movies and was flatly denied. I wondered what they would say now and did not feel like letting myself in for further rejection. But I was desperate and had to try. They had never hit me. They had provided food, not enough to feel full but enough to live on. They had provided clothes that were too big but could be grown into. They had provided shelter, but the neighborhood was violent and they left me alone to deal with it. They loved me but hadn't shown it.

Then again, I had left home when I was seventeen and never once asked them for anything from that day forward. Although I had not been a model son I paid for their cruise to Alaska and trips to Lake Tahoe and the Bahamas. I bought my mother expensive jewelry. When I had money I wanted my parents to have things they never would have bought for themselves. Now I really needed help. I had my own family and for years had been a good husband and father. How was I going to ask my parents for help? I guess I would just call them and ask. I waited for a time to be alone. I gathered my courage fully expecting them to blame me and say "No, you got yourself into this, you get yourself out."

My father answered the call. We talked for an hour or so. I was very emotional, close to tears as I explained how I had let my family down. I told him how much I loved my son and how important it was to us that he go to college. I let him know none of the money was for me, but for my family. He agreed to help out by lending me the money. I could not thank him enough. He told me that my mother did not agree with helping me in any way, but he would take the lead in not letting me suffer over this.

I kept in touch with my parents sporadically after that.

With the financial help of my sister and father, Claudia and I decided to move to Washington, D.C. Claudia had worked there before I met her and Adam would be starting college there in the fall. We had nothing keeping us in Southern California so we made the decision to move back to the East Coast. We put our furniture into storage, packed a few suitcases, and left. I had been away for more than twenty-five years. It was time to go home.

A few years later my parents were in a car accident in Boston and my mother talked to me on the phone from the emergency room.

She said, "David, I am not doing well."

Those were the last words I heard from her. By the time had I traveled from Washington, D.C., to the hospital she was on life support. The doctor explained there was no hope of her recovering and recommended we let her die peacefully. We went back to my parents' house not saying much. This was the first time I'd been there in years. The next morning my father and I drove to the hospital. On the drive I could sense my dad was focused on the tasks ahead. We walked into her room and sat down. They took her off of life support. I held one hand, my dad held the other, and she died within minutes. At the funeral parlor before the service, her body was in a casket in the back room. No one wanted to go in to see her but I did. I went in and looked at her swollen and cold body. I bent down and kissed her cheek and told her, "I love you Mom, and always have."

FIFTEEN

Moral Dilemmas

From the time I was a small child, I believed I always knew the difference between right and wrong, the simple truths. It is wrong to steal something that is not yours. It is wrong to lie. It is wrong to take advantage of someone because you are bigger, stronger, richer, or smarter. These simple truths seemed like they should be absolute in their understanding, rules for living a morally correct life. The reward would be feeling good about yourself, breeding happiness and confidence.

As a child growing up I did not lie. I told the truth to my friends and they understood me and accepted what I said with without question. With my mother, I learned the only truth she wanted to hear was good news. If the truth was that I had knocked out a tooth or that I was worried about being beat up on the way home my mother would minimize what I told her or blatantly call me a dreamer with a vivid imagination. After years of this I just stopped telling her anything that would cause her to attack the validity of what I had to say. I very seldom talked with my dad, if at all. My aunts and uncles had little to say other than "How are you? How's school?" I learned the one-word answers that would please them.

Those truths got complicated for me as I got older. I was alone to face the consequences of decisions I made that would not work out in my favor if I followed those rules. When I was attacked in my backyard and beaten up, I could have run away or I could have stood there and fought. If I had run away I might have avoided that beating, but those kids would have returned to finish the job, and I would have gotten the reputation of being a coward. I could have gone to some-one of authority for protection but that was not an option because that person did not exist. I could have carried a knife with me from then on, giving me a little edge if a fight like that were to take place again. I could have allied myself with the gangs in my neighborhood but that would have meant I had to join them and be like them and there would be no getting out.

I made the decision to maintain a heightened awareness of pending danger like an animal stalked as prey and avoid trouble be-fore it could play out. I thought of revenge toward those kids who beat me up. At some unsuspecting moment I would pick them apart one at a time, when they were not with their gang. If I did that it would turn into a long-term feud, me against the gang. Parents tell their children "Run away from fights. Nothing is worth getting hurt over." That is a lie. There are some causes worth getting hurt for. In my neighborhood there were lots of reasons to fight: your reputa-tion, your food, your clothes, your basketball, your bike, your sur-vival. So in what world is nothing worth getting hurt for? Not mine. I had no thoughts of my community. The only worthwhile actions were the ones that I benefited from. Finally my moral code was being formulated on a conscious level. But none of this felt good. I was not happy. I was disconnected, yet I was alive. This dilemma was present in my life every day. Should I do what serves me or what is best for everyone and at what expense?

When I was pushed into the circle of kids and forced to fight Joseph Podeko in middle school, I could have yelled out to the specta-tors, "I won't fight a perfect stranger who has done nothing to me, a kid I don't even know. You should all be ashamed of yourselves for wanting to see someone get hurt." They would've retorted in unison "Who the fuck do you think you are? This is what we do, if you don't like it, we will humiliate you every minute of your weak life." I could have stopped the fight when I knew Podeko couldn't possibly beat me. I could have said, "Fight's over. You can see he doesn't know how to fight. His eye is swollen shut. He can't even see who is beating him.

His clothes are ripped and bloody. He'll have to walk home naked."

If I did that then my peer group would think I was weak. Being weak meant being vulnerable to abuse. This was not about fair; this was about a pecking order. The collective mentality demanded I prove my aggressive instinct, prove I could hold the other kid down and keep myself up. People think society has evolved past resorting to violence to show dominance but it really has not.

So how does that fit into a moral code? The gray areas are places between right and wrong. Does the gray area principle apply to everyone or am I the only one who sees the need for it? If I'm the only one who makes such a distinction, at least consciously, should I tell everyone I meet to expect that my moral code will be different than theirs? When I saw that kid getting raped in the bathroom, I could have stopped it and gotten my ass kicked or possibly worse. Then I would be seen as his friend. I could not protect him every day at school. Should I just say too bad for him and let this part of his life continue on, protecting only myself? The bad news for me was that every time I did not act in good conscience or defend someone when they were being attacked or at a disadvantage I felt bad as if I had done something wrong. Intellectually I knew I had to protect myself but those feelings of guilt and shame added up.

When I was twelve years old the woman who gave me my first hand job was a patient at a mental institution. I knew that when she was jerking me off, but I let it continue because I liked the way it felt. I could have put my dick in my pants and walked away. No one would ever have known. But I didn't. Who was taking advantage of whom? She was older and on some level probably knew what she was doing. I had no idea what was happening and let it continue while a part of me growled no, this is wrong.

At seventeen, while living in a junkie-infested apartment building, I didn't have to push the guy who stole two stereos from me out the window. I understood he was a junkie. He was doing what junkies do. But if I had let him get away with it all the junkies in the neighborhood would have known and my apartment would be marked as an easy place to steal from. Why was I God, making life and death judgments on other people and then punishing them for hurting me?

When the hippie in the Boston Commons asked me if I wanted to sell pot for him, I knew it was wrong. I knew there could be serious consequences, but I didn't care because by that time my moral code had fused with my self-interest. I could have said no thanks and looked for a job to make money while going to school. I made decisions for my own survival, so selling his pot meant making money immediately.

Oh wait a minute, let's take the moral high ground. Have no money and stay hungry but then they say "Oh, but you better go hide in an alley so your hunger doesn't annoy us happy-faced people walking by. Hell, stay hungry long enough to get sick. Don't bathe. At the same time don't bother anyone because their worlds are just fine."

Okay, so I sold some pot to make money. I didn't get caught so I wanted more.

When Peter got busted in Amsterdam I felt guilty. He would pay the price for the both of us. He never once tried to bargain his way out of prison by turning me in. He protected me. He lied to the courts and told them he was acting alone. He had a code. He made a mistake, took responsibility for it, and was honorable. He violated one of the simple rules of survival. Don't put others before yourself. He broke that rule because he found a truth greater than self-interest, the truth of his honor and his bond to me. Had he negotiated with the courts by sacrificing me he would have benefitted but dishonored himself. Although I had never ratted on anyone, I was surprised that someone would do it for me. That was a first.

On my first trip to Nepal the hash dealers I bought from had sent back empty hollowed out fake museum artifacts. When I returned with John to confront them we wanted to show a threat of violence. John's sheer physical presence was enough to get the truth from those dealers. I had learned that lesson back in Dorchester at the pool hall. When I won at eight-ball, the guy said "Take the money if you can."

It was not enough to win the game, I needed the leverage to collect. The dealers were so shocked when we barged into their office I thought they might implode. They told us straight up they had sent empty containers. Foreigners fell for this scam all the time but either didn't have the funds or didn't want to take the trouble of going all the way back to Nepal. Then again, they could have been afraid of a confrontation. Those dealers never tried to steal from us again.

I could have said when I had first gotten back from Nepal laying in my bed recovering from bacillary dysentery, "I can't go back. I could die of disease. The trip is too long. I'll never get my money back." Actually there were lots of reasons not to go back to Nepal. But I did. This was now a fight and my code told me I had to finish it.

My godfather in Colombia sent me on a mission where I was told to shoot someone I did not know in the head if he did not take the bribe I offered him. His life depended on making the right choice and he didn't know it. The border guard's decision allowed my convoy of trucks to carry food and clothes to a poor village in the mountains of Venezuela. If he decided not to allow the convoy through, he would be dead and the convoy would go through anyway. By his moral code he had to violate the duty he was sworn to uphold in order to live. For him it was easy. He took some money and let us through. I wondered if he felt guilty, if he shared the money, and how he reconciled this act within himself. A moral code comes after your survival is ensured. That's what happened here. I thought that must happen everywhere. Does the end justify the means?

My family in Colombia was in the pot and cocaine business to make money to feed and clothe impoverished villagers in the mountains of Northern Colombia and Venezuela. Of course they had more than enough money for themselves, but beyond that they did not have to support the villagers believe what they did was justified. Right and wrong are presented as opposites in fairytales but are often intertwined in reality. Nothing is for free in the real world. Everything takes sacrifice. Is selling drugs worth feeding children? In their world it was. In my world it was. I only wish my motives had been as pure.

When I was in a Bolivian military prison handcuffed to a bed for months, I would periodically be brought to a dungeon where I was beaten and tortured, always with the same theme, "Who do you work for?" After getting nowhere with this technique they continued to take me to the dungeon but stopped the torture. They asked the same question but in a civil manner like the way a waiter in a restaurant asks, "Are you ready to order?" My family in Colombia had treated me so honorably; I could not have lived with myself if I had betrayed that trust. When the U.S. Marshal, the DEA, and the federal prosecutor tried to get me to exchange my prison sentence for their identities and locations. I told them the truth.

I said, "You caught me. I am guilty. I will not deny that, but you have not caught them and, if you do, it will be because you did your job. I am not doing it for you. Have some self-respect. Stop trying to get me to do your work for you. They never bothered me with those questions again and in a strange way they may have recognized a value in me that was lost in mainstream society, honor.

My parole officer was a good man. I could tell he was hardened by his job, yet at the same time very clear and truthful about his expectations. My worst drinking and drug taking took place the minute I left prison. I was always stoned and drunk when I saw him and he knew it. I gave him six dirty drug tests and told him in advance they were dirty. In another life I could have been friends with this man. I was honorable with him and he with me. When I was in treatment he told me he might revoke my parole, that I could go back to prison for eight years. I told him, "Fine, I'll take what I have coming." The truth did not serve my self-interest, but I told the truth anyway. My plan was to be an advocate for people like me in prison, from prison. I was thinking of them. I was on parole for two years. When he visited me in treatment and tested me I told him the tests were clean. When he asked me what would happen when I left the safety of the hospital I told him I did not know.

There is no issue of morality when you are living on Mars. Moral dilemmas don't exist. The only thing that matters is staying there.

Whether you got there by drugs, alcohol, gambling, or whatever addiction, it's the same story. You like the way you feel because you don't feel. I know now if I were to be drunk or high the decisions I would make would result in self-destruction while at the same time make feelings of loneliness and self-loathing disappear. This must be the secret to avoiding moral dilemmas: take action based only upon your point of view, only do things that serve you, and stay unconscious to your feelings. They are the enemy. Turn them off.

Being in debt led me to become a liar. This was the worst place I could have been in my life. I lied to my wife, making up stories of offshore bank accounts and hidden monies all to give her hope that we would be okay. Telling the truth would have taken courage but I was a coward not wanting to face my failures and weaknesses. I wanted to be her hero but instead became a villain. I gave her false hope, the worst thing you can do to someone you love. Lying is the quickest way back to Mars. One lie feeds on another and the feelings of worthlessness, loneliness, and despair come right back and start taking over. It's like the lies are stones. First a small lie as heavy as a pebble is put into a sack you carry on your back, the big lies are heavier stones, and before you know it you are bent over from the weight of the lies accumulating in the sack on your back. The light of your spirit goes out and your body internalizes the pain until it feels like your heart will explode. The Martian lifestyle takes over—dull the pain with drugs, alcohol, gambling, sex, food, whatever works—it's a planet without feelings.

During my teenage years up until the time I started dealing pot, I was very verbal and naively thought everything I said had meaning. I engaged in a lot of debates, but when it came to my own feelings or reporting back the incidents of my day I was truthful. When I started dealing pot to make money is when I became guarded and learned to be creative with words. I could not be honest about how I was earning money. The consequences would be too harsh. As I got deeper into the dealing and smuggling world, I gave great thought to my cover stories, creating lie-based truths for the world to see. At the same time I never lied to myself or to the people in my inner circle. When I decided to be a ghost, it meant to me that I no longer had any connection to my past. I had no one to be responsible to or for, only to myself whatever I would be. So as I created one story after another to fit into wherever I lived, the only one who could get hurt was me. The only one I could destroy was myself. I made that decision on my own. Lying just took over and became my way of life. I did not feel guilt or shame. I was proud of my smuggling career.

Imagine if I had a guest at my house, a nice, normal member of society, and they asked, "What do you do? This property is amazing. How could you afford it?"

I would truthfully look them in the eye and say, "I am a drug smuggler. I have had a pretty good year."

Then they would ask, "Well, isn't that dangerous?"

To which I would say, "You know the risks when you make the decision to join this world. I won't lie to you about it."

After I was arrested for importing thirty-seven tons of marijuana I was invited to be a guest on a San Francisco radio talk show. The drug culture in the '70s was pervasive, from Studio 54 in New York to Haight-Ashbury in San Francisco and the topic was on everyone's minds.

A caller asked if I felt responsible for the downfall of people who got addicted to drugs.

"No, I started out in the pot business because I smoked pot and liked making money. I liked the effect it had on me and my friends liked being stoned too. In the late '70s prescription pills such as Quaaludes became a fad in the States. So in Colombia a number of pills factories were set up to make counterfeit pills. I was offered the opportunity to capitalize on that business with my Colombian family, but we turned it down. There was a question of the quality and safety of the different manufactures. We were also offered the transportation contract for the shipping of heroin from Cambodia to the U.S. and Europe but we also turned that down because heroin crossed a line we were not willing to cross.

One of the callers had said he was a pot smoker as was everyone else he knew. He asked me why I would break the law by smuggling such a huge amount of pot into the country. Why didn't I just buy some and smoke it like everyone else? I asked him "Where do you think the pot you and your friends smoke comes from?"

There was no answer.

My experience as a drug addict and alcoholic and as someone who has worked in the treatment field has led me to believe that drugs and alcohol are not the problem. The problem lies within the addict. Statistics vary from twelve to sixteen percent of Americans are currently addicted to drugs and alcohol. Another twenty percent are in some form of recovery. That leaves about two hundred million people who may drink or smoke pot as a form of recreation. This has been going on since recorded history. People like to use drugs. It is not going to stop because some politician in Washington decides smoking a joint is morally worse than taking a shot of alcohol. And the reason either ruins your life is implicit in you, not the glass of liquid or dried plant pulp you are trying to claim is controlling your life. The drug doesn't control you. You use it to allow yourself to be out of control.

Later when I was a drug addict I acknowledged my addiction to myself. I was overt in my drug addict behavior displaying the truth about destroying my body and soul to anyone who cared enough to notice. That was pretty much my best friend Eric and my dog, Ainge. Everyone else was okay with it because I still made them a lot of money. I never denied being stoned. As a matter of fact, I encouraged it.

My first five years of being drug and alcohol free the other Martians whom had formed a fellowship on Earth told me anytime my lips moved I would be lying.

They said, "You have been lying for so long it will take time for you to even understand what the truth is."

I watched my words carefully when I spoke at these meetings, I wanted to tell the truth and paid attention to my mind as words formed into sentences to double check that what I was saying was the truth. As a businessman I used words to motivate people I worked with to have enthusiasm toward our business venture. I chose those words carefully never lying, not exaggerating but being as factual as possible, based on the data I had collected. If I did not know something I would say, "I don't know. It's not my area of expertise."

If they countered with "Well, what do you think?" I would answer, "What I think is not important."

For me most insidious addiction is gambling. With that addiction you can be assured of a life of lying, self-degradation, and misery. During my gambling period, I lied from the second I woke up until the time I went to sleep. My character was lost to me and anyone who depended on me. I had a wife and son, employees, and acquaintances whom I respected and I could not let them know what I was doing. My life became a total lie and for the first time I gave thought to suicide—enough suffering, enough pain, let it all end. Who cares? Well, my wife cared and so did my son. I would have to try to undo the damage and make this right.

■ ■ ■

A thirty-five-year-old man is an avid Boston Red Sox fan. He has saved his money to purchase tickets to a Red Sox versus the New York Yankees game at Fenway Park, the game of the year. As he approaches his seat he is filled with the anticipation of a great game. He sits down and hears a voice yell out "Hey, Dave." He looks around but sees no one he knows. As the game progresses he hears the voice again, "Hey, Dave," only this time it sounds closer, so he stands up and looks around. Once again he can't identify where the voice is coming from. Now he's frustrated and getting angry. Someone is disrupting his perfect afternoon. The seventh inning approaches and he decides to get himself a large popcorn and a beer. On his return just before sitting down he hears the voice again, this time louder, "Hey Dave!" Now infuriated he throws his arms up in frustration, spilling the popcorn and beer on the woman sitting in front of him. He puts his hand in front of his mouth making a temporary loudspeaker and yells back, "My name is not Dave."

This story epitomizes my attitude from early on. I thought everything in life was about me. I tried to make life's circumstances work out in my favor, often overlooking the consequences to other people. As I traveled to remote parts of the world I was looking for opportunity to get more for myself. I took more money than I needed. I bought more houses, cars, and clothes than I could ever use in three lifetimes. I took extreme risks with my freedom and life to have more. I never had an idea of what was enough so I could never reach the goal and be content. During this period of my life I was generous with what I had, but I had a lot to be generous with. If I had had less would I have been so generous or was I just serving my own interest by giving a little when I had a lot?

As I entered my thirties I became a sober member of society. More about my character was revealed to me. Starting from the disadvantage of being an ex-con with a multitude of newspaper stories describing me as everything from a drug smuggler, fugitive, and drug kingpin, I had to build a life in the real world. I needed a job that might lead to a career. I had to learn about business and the ethics and morality that govern that world. I had to accept civil law whether I agreed with it or not. As I saw it at the time, I had to compromise myself and work for the interest of others. I did not fit into that norm. Prospective employers believed the newspaper stories about me and steered away.

So I ended up creating and building my own companies. I worked hard and was successful, once again making more money than I needed only in the legal way. I was fair to my employees and wanted them to share in the success of the company. I set up a program where they could borrow money at no interest for a down payment on a house. I paid them double what the market rate was for similar jobs and when the company was sold they got twenty-five percent of what I got. Now at age sixty-three, by writing my life story, I wanted to share some hard earned wisdom with others. I spend time speaking to groups of emotionally wounded people, broken by a combination of life circumstances and bad choices. I look into the faces of my audience studying each one and I see the pain and disappointment they are feeling. None of these people had the life goal of ending up in homeless shelters or group homes. They did not dream of being addicts or criminals. I tell them about my life and how I am able to achieve peace with myself, how I have accepted and taken responsibility for my past and have new dreams for my future.

I explain how most of my life I imagined myself as a large black wolf with a mission to survive at any cost. I also talk about the smaller white wolf that went into hiding by the time I was fourteen. Now when I hear the voice of the black wolf I tell him "I know you. I recognize your voice. I want you to be patient. Calm down, I love you. You are a part of me." The white wolf now is more confident willing to show himself to people he trusts. He is gentle and just wants to be safe and have his voice heard. Both of these wolves have equal say in my mind. Together they have found peace.

Made in the USA
Middletown, DE
14 October 2021